Intermediate Microeconomics:
The Science of Choice

Dr. Jeremy Petranka
UNC - Chapel Hill

December, 2011

Contents

Chapter 1

What is Microeconomics?

Task: Consider what each of these questions have in common.

- What is likely to happen if AT&T merges with T-Mobile? Will cell-phone costs go up? Will fewer poor individuals be able to connect to the internet, potentially widening the digital divide? Should the government block this merger?

- Do people tend to be more prone to relationships with people who are similar to themselves? If so, can this help explain lower employment rates in specific demographic groups? Could enacting school policies to increase friendship diversity initiatives possibly help alleviate persistent employment disparities?

- How should Facebook respond to Google+'s entry into the social networking market? Would you advise Facebook to encourage interactivity with Google+, or block the ability for Google+ updates to appear in Facebook?

- Which is more important in explaining differences in NFL wide receivers, popularity or performance?

Answer: They each ask a question about individuals making choices.[1]

Engineers and physicists answer questions about how the world works. Physicians answer questions about how the human body works. Philosophers answer questions about how the human mind works. Economists answer questions

---

[1] They also have been addressed, to some extent, in the Economics literature. Please see Crémer et al. (2000), Motta (2004), Prince and Goldfarb (2008), Calvó-Armengol and Jackson (2004), Treme and Allen (2011)

about how individuals make choices, given the constraints of the world around us, the frailties of our bodies, and the limitations of our minds.

While the separation between the fields is far from rigid, Economics is generally divided into three major subcategories.

Definition 1.1 (Microeconomics):
The theoretical study of individual decision-making. An "individual" can be a person, a firm, or a group, as long as the "individual's" preferences can be identified.

Definition 1.2 (Macroeconomics):
The theoretical study of aggregate decision-making, oftentimes at the national economic level. A large group's preferences need not be identifiable, as long as its behavior is predictable.

Definition 1.3 (Econometrics):
The empirical study of Economic issues using real-world data to make statistical inferences.

In this text, we will focus on Microeconomics, and develop a theory to help explain individual decision-making. If you have been around other humans for any amount of time, you have undoubtedly recognized the fact that predicting behavior is not an easy task. How many times have you found yourself thinking "what in the world is that person thinking?"

Economists can attempt to predict human behavior using a myriad of tools. We could use statistical forecasting, computer simulation, survey analysis, etc. As it turns out, the tool Economists use most frequently is mathematics. Mathematics allows us to "put ourselves in the shoes" of the individuals we are studying and analyze how they are likely to behave in a very formal framework. To understand why mathematics is our method of choice, we must first take a few detours into what "thinking about a problem" really entails, and how mathematics fits into the process.

1.1 A Brief Detour into the Mind

1.1.1 What is Thought?

What is "thinking"? What is that glimmer of "something" I see behind my dog's eyes, but is seemingly quite different than the glimmer I see in my niece's eyes? Why can two seemingly "intelligent" individuals develop drastically contrasting viewpoints on issues ranging from gun control to tax policy to the best type of music? Why do we consider computers as "unthinking" machines?

Cognitive science has been attempting to answer these questions for years. While a consensus has not been reached, a general agreement has been reached that thought involves something "beyond" the strict operation of neural networks. Marr (1982), for instance, argues that an information-processing system (a "thinker") consists of three levels.

> **Implementation Level:** The structure of the system. i.e. the brain's physiological makeup
>
> **Algorithmic Level:** The problem-solving algorithms of the system. i.e. the methods by which the brain solves a problem. What chemicals/electric charges get produced and in what order when a particular problem is being solved?
>
> **Computational/Semantic Level:** The interpretation of the problem and the solution.

To demonstrate these levels, consider the following scenario

> You just graduated and you start work at your first job. While you will no doubt be CEO of your company very shortly, you start as a call-center representative, answering computer questions for die-hard computer programmers. Unfortunately, you know nothing about computers. As most of the questions are written in a computer language you have never seen, you have no idea what you are being asked, much less the answer. Luckily for you, you have been given a very impressive training manual that tells you how to respond to every question you might receive! Even better, it gives you the answer in the same computer language so the die-hard computer programmers can understand your response. Of course, you have no idea what these responses mean, but you are very good at matching the questions with the correct answers.

The question I pose to you is this: From the point of view of a die-hard computer programmer, do you understand the computer language?[2] You are able to answer every question in the language the computer programmer understands. You use an algorithm that ensures the correct answer is given. However, are you really "thinking"?[3] Could you answer a question that is almost identical to a question in your training manual, but ever-so-slightly different?

In terms of Marr's Tri-Level hypothesis, you were not thinking about the actual problems because you were missing the fundamental third level, the Semantic Level. You had an algorithm and a system to implement it, but you were not able to semantically understand the problems you were solving. It is interesting to note that you were, in fact, thinking about a different problem that you did semantically understand. Specifically, "how do I match up a given question with a specific answer". For instance, you semantically understood that "I solved the problem of matching up question A with answer B". Thus, you understand how to match up questions and answers, but you do *not* understand the computer language itself.

There is lively debate over whether this third level should be viewed as separate from the first two levels, but there tends to be agreement that the concept of "thinking" needs to include some hierarchical basis, in which a given neural response is given "meaning". Put another way, "thinking" is not the creation of neural patterns in the brain. It is the mapping of specific neural patterns to non-neural events. It is the ability to respond to the analogy that a particular neural pattern represents. It is the ability to combine neural patterns into new neural patterns which have their own host of non-neural interpretations. As Hofstadter (2007, p. 177) states,

> By our deepest nature, we humans float in a world of familiar and comfortable but quite impossible-to-define abstract patterns, such as: "fast food" and "clamato juice", "tackiness" and "wackiness", "Christmas bonuses" and "consumer service departments",..., "goals" and "lies", "dreads" and "dreams", "she" and "he" - and last but not least, "you" and "I".

In more mathematical terms, thinking can be seen as the ability to create infinitely extendable isomorphisms (formalized analogies) between neural patterns

---

[2]This is the classic Searlean "Chinese Room" thought experiment.

[3]If you answered yes, consider the last time you called a help-desk in which the representative was reading answers off a script. Any chance you thought to yourself "why won't this person think for a minute and help me with my problem?"

and "real-world" events. A computer does not "think" because it does not map its series of 1's and 0's to "real-world" events. When you see a digital TV produce a specific pattern of pixels that cause your eyes to stimulate a specific pattern of neurons, you are able to recognize that pattern as not just a pattern of colors. You are also able to map that pattern to the higher level, "NCAA basketball championship game". That higher-level interpretation can then cause other patterns to emerge, such as "National Champions", "pride", "Carolina blue", "Duke", "evil", ad infinitum. Unfortunately for the TV, it does not have these higher-level interpretations. The 1's and 0's are only 1's and 0's and it will never experience the pattern representing "rushing Franklin street with 100,000 of my closest friends".

To continue with our diversion, consider what happens in your brain as you answer two different questions:

Question 1: In what U.S State are you currently residing?

Question 2: Think about the person you love the most. What could you do today that would make them the most happy without spending any money?

For the first question, you likely bypassed higher-level "thinking". While your brain recalled the name of the state, you likely did not create higher-level patterns, forming new analogies of real-world events. For the second question, your brain had to form higher-level patterns. It needed to combine the concepts of "today","love", "money", and "happy", which are themselves based on other concepts. Your brain needed to form analogies "the happiness of the person you love the most if you did x for them" and "the happiness of the person you love the most if you did y for them". It even had to go so far as combining these analogies by incorporating the concept of "most happy". It likely took you longer to come up with an answer to Question 2, since your brain had to do so much more work. And given the amount of analogies you had to produce in your brain, you are most likely less sure of your answer. Is that person the person you love *the most*? Did you not think of something you could have done that would have made them happier? Put more elegantly, Hofstadter (2007, p. 247) asks,

What is *really* going on when you dream or think more than fleetingly about someone you love?...The symbol for that person has been activated inside your skull, lurched out of dormancy, as surely as if it had an icon that someone had double-clicked. And the moment this happens, much as with a game that has opened up on your screen, your mind starts acting differently from how it acts in a "normal" context. You have allowed yourself to be invaded by an "alien universal being", and to some extent the alien takes charge inside your skull, starts pushing things around in its own fashion, making words, ideas, memories, and associations bubble up inside your brain that ordinarily would not do so. The activation of the symbol for the loved person swivels into action whole sets of coordinated tendencies that represent that person's cherished style, their idiosyncratic way of being embedded in the world and looking out at it.

While the exact concept of "thinking" is still an open area of research, it is clear that a key foundation is the ability to make analogies that represent the real world. The better the analogy, the better the "thinking".

Example 1.1 (Thinking as Analogy):
   Task: Implement your solution to Question 2, above. Was the analogy formed by your brain consistent with the real-world result?

1.1.2 Thinking vs. Recall

Having established that "thinking" involves the formation of analogies from neural patterns, it is not surprising that some of the most effective learning also comes from the use of analogies. Consider the scenario in which you take a bus to a new city, and are dropped off in an unfamiliar area. Without any knowledge of the city, learning what direction will take you to hotels, restaurants, and friendly faces could prove quite difficult. You are effectively reduced to the insight of a young child, processing a new experience using primitive sensory cues. Now imagine if someone walked up to you and said "You look lost. Just so you know, this street is just like Franklin street. Where you are standing is equivalent to the East End, and that direction would take you towards the West End." Suddenly, all the concepts you have developed of Franklin Street are analogous to the street on which you find yourself. Because the analogy is so strong, in one sentence you have learned "are there a lot of restaurants in this town?", "can I find a diverse business district?", "can I find a hotel?", etc.

The ability to think and learn is the ability to form analogies that closely relate to the real-world and correctly "work through" the analogy. This is fundamentally different from the steps taken by our call-center example, in which simple recall is being performed with no higher-level thinking. Specifically, "thinking" requires four steps,[4]

1. **Identify the Problem**

2. **Create an Analogy**

3. **Algorithmically Work through the Analogy**

4. **Relate the Results Back to Reality**

Figure (1.1) shows the differences between thinking and recalling facts. "Recall" only requires the ability to match questions with pre-defined answers, as in our call-center example. It does not require the ability to "build an analogy" from pre-existing concepts. And unfortunately, the human brain has become obsolete when it comes to recall. Computers are faster, more reliable, and cheaper to feed. This was strikingly demonstrated in February 2011, when Watson, IBM's artificial intelligence computer system, squared off against Ken Jennings and Brad Rutter in a two-day game of Jeopardy.[5] At the end of the two days, the final scores were Watson: $77,147; Jennings: $24,000; Rutter: $21,600.

1.2 A Brief Detour into Mathematics

Having hopefully convinced you that thinking involves the use of analogy, the question remains, "what makes a good analogy?". Literature, for instance, can provide a very rich analogy for human behavior. The algorithmic "solution" to a given problem is provided by consistent character development throughout a novel. Many lessons we teach our children are based on narrative analogies, such as *The Frog Prince's* lesson that we should not judge an individual by his outside appearance. Other forms of analogy include computer simulations, statistical inference, and outright guessing (not a very good analogy, but an analogy nonetheless). Even music can form analogies in our minds, as you will likely encounter the next time you hear the first song to which you slow-danced.

When faced with different options for forming analogies, which is best for thinking through a new problem? Literature, unfortunately, works through problems

---

[4]Note these steps are essentially a reformulation of the Tri-Level hypothesis, with steps 1, 2, and 4 constituting the Semantic Level.

[5]Ken Jennings has the longest championship streak and Brad Rutter is the biggest all-time money winner in Jeopardy history.

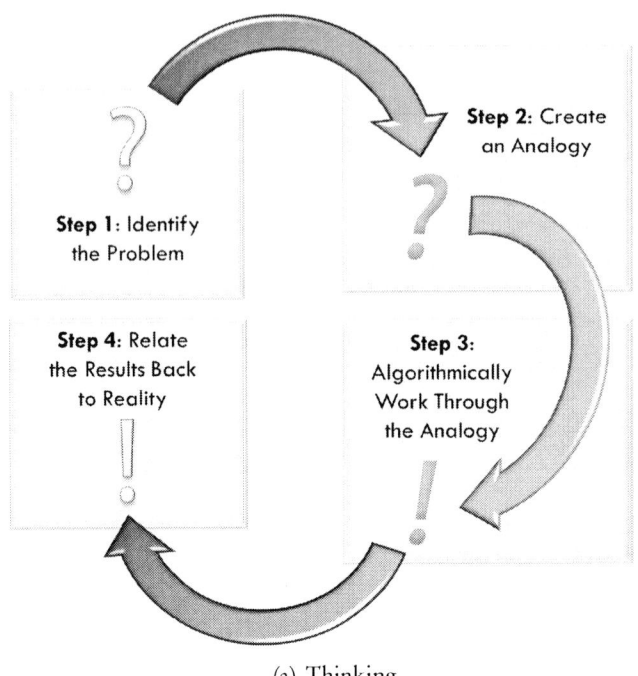

(a) Thinking

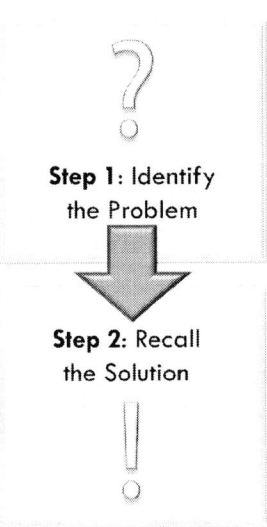

(b) Recalling Facts

Figure 1.1: Thinking vs. Recall

very slowly. Ayn Rand's *Atlas Shrugged* works through the core tenants of objectivism, but takes over 1000 pages to do so. In addition, as assumptions underlying a piece of literature change, it is not immediately clear how the results would change.[6] Computer simulations, another option, can be extremely costly to code, even if the results are highly accurate.

Figure 1.2: Kurt Gödel

In 1931, the young mathematician Kurt Gödel helped us identify a highly useful option for forming analogies, changing the nature of analogic thinking through his concept of Gödel numbering. In particular, Gödel found that any pattern can be represented using only integers. Language, weather, your favorite sports team...if it follows a pattern, there is a perfect analogical representation using only integers. As Hofstadter (2007, p. 161) states

> Kurt Gödel was the first person to realize and exploit the fact that the positive integers, though they might superficially seem to be very austere and isolated, in fact constitute a profoundly rich representational medium. They can mimic or mirror any kind of pattern. Like any human language, where nouns and verbs (etc.) can engage in unlimitedly complex dancing, the natural numbers too, can engage in unlimitedly complex additive and multiplicative (etc.) dancing, and can thereby "talk", via code or analogy, about events of any sort, numerical or non-numerical.

While at the time (and even now), this might have seemed fairly unbelievable,

---

[6]What if Ahab suddenly decided he liked white whales? What new lessons would we learn?

we are closely approaching the full realization of this astounding fact. Turn on a computer and look at the weather forecast. Then open Rosetta Stone™ software and teach yourself a foreign language. After that, play Madden 2012™ and predict how your favorite football team will fare this season. Your computer can make analogies (in some cases almost perfectly) of each of these concepts, using only "1's" and "0's".[7]

Kurt Gödel showed us that numbers can be used to represent any scenario that follows a pattern. The implication is that using numbers to create mental analogies ensures that we will never face a real-world pattern that we cannot mathematically analyze. In addition, and possibly more importantly, centuries of mathematics has given us the tools to fully work through these numerical analogies!

1.3 Goals of Microeconomics

We are now able to return to our original question: "How can Economists approach the task of predicting what decisions humans will make?" We clearly cannot rely solely on recalling facts, since humans are so complex. We must be able to study scenarios we have never encountered, and possibly incorporate lessons we have learned from similar, but different, situations. We must be able to analyze "what if" questions and determine the best course of action. In short, we must think.

As we have established, mathematics can not only represent every kind of pattern, but we have centuries of mathematical tools to help us work through potentially new scenarios. As such, it is a perfect candidate for creating analogies and working through them. Specifically, using mathematics as our algorithm of choice, our four steps to thinking outlined above become:

Definition 1.4 (Steps of Quantitative Economic Thinking):

1. Identify the Problem

2. Create a Mathematical Model (the Analogy)

3. Solve the Mathematical Model (Work through the Analogy)

4. Relate the Results Back to Reality

---

[7]The algorithmic processing of virtually all modern computers is based on a series of electronic switches that get set to "on" (1) or "off" (0).

With that in mind, we now have a framework for studying individual choice. While mathematics is not the only analogical tool that can be used to represent human decision-making, it is the most common tool in the Economist's toolkit. As such, we will be focusing on this framework, with two major goals in mind.

1. Introduce the basic concepts of Microeconomics on which more advanced concepts are built. While we will occasionally analyze more complicated problems, the majority of this book is devoted to teaching a few standard concepts used throughout the Economics literature, including consumer choice, profit maximization, and game theory.

2. Teach you to "think". Go beyond fact recall, and develop the ability to quantitatively analyze a situation using mathematical methods. Learn to not just solve a mathematical problem, but recognize how your results can represent a real-world phenomenon.

As computers have far surpassed us in the ability to recall, we must be able to think to add value to an organization. We must be able to consider previously unexplored options and determine which is theoretically best. We must be able to take a new concept and apply previously learned lessons.

Unfortunately, thinking cannot be taught. Instead, it must developed through practice.[8] Like a basketball player who develops "court vision" over many years, developing the skills to quantitatively analyze a given problem takes practice. Luckily, like many skills, learning to mathematically represent a given problem makes analyzing similar problems much easier. Developing a high-level of skill in one sport makes you more amenable to learning a new sport. Being fluent in multiple languages makes you more easily learn a new language. Developing a talent for one musical instrument makes you more quickly become proficient with another instrument. Practicing the skills developed in Microeconomics will make you be able to analyze quantitative scenarios much more easily. Whether it be interpreting financial statements, interpreting customer analytics, or considering the optimal contract to sign with your employer, developing the skill to think using numerical representations of economic scenarios will improve your skills in many other disciplines.

As a final note, you might have noticed that neither of the two objectives were "learn a bunch of facts you can learn later". While we will introduce some principles that can be easily applied to real-world scenarios, for the most part this

---

[8]Please refer to Bellemare (2010) for a recommendation on how, exactly, you should practice.

course is about learning the techniques to reasonably answer questions you have not encountered. As stated by Bellemare (2010),

> In fact, my own experience is that preparing for an economics exam has more to do with preparing for a musical performance than with preparing for an exam in the humanities.

In other words, the course is not about "memorizing the music". It is about "mastering the musical instrument".

Chapter 2

Math Review

If we revisit Definition (1.4), we note that "Solving the Math" is only one step of the Economic process. While it allows us to logically work through our mathematical analogy, equally important is identifying the relevant problem, creating a valid mathematical model, and relating our mathematical results back to human behavior.

As your pre-reqs for this course include mathematics classes that cover most all of the techniques we will be using, we will not focus explicitly on "Solving the Math". Instead, we will work to develop our skills in creating and interpreting Economic models. That being said, if you have difficulty working through the mathematics, the process of thinking illustrated in Figure (1.1(a)) will prove extremely difficult at almost every step, from creating a mathematical model to interpreting our analogical results back to reality.

To allow us to more effectively achieve the goals of the course, we will focus on a few mathematical techniques that are used throughout the Economics literature. These are far from the only mathematical techniques professional economists use, but a proficiency in these techniques will give you a strong basis for more advanced material. The mathematical techniques we use are generally calculus-based, but as we will see, only a few concepts are needed to develop quite rich models of Economic behavior. I strongly encourage you to review this Chapter prior to continuing with the text. If you feel you have a strong proficiency in a specific topic and can solve the Example problems within a Section with ease, I encourage you to spend your time on more rewarding pursuits. If you do not have a strong proficiency in a topic or are having trouble with the Example problems, please review the material closely, and refer to your pre-req mathematics courses as needed. For the most part, we will not use any mathematics that is significantly more difficult than the material within this Chapter.

2.1 Algebra

It is expected that you are proficient in algebraic simplification. We will not use any trigonometric functions (sine, cosine, etc.), but will rely heavily on polynomial functions. A few facts that you have doubtless encountered, but will prove useful to keep in mind throughout the course:

2.1.1 Simplifying Fractions

To simplify a complex fraction, use the formula $\frac{\frac{a}{b}}{\frac{c}{d}} = \frac{ad}{bc}$. In other words, multiply the fraction in the numerator by the inverse ("flip") of the fraction in the denominator. If the numerator or denominator is a whole number, change the whole number to its equivalent fractional form (i.e. $a = \frac{a}{1}$) and perform the division as normal.

> **Example 2.1 (Simplifying Fractions):**
> **Task:** Simplify the fraction
>
> $$\frac{3}{\frac{2}{3}}.$$
>
> **Answer:** 3 can be rewritten $\frac{3}{1}$. Using the above procedure,
>
> $$\frac{3}{\frac{2}{3}} = \frac{\frac{3}{1}}{\frac{2}{3}} = \frac{3*3}{1*2} = \frac{9}{2}$$

When facing compound fractions in which the numerator or denominator of one fraction is itself a fraction, start with the innermost fractions, and work your way out using the above formula.

> **Example 2.2 (Simplifying Compound Fractions):**
> **Task:** Simplify the fraction
>
> $$\frac{\frac{2}{3}}{\frac{3}{4+\frac{1}{3}}}.$$

Answer: Facing a compound fraction, we must first start with the innermost fractions. In this case, $\frac{3}{\frac{4}{3}}$ is a fraction in the denominator of another fraction.

Thus, $\frac{3}{\frac{4}{3}}$ is the innermost fraction. Simplifying this using our technique, above,

$$\frac{3}{\frac{4}{3}} = \frac{\frac{3}{1}}{\frac{4}{3}} = \frac{3*3}{1*4} = \frac{9}{4}$$

We can now use this simplification in the outermost fraction to complete our simplification.

$$\frac{\frac{2}{3}}{\frac{3}{\frac{4}{3}}} = \frac{\frac{2}{3}}{\frac{9}{4}} = \frac{2*4}{3*9} = \frac{8}{27}$$

As $\frac{8}{27}$ cannot be reduced further, we have fully simplified our original fraction.

2.1.2 Multiplying by the Same Variable

When multiplying a variable raised to a power and the same variable raised to another power, use the formula

$$x^a x^b = x^{a+b}. \tag{2.1}$$

Example 2.3 (Multiplying by the Same Variable - Simple):
Task: Simplify the term $x^3 x^2$

Answer: Directly using the above procedure,

$$x^3 x^2 = x^{3+2} = x^5$$

Note this procedure can be used with other properties of multiplication, such as the commutative, associative, and distributive properties.

Example 2.4 (Multiplying by the Same Variable - Complex):
Task: Simplify the term $x^3 a x^2 (2x^2 + 3)$ where a is a constant.

Answer: To simplify the term, we will use the multiplicative properties along with Eqn. 2.1. Using the commutative property,

$$x^3 a x^2 (2x^2 + 3) = a x^3 x^2 (2x^2 + 3)$$

Using the associative property,

$$ax^3x^2(2x^2+3) = a(x^3x^2)(2x^2+3)$$

Using Eqn. 2.1,

$$a(x^3x^2)(2x^2+3) = a(x^{3+2})(2x^2+3) = a(x^5)(2x^2+3)$$

At this point, the term is simplified to an acceptable level. Depending on our need, we could further simply the term. Using the associative property,

$$a(x^5)(2x^2+3) = a((x^5)(2x^2+3))$$

Using the distributive property,

$$a((x^5)(2x^2+3)) = a(2x^2x^5+3x^5)$$

Using Eqn. 2.1,

$$a(2x^2x^5+3x^5) = a(2x^7+3x^5)$$

As a quick aside, note that $\sqrt{x} = x^{\frac{1}{2}}$, and can therefore be used with Eqn. 2.1 in the same manner as any variable raised to a power.

2.1.3   Dividing by the Same Variable

When dividing a variable raised to a power by the same variable raised to another power, use the formula

$$\frac{x^a}{x^b} = x^{a-b}.$$

An important point to note is that there is no need to memorize this equation. In particular, you should recognize that $\frac{1}{x^b} = x^{-b}$. Thus,

$$\frac{x^a}{x^b} = x^a \frac{1}{x^b} = x^a x^{-b}$$

Using Eqn. 2.1, this simplifies to x^{a-b}, our formula from above. We will see a similar technique used when discussing the quotient rule for differentiation.

2.1.4   Raising a Variable to a Power

When raising a variable raised to a power to another power, use the formula

$$(x^a)^b = x^{a*b}.$$

Example 2.5 (Raising a Variable to a Power):
   Task: Simplify the term $(x^3)^5$

   Answer: Directly using the above procedure,

$$(x^3)^5 = x^{3*5} = x^{15}$$

2.1.5   Solving for a Variable

Essentially, solving for a variable in an equation is simply a matter of performing operations to the equality and simplifying the results in an effort to leave the variable by itself on one side of the equality. Operations that are generally used are:

- addition/subtraction

- multiplication/division

- raising to a power

- taking the logarithm/exponential function

The key to solving for a variable is recognizing the left side of the equality is identical to the right side of the equality. Thus, any operation performed to the left side of the equality must also be performed to the right side.

Example 2.6 (Solving for a Variable):
   Task: Given $(x^3 + 3)^2 = 4$, solve for x.

   Answer: We will solve for x using the following operations and the corresponding simplifications they allow:

   Operation: Raise to the power $\frac{1}{2}$ (in other words, take the square root of both sides of the equality).

$$(x^3 + 3)^2 = 4 \Rightarrow \left((x^3 + 3)^2\right)^{\frac{1}{2}} = 4^{\frac{1}{2}}$$

Simplifying,

$$(x^3 + 3)^{2*1/2} = (2, -2)$$
$$\Rightarrow x^3 + 3 = (2, -2)$$

Note because $4^{1/2}$ equals 2 and -2, this solution will have two answers. We first solve using $x^3 + 3 = 2$.

Operation: Subtract by 3.

$$x^3 + 3 = 2 \quad \Rightarrow \quad x^3 + 3 - 3 = 2 - 3$$
$$\Rightarrow x^3 = -1$$

Operation: Raise to the power $\frac{1}{3}$.

$$x^3 = -1 \quad \Rightarrow \quad (x^3)^{\frac{1}{3}} = -1^{\frac{1}{3}}$$

Simplifying,

$$x^{3*\frac{1}{3}} = -1$$
$$\Rightarrow x = -1$$

We can now solve for the second equation using $x^3 + 3 = -2$.

Operation: Subtract by 3.

$$x^3 + 3 = 2 \quad \Rightarrow \quad x^3 + 3 - 3 = -2 - 3$$
$$\Rightarrow x^3 = -5$$

Operation: Raise to the power $\frac{1}{3}$.

$$x^3 = -1 \quad \Rightarrow \quad (x^3)^{\frac{1}{3}} = -5^{\frac{1}{3}}$$

Simplifying,

$$x^{3*\frac{1}{3}} = -5^{\frac{1}{3}}$$
$$\Rightarrow x = -5^{\frac{1}{3}} \approx -1.71$$

Thus, our two solutions are $x = -1$ and $x = -5^{\frac{1}{3}}$.

Example 2.7 (Solving for a Variable):
Task: Given $\ln(y^2) = 10$, solve for y.

Answer: We will solve for y using the following operations and the corresponding simplifications they allow:

Operation: Raise the exponential function by each side of the equality.

$$\ln(y^2) = 10 \Rightarrow \exp^{\ln(y^2)} = \exp^{10}$$

Recognizing that $\exp^{\ln(y^2)} = y^2$, this simplifies to

$$y^2 = \exp^{10}$$

Operation: Raise to the power $\frac{1}{2}$.

$$y^2 = \exp^{10} \quad \Rightarrow \quad (y^2)^{\frac{1}{2}} = \pm\left(\exp^{10}\right)^{\frac{1}{2}}$$

Simplifying,

$$y^{2*\frac{1}{2}} = \pm\exp^{10*\frac{1}{2}}$$
$$\Rightarrow y = \pm\exp^5$$

We could use a calculator to determine a numerical value for $\pm\exp^5$ if we were so inclined.

Example 2.8 (Solving for a Variable):
Task: Given $\frac{1}{x} + 3x = \frac{6}{x}$, solve for x.

Answer: In order to simplify the problem, we will first recognize that $\frac{1}{x} = x^{-1}$ and $\frac{6}{x} = 6x^{-1}$. Thus, our problem can be rewritten

$$x^{-1} + 3x = 6x^{-1}$$

We will now solve for x using the following operations and the corresponding simplifications they allow:

Operation: Multiply by x.

$$x^{-1} + 3x = 6x^{-1} \Rightarrow x^{-1}x + 3xx = 6x^{-1}x$$

Simplifying,

$$x^{-1+1} + 3x^{1+1} = 6x^{-1+1}$$
$$\Rightarrow 1 + 3x^2 = 6$$

Operation: Subtract by 1.

$$1 + 3x^2 = 6 \quad \Rightarrow \quad 1 + 3x^2 - 1 = 6 - 1$$
$$\Rightarrow 3x^2 = 5$$

Operation: Multiply by 3^{-1} (in other words, divide by 3).

$$3x^2 = 5 \quad \Rightarrow \quad 3^{-1}3x^2 = 3^{-1}5$$
$$\Rightarrow x^2 = \frac{5}{3}$$

Operation: Raise to the power $\frac{1}{2}$.

$$x^2 = \frac{5}{3} \quad \Rightarrow \quad (x^2)^{\frac{1}{2}} = \left(\frac{5}{3}\right)^{\frac{1}{2}}$$

Simplifying,

$$x^{2*\frac{1}{2}} = \left(\frac{5}{3}\right)^{\frac{1}{2}}$$
$$\Rightarrow x = \sqrt{\frac{5}{3}}$$

2.1.6 Solving for Multiple Variables

Solving for multiple variables in multiple equations is not much more difficult than solving for one variable in a single equation. Essentially, it requires solving a series of single-variable equations. The specific steps are:

1. Select an equation and a variable. Solve for that variable in that equation.

2. Plug the solution to that variable into the remaining equations.

3. Select another equation and another variable. Solve for that variable in that equation. Plug the solution to that variable into the remaining equations.

4. Repeat the process until you are left with a single equation and a single variable. Solve for that final variable.

5. Plug the solution to the final variable into the remaining solutions. Solve the penultimate (second to last) solution to solve for the penultimate variable.

6. Repeat this process until all variables have been solved.

7. Check your work by plugging your solutions into the original equations.

Example 2.9 (Solving for Multiple Variables):
Task: Solve for x_1, x_2, and x_3 given the equalities:

$$2x_1 + x_2 + x_3 = 5$$
$$x_1 + x_2 + x_3 = 3$$
$$x_1 + x_2 - x_3 = 4$$

Answer:

1. **Select an equation and a variable. Solve for that variable in that equation.** We will start by selecting the first equation and solving for x_1. Using the techniques for solving a single equation for a single variable, we find

$$x_1 = \frac{5 - x_2 - x_3}{2}$$

2. **Plug the solution to that variable into the remaining equations.** Plugging our solution for x_1 into the remaining two equations, we find

$$\frac{5 - x_2 - x_3}{2} + x_2 + x_3 = 3$$
$$\frac{5 - x_2 - x_3}{2} + x_2 - x_3 = 4$$

3. **Select another equation and another variable. Solve for that variable in that equation. Plug the solution to that variable into the remaining equations.** We will select the second equation and solve for x_2. Using the techniques for solving a single equation for a single variable, we find

$$x_2 = 1 - x_3$$

Plugging this into the final equation, we find

$$\frac{5 - (1 - x_3) - x_3}{2} + (1 - x_3) - x_3 = 4$$

4. **Repeat the process until you are left with a single equation and a single variable. Solve for that final variable.** Note we have only one equation left and one variable. Solving this equation for x_3, we find

$$x_3 = -\frac{1}{2}$$

5. **Plug the solution to the final variable into the remaining solutions. Solve the penultimate (second to last) solution to solve for the penultimate variable.** Recall our solutions were

$$x_1 = \frac{5 - x_2 - x_3}{2}$$
$$x_2 = 1 - x_3$$

Plugging in $x_3 = -\frac{1}{2}$,

$$x_1 = \frac{5 - x_2 - (-\frac{1}{2})}{2}$$
$$x_2 = 1 - (-\frac{1}{2})$$

Solving the penultimate solution, we find $x_2 = \frac{3}{2}$.

6. **Repeat this process until all variables have been solved.** Plugging $x_2 = \frac{3}{2}$ into the final solution,

$$x_1 = \frac{5 - \frac{3}{2} - (-\frac{1}{2})}{2}$$

Solving this equation, $x_1 = 2$. Thus, our final solution is

$$x_1 = 2$$
$$x_2 = \frac{3}{2}$$
$$x_3 = -\frac{1}{2}$$

7. **Check your work by plugging in your solutions to the original equations.** Plugging these values into the original equalities,

$$2*2 + \frac{3}{2} + (-\frac{1}{2}) = 5$$
$$2 + \frac{3}{2} + (-\frac{1}{2}) = 3$$
$$2 + \frac{3}{2} - (-\frac{1}{2}) = 4$$

Since the equalities hold, we have correctly solved the system of equations.

While this technique will always work if a solution exists, it is important to realize this might not always be the case. Consider the system of equations

$$
\begin{aligned}
x_1 + x_2 &= 1 \\
x_1 + x_2 &= 2
\end{aligned}
$$

It should be obvious that there are no values of x_1 and x_2 such that $x_1 + x_2$ equals both 1 and 2 simultaneously. In such cases, there is nothing we can do besides state that no solution exists.

In addition, note that while this technique will always ensure the correct answer, it is not always the most efficient method. Consider the following example.

Example 2.10 (Solving for Multiple Variables):
   Task: Solve for x_1, x_2, and x_3 given the equalities:

$$
\begin{aligned}
x_1 + 2x_2 - x_3 &= 5 \\
-x_1 - x_2 + x_3 &= -1 \\
x_2 + x_3 &= 2
\end{aligned}
$$

Answer: We could correctly use the above technique to solve this system of equations. However, there is a faster method. It relies on the fact that adding two equations together will maintain the equality. The reason stems from the fact that if $A = B$ and $C = D$, then $A + C = B + D$. If we use this fact and add the first two equations together, we find

$$
\begin{array}{rcl}
x_1 + 2x_2 - x_3 & = & 5 \\
+ & & + \\
-x_1 - x_2 + x_3 & = & -1 \\
\hline
x_1 + 2x_2 - x_3 + (-x_1 - x_2 + x_3) & = & 5 + (-1)
\end{array}
$$

Simplifying this equality, we immediately find that $x_2 = 4$. We can then plug this directly into the third equation to find

$$
4 + x_3 = 2
$$

Simplifying, this tell us $x_3 = -2$. Finally, we can plug this into the first equation to find

$$x_1 + 2(4) - (-2) = 5$$

which tells us $x_1 = -5$. Thus, our final solution is

$$
\begin{aligned}
x_1 &= -5 \\
x_2 &= 4 \\
x_3 &= -2
\end{aligned}
$$

Checking our work,

$$
\begin{aligned}
-5 + 2(4) - (-2) &= 5 \\
-(-5) - 4 + (-2) &= -1 \\
4 + (-2) &= 2
\end{aligned}
$$

To know the most efficient manner to approach a problem simply takes practice. If you would like additional practice performing algebraic manipulations, please refer to an introductory algebra book such as Huettenmueller (2003).

2.2 Derivative - Single Variable

2.2.1 Derivative - Definition

Because we are more concerned with "how calculus can be used to represent Economic behavior" as opposed to the rigorous treatment of the underlying mathematical concepts, we will bypass the formal treatment of derivatives involving limit definitions, and will instead focus on its intuitive meaning and techniques to solve for a derivative. Consider the function shown in Figure 2.1.

At point a, the value of the function is $f(a)$ (labeled P in the figure). At point x, the value of the function is $f(x)$ (labeled Q in the figure). Consider the secant line connecting the two points P and Q. The slope of this line is equal to $\frac{f(x)-f(a)}{x-a}$. This is the standard formula for "rise over run", which is the amount the function changes per a unit change in the parameter value (in this case, the x value). Let us now consider the slope of the secant line between P and Q as we move Q closer to P, as shown in Figure 2.2.

As seen in the Figure, the slope of the secant line approaches the slope of the line tangent to the function at point P, labeled "t" in the Figure. In other words, if we

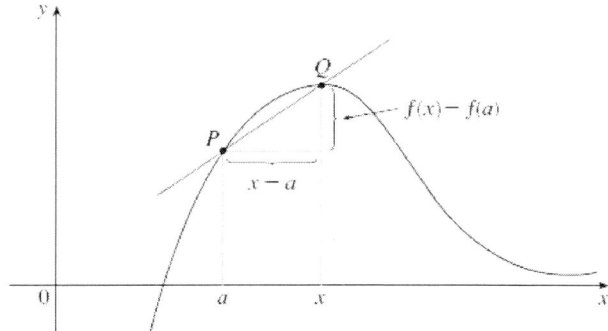

Figure 2.1: Secant Line between points P and Q

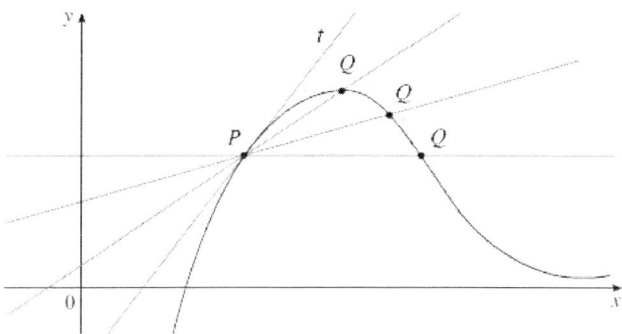

Figure 2.2: Secant Line as Q approaches P

can determine the slope of the secant line at points extremely close to P, we will have determined the slope of the tangent line to the function at P. This is exactly what the derivative tells us.

Definition 2.1 (Derivative):
The *derivative* of a function, $f(x)$, at a given point, P, is

1. The slope of the secant line between P and a point infinitely close to P.

2. The slope of the tangent line of $f(x)$ at P.

3. The ratio $\frac{f(x)-f(a)}{x-a}$ where $P = (x, f(x))$ and $(a, f(a))$ is a point infinitely close to P.

4. **(Informal)** The amount $f(x)$ increases as x increases by 1.

5. **(Informal)** The amount $f(x)$ decreases as x decreases by 1.

Note that if the derivative is negative, then $f(x)$ will be decreasing as x is increasing and vice versa. Also note that not every point on every function has a derivative. If, for instance, the function has a "kink" in it (the absolute value function, for instance), then no derivative will exist at the "kink".

Notationally, the derivative of a function can be written in a few ways. Note these are written in functional notation. To determine the derivative at a specific point, P, simply plug P in for x, in the same manner the value of a function at a specific point is determined.

Definition 2.2 (Derivative Notation):
The derivative of a function, $f(x)$, is written

1. $f'(x)$

2. $\frac{df(x)}{dx}$

3. $f_x(x)$

Since the derivative is itself a function, we can take the derivative of a derivative, the derivative of a derivative of a derivative, etc. These are referred to as the "second derivative, third derivative", etc. The notation for higher order derivatives is similar to that of first-order derivatives.

Definition 2.3 (Higher-Order Derivative Notation):
The higher order derivatives of a function, $f(x)$, are written

1. $f'(x), f''(x), f'''(x), \ldots$

2. $\frac{df(x)}{dx}, \frac{d^2f(x)}{dx^2}, \frac{d^3f(x)}{dx^3}, \ldots$

3. $f_x(x), f_{xx}(x), f_{xxx}(x), \ldots$

As a final note, it is extremely important to intuitively understand what a derivative is. We will repeatedly return to this concept, and a thorough understanding is key to understanding the tools we will be developing. If you would like a more robust treatment of derivatives, please refer to an introductory calculus textbook, such as Krantz (2003).

2.2.2 Derivative - Calculation

While the concept of a derivative can be a bit abstract, calculating a derivative turns out to be reasonably straightforward. In particular, there are a few basic rules of differentiation that will allow you to solve for the derivative of most functions.

2.2.3 Derivative of a Constant

$$\frac{d}{dx}(c) = 0, \text{ where } c \text{ is a constant}$$

In other words, the derivative of a constant is 0. This concept should be obvious given our intuitive definition of a derivative. Consider, for instance, the constant function, $f(x) = 5$. Intuitively, we know a derivative is the amount $f(x)$ increases as x increases by 1. In this case, $f(x)$ never changes. It always equals 5. Thus, increasing x by 1 causes no change in $f(x)$. Thus, the derivative equals 0.

2.2.4 Derivatives of Powers of x (The Power Rule)

$$\frac{d}{dx}(x^n) = nx^{n-1}$$

Example 2.11 (Derivatives of Powers of x):
  Task: What is the derivative of x^9?

Answer: Using the above equation and recognizing $n = 9$,

$$\frac{d}{dx}(x^9) = 9x^8$$

One extremely important aspect of the Power Rule is that it shows us how to handle fractions. Specifically, recall that $\frac{1}{x^n} = x^{-n}$. For instance, $\frac{1}{x} = x^{-1}$, $\frac{1}{x^2} = x^{-2}$, etc. This is exactly the form required by the Product Rule, which means we can directly apply it as shown in the following example.

Example 2.12 (Derivatives of Powers of x):
   Task: What is the derivative of $\frac{1}{x^2}$?

   Answer: Recall that $\frac{1}{x^2} = x^{-2}$. Using the Product Rule with $n = -2$,

$$\frac{d}{dx}(x^{-2}) = -2x^{-3} = -\frac{2}{x^3}$$

2.2.5   Derivatives of a Sum (The Sum Rule)

$$\frac{d}{dx}(f(x) \pm g(x)) = \frac{df(x)}{dx} \pm \frac{dg(x)}{dx}$$

In other words, the derivative of a sum of functions is the sum of the derivatives of the functions.

Example 2.13 (Derivatives of a Sum):
   Task: What is the derivative of $x^9 + 5$?

   Answer: The derivative of the sum of the two functions, $f(x) = x^9$ and $g(x) = 5$ is simply the sum of the derivatives of the two functions. We have already established that $\frac{d}{dx}(x^9) = 9x^8$ and $\frac{d}{dx}(5) = 0$. Thus,

$$\frac{d}{dx}(x^9 + 5) = 9x^8 + 0 = 9x^8$$

Example 2.14 (Derivatives of a Sum):
Task: What is the derivative of $x^3 + \sqrt{x}$?

Answer: The derivative of the sum of the two functions, $f(x) = x^3$ and $g(x) = x^{1/2}$ is simply the sum of the derivatives of the two functions. Using the power rule, we know that $\frac{d}{dx}(x^3) = 3x^2$. By recognizing $\sqrt{x} = x^{1/2}$, the power rule tells us and $\frac{d}{dx}(x^{1/2}) = \frac{1}{2}x^{-1/2}$. Thus,

$$\frac{d}{dx}(x^3 + \sqrt{x}) = 3x^2 + \frac{1}{2}x^{-1/2} = 3x^2 + \frac{1}{2\sqrt{x}}$$

2.2.6 Derivatives of a Product (The Product Rule)

$$[f(x)g(x)]' = f'(x)g(x) + f(x)g'(x)$$

Example 2.15 (Derivatives of a Product):
Task: Using the product rule, show that the derivative of x^3x^2 is the same as the derivative of x^5.

Answer: Using the power rule, we know $\frac{d}{dx}(x^5) = 5x^4$. To determine if the derivative of x^3x^2 is the same, we will use the product rule with $f(x) = x^3$ and $g(x) = x^2$. Note $f'(x) = 3x^2$ and $g'(x) = 2x$. Plugging these values into the product rule,

$$
\begin{aligned}
[f(x)g(x)]' &= f'(x)g(x) + f(x)g'(x) \\
\left[x^3x^2\right]' &= (3x^2)(x^2) + (x^3)(2x) \\
&= 3x^4 + 2x^4 \\
&= 5x^4
\end{aligned}
$$

2.2.7 Derivatives of the Exponential and Natural Log Functions

Quite possibly the easiest rule of differentiation is

$$\frac{d}{dx}(e^x) = e^x$$

In other words, the derivative of the exponential function is the exponential function itself. The derivative of the natural log function, on the other hand, is

$$\frac{d}{dx}(\ln(x)) = \frac{1}{x}$$

2.2.8 Derivatives of Composite Functions (The Chain Rule)

$$[f(x) \circ g(x)]' = f'(g(x))g'(x)$$

By far, the Chain Rule is the most important rule when taking derivatives. It can be used to derive the power rule, the product rule, and, as we will see later, the quotient rule. Generally, the Chain Rule is the most troublesome for inexperienced calculus practitioners, and even occasionally for highly experienced users. The trouble generally stems from two areas. First, students tend to not understand what a composite function is. As such, it is difficult to recognize what function plays the role of $f(x)$ and what function plays the role of $g(x)$ in the above equation. Second, students tend to make mistakes utilizing the above equation, especially when it comes to substituting $g(x)$ into $f(x)$.

Luckily, the Chain Rule can be broken down into two fundamental concepts. If you are able to master these, you will be able to take the derivative of any "well-behaved" function.

Concept 1: Composite Functions

Consider the following scenario:

> You make extra money for college by working at an animal kennel. While performing your daily duties, you have noticed a strange occurance. Specifically, you have noticed that every time you clap your hands, a specific dog barks twice. You also noticed that every time this dog barks once, a neighboring cat meows three times. As you are changing the cat's litter box, you wonder to yourself, "If I clap my hands once, how many times will this cat meow?". Being that you find derivatives fascinating, you notice that this question is extremely similar to the question "If I increase my level of hand claps by 1, how much will the level of cat meows increase?". And having just read Definition 2.1, you know that this question is the informal interpretation of the question "What is the derivative of cat meows with respect to hand claps?".

Hopefully, without too much effort, you are able to determine that each hand clap results in six cat meows. The method you used to determine this is the intuitive interpretation of the Chain Rule. Specifically, you first determined that an

additional hand clap would result in two additional dog barks. You then determined that each additional dog bark would result in three additional cat meows.
Finally, to determine how many cat meows would result from an extra hand clap,
you just multipied these two values together. Or, in a (slightly) more elegant
form:

$$\frac{\text{Change In Cat Meow}}{\text{Change In Hand Clap}} = \frac{\text{Change In Cat Meow}}{\text{Change In Dog Bark}} \cdot \frac{\text{Change In Dog Bark}}{\text{Change In Hand Clap}}$$

Hoefully you have an intuitive understanding of the above equation. If not, note
that mathematically "Change in Dog Bark" cancels out of the fractions, making
the two sides of the equations identical. We can write the above equation even
more elegantly as

$$\frac{\Delta \text{ Cat Meow}}{\Delta \text{ Hand Clap}} = \frac{\Delta \text{ Cat Meow}}{\Delta \text{ Dog Bark}} \cdot \frac{\Delta \text{ Dog Bark}}{\Delta \text{ Hand Clap}}$$

And finally, if we recognize this is the intuitive definition of a derivative and
assume everything stays roughly the same if I am able to increase my level of
hand claps by a very small amount, then we can write

$$\frac{d \text{ Cat Meow}}{d \text{ Hand Clap}} = \frac{d \text{ Cat Meow}}{d \text{ Dog Bark}} \cdot \frac{d \text{ Dog Bark}}{d \text{ Hand Clap}}$$

Let's put this to the test. The above scenario can be mathematically described by
the equations

$$m(b) = 3b$$
$$b(c) = 2c$$

where $m(b)$ is the number of cat meows (as a function of barks), b is the number
of dog barks (as a function of claps), and c is the number of hand claps.

Note that since barks are a function of claps, the number of cat meows can also
be written as a function of claps. Specifically,

$$m(b) = 3b$$
$$m(c) = 3(2c) = 6c$$

It is clear that $\frac{dm(c)}{dc} = 6$. What is more important is that we get the same result if we use our above equation

$$\frac{d \text{ Cat Meow}}{d \text{ Hand Clap}} = \frac{d \text{ Cat Meow}}{d \text{ Dog Bark}} \cdot \frac{d \text{ Dog Bark}}{d \text{ Hand Clap}}$$

$$\frac{dm(c)}{dc} = \frac{dm(b)}{db}\frac{db(c)}{dc}$$

$$\frac{dm(c)}{dc} = \frac{d(3b)}{db}\frac{d(2c)}{dc}$$

$$\frac{dm(c)}{dc} = (3)(2) = 6$$

Let's use this concept to solve for more "difficult" composite functions.

Example 2.16 (Chain Rule Concept 1):
Task: What is the derivative of $\ln(c^2)$ with respect to c?

Answer: This might look different than our cats and dogs example, but at its core we use the same methodology. To show this, let us assume that the cats and dogs in our example behave according to the following functions

$$m(b) = \ln(b)$$
$$b(c) = c^2$$

As above, since barks are a function of claps, the number of cat meows can also be written as a function of claps. Specifically,

$$m(b) = \ln(b)$$
$$m(c) = \ln(c^2)$$

In this case, it is not immediately or intuitively clear what $\frac{dm(c)}{dc}$ should equal. However, if we use the Concept we just developed,

$$\frac{dm(c)}{dc} = \frac{dm(b)}{db}\frac{db(c)}{dc}$$

$$\frac{dm(c)}{dc} = \frac{d(\ln(b))}{db}\frac{d(c^2)}{dc}$$

$$\frac{dm(c)}{dc} = \frac{1}{b} \cdot 2c = \frac{2c}{b}$$

and recognizing $b = c^2$,

$$\frac{dm(c)}{dc} = \frac{2c}{c^2} = \frac{2}{c}$$

Example 2.17 (Chain Rule Concept 1):
Task: What is the derivative of $h(x) = \ln(x^3 + 2)$ with respect to x?

Answer: Moving away from the cats and dogs example and using the standard notation of the Chain Rule,

$$\begin{aligned} f(g) &= \ln(g) \\ g(x) &= x^3 + 2 \end{aligned}$$

Using Concept 1,

$$\begin{aligned} \frac{dh(x)}{dx} &= \frac{df(g)}{dg}\frac{dg(x)}{dx} \\ \frac{dh(x)}{dx} &= \frac{d(\ln(g))}{dg}\frac{d(x^3 + 2)}{dx} \\ \frac{dh(x)}{dx} &= \frac{1}{g} \cdot 3x^2 = \frac{3x^2}{g} \end{aligned}$$

and recognizing $g = x^3 + 2$,

$$\frac{dh(x)}{dx} = \frac{3x^2}{x^3 + 2}$$

Let's now extend our example to assume that whenever a cat meows, a bird chirps 5 times. Without going through the formal steps, it should be clear that one hand clap will result in 30 bird chirps. It should also be fairly clear that our Concept can easily be extended to composite functions of composite functions as demonstrated in the next example.

Example 2.18 (Chain Rule Concept 1):
   Task: What is the derivative of $l(x) = \ln\left((x^4 + 7)^2\right)$ with respect to x?

Answer: Using the same Concept,

$$
\begin{aligned}
h(f) &= \ln(f) \\
f(g) &= g^2 \\
g(x) &= x^4 + 7
\end{aligned}
$$

Using Concept 1,

$$
\begin{aligned}
\frac{dl(x)}{dx} &= \frac{dh(f)}{df}\frac{df(g)}{dg}\frac{dg(x)}{dx} \\
\frac{dl(x)}{dx} &= \frac{d\left(\ln(f)\right)}{df}\frac{d(g^2)}{dg}\frac{d(x^4+7)}{dx} \\
\frac{dl(x)}{dx} &= \frac{1}{f}\cdot 2g \cdot 4x^3 = \frac{8gx^3}{f}
\end{aligned}
$$

and recognizing $g = x^4 + 7$ and $f = g^2 = (x^4 + 7)^2$,

$$
\frac{dl(x)}{dx} = \frac{8(x^4+7)x^3}{(x^4+7)^2} = \frac{8x^3}{x^4+7}
$$

If you are unsure of this Concept, you should write out the functions as we have done in these examples. As you gain confidence, you will find you no longer need to write out the explicit functions.

Concept 2: Multiple Instances of the Choice Variable

As the intuition for Concept 2 is more subtle than Concept 1, we will instead skip straight to the result. Specifically,

> *If your choice variable shows up multiple places, take the derivative of each place separately, **while keeping the other instances constant** then add everything up.*

Essentially, this Concept states that if you have multiple instances of your choice variable, deal with each instance as if you are taking a partial derivatiee with respect to only that instance of the variable, then add up all the "partials".[1] If you have not been introduced to partial derivatives, you mind find it useful to revisit this Concept after reading Section 2.4.

In the next two examples, we will demonstrate that the Power Rule and Product Rule are specific applications of this Concept. You should check for yourself that this also holds for the Sum Rule.

Example 2.19 (Chain Rule Concept 2):
Task: Find the derivative of $f(x) = x^3$ with respect to x using Concept 2.

Answer: Note $f(x) = x^3$ can be written $f(x) = x \cdot x \cdot x$. We will use the above Concept on each instance of x.

There are three instances of x. We need to take the partial with respect to each term, while keeping the other terms constant. For the first instance of x, it helps to write the function as $f(x) = \mathbf{x} \cdot x^2$. Taking the partial with respect to $\mathbf{x}$ while keeping x^2 constant gives us x^2 (since the partial of $\mathbf{x}$ times a constantt is just the constant itself). For the second instance of x, it helps to write the function as $f(x) = x \cdot \mathbf{x} \cdot x$. Rearranging, we once again have $f(x) = \mathbf{x} \cdot x^2$. Taking the partial with respect to $\mathbf{x}$ while keeping x^2 constant once again gives us x^2. Not surprisingly, for the third instance we also get a partial equaling x^2.

Concept 2 states that once we have taken the partial derivative of each term, we must then add them to find the derivative of the original function. Adding up the three "partials", we have $f'(x) = x^2 + x^2 + x^2 = 3x^2$, exactly as predicted by the Power Rule.

Example 2.20 (Chain Rule Concept 2):
Task: Find the derivative of $f(x) = x^2 \ln(x)$ with respect to x without using the Product Rule.

Answer: As before, we will use Concept 2 on each instance of x.

There are two terms[2] containing x, x^2 and $\ln(x)$. We need to take the partial with respect to each term, while keeping the other terms constant. For the first instance of x, it helps to write the function as $f(x) = \mathbf{x}^2 \ln(x)$. Taking the

---

[1] I will severely abuse the formal definition of "partial derivative" throughout this section as the intuition is extremely illustrative.

partial of $\mathbf{x}^2$ with respect to $\mathbf{x}$ while keeping $\ln(x)$ constant gives us $2x\ln(x)$ (since the partial of x^2 times a constant is just the constant times the derivative of x^2, which is $2x$). For the second instance of x, it helps to write the function as $f(x) = x^2\ln(\mathbf{x})$. Taking the partial of $\ln(\mathbf{x})$ with respect to $\mathbf{x}$ while keeping x^2 constant gives us $x^2 \frac{1}{x} = x$.

Concept 2 states that once we have taken the partial derivative of each term, we must then add them to find the derivative of the original function. Adding up the two "partials", we have $f'(x) = 2x\ln(x) + x$, exactly as predicted by the Product Rule.

Example 2.21 (Chain Rule Concept 2):
  Task: Find the derivative of $f(x) = x^2\ln(x) + x$ with respect to x without using the Product Rule.

  Answer: As before, we will use Concept 2 on each instance of x.

  $f(x)$ is identical to the last example, with one additional instance of x (the "$+x$" at the end). We just calculated the "partial" derivative of $x^2\ln(x)$. As such, we need only determine the partial with respect to the last x while keeping the other instances constant and add that result to the result from our last Example. As before, it helps to write the function as $f(x) = x^2\ln(x) + \mathbf{x}$. Taking the partial of $\mathbf{x}$ with respect to $\mathbf{x}$ while keeping $x^2\ln(x)$ constant gives us 1. (since the partial of x plus a constant is just the the derivative of x, which is 1). Please make sure you understand this step. Oftentimes students are hesitant to treat a "complicated" function as a constant in this scenario, since the derivative of a constant is 0. However, this is absolutely correct.

  Concept 2 states that once we have taken the partial derivative of each term, we must then add them to find the derivative of the original function. As shown in the last example, the first two instances of x give us $2x\ln(x) + x$. Adding the term we just calculated, we find $f'(x) = 2x\ln(x) + x + 1$

---

[2]If you write $f(x) = x \cdot x \cdot \ln(x)$, you will note that there are actually three instances of x. However, as we knew the derivative of x^2, we shortened the process instead of dealing with each instance separately. You should check that if you applied Concept 2 to each instance of x (x, x, and $\ln(x)$), you would get an identical answer.

Putting the Concepts Together

To take the derivative of any "well-behaved" function, you need only Concepts 1 and 2. Thus, instead of memorizing every derivative rule, you need only these two Concepts. That being said, feel free to use any of the Derivative Rules if it is faster for you. As they are all based on the same concepts, they will all give you correct answers if applied correctly.

Example 2.22 (Chain Rule):
Task: Find the derivative of $f(x) = x^2 \ln(x^3 + x^2 - 1)$ with respect to x without using the Product Rule.

Answer: We have two terms containing x, x^2 and $\ln(x^3 + x^2 - 1)$. We will use Concept 2 on each term, at which point we will need to also use Concept 1.

We need to take the partial with respect to each term, while keeping the other terms constant. For the first instance of x, it helps to write the function as $f(x) = \mathbf{x^2} \ln(x^3 + x^2 - 1)$. Taking the partial of $\mathbf{x^2}$ with respect to $\mathbf{x}$ while keeping $\ln(x^3 + x^2 - 1)$ constant gives us $2x \ln(x^3 + x^2 - 1)$. (since the partial of x^2 times a constant is just $2x$ times the constant).

For the second instance of x, it helps to write the function as $f(x) = x^2 \ln(\mathbf{x^3 + x^2 - 1})$ Taking the partial of $\ln(\mathbf{x^3 + x^2 - 1})$ with respect to $\mathbf{x}$ while keeping x^2 constant gives us x^2 times the derivative of $\ln(x^3 + x^2 - 1)$. It is at this point that we need Concept 1, as $\ln(x^3 + x^2 - 1)$ is a composite function.

$$
\begin{aligned}
f(g) &= \ln(g) \\
g(x) &= x^3 + x^2 - 1
\end{aligned}
$$

Using Concept 1,

$$
\begin{aligned}
\frac{d \ln(x^3 + x^2 - 1)}{dx} &= \frac{df(g)}{dg} \frac{dg(x)}{dx} \\
\frac{d \ln(x^3 + x^2 - 1)}{dx} &= \frac{d(\ln(g))}{dg} \frac{d(x^3 + x^2 - 1)}{dx} \\
\frac{d \ln(x^3 + x^2 - 1)}{dx} &= \frac{1}{g} \cdot 3x^2 + 2x = \frac{3x^2 + 2x}{g}
\end{aligned}
$$

and recognizing $g = x^3 + x^2 - 1$,

$$\frac{d\ln(x^3 + x^2 - 1)}{dx} = \frac{3x^2 + 2x}{x^3 + x^2 - 1}$$

Which means that the "partial" of the second instance of x is

$$x^2 \frac{d\ln(x^3 + x^2 - 1)}{dx} = x^2 \frac{3x^2 + 2x}{x^3 + x^2 - 1}$$

Now that we know the "partial" of the second x term, we can once again refer to Concept 2, which states that once we have taken the partial derivative of each term, we must then add them to find the derivative of the original function. Adding up the two "partials", we have $f'(x) = 2x \ln(x^3 + x^2 - 1) + x^2 \frac{3x^2 + 2x}{x^3 + x^2 - 1}$.

Example 2.23 (Chain Rule):
  Task: Find the derivative of $f(x) = \ln\left(x \exp(5x^2)\right)$ with respect to x.

  Answer: We have two terms containing x, x and $\exp(5x^2)$. We will use Concept 2 on each term, at which point we will need to also use Concept 1.

We need to take the partial with respect to each term, while keeping the other terms constant. For the first instance of x, it helps to write the function as $f(x) = \ln\left(\mathbf{x}\exp(5x^2)\right)$. Taking the "partial" with respect to $\mathbf{x}$ requires us to use Concept 1.

$$f(g) = \ln(g)$$
$$g(x) = \mathbf{x}\exp(5x^2)$$

Using Concept 1,

$$\frac{d\ln\left(\mathbf{x}\exp(5x^2)\right)}{d\mathbf{x}} = \frac{df(g)}{dg}\frac{dg(x)}{dx}$$

$$\frac{d\ln\left(\mathbf{x}\exp(5x^2)\right)}{d\mathbf{x}} = \frac{d\left(\ln(g)\right)}{dg}\frac{d\mathbf{x}\exp(5x^2)}{d\mathbf{x}}$$

$$\frac{d\ln\left(\mathbf{x}\exp(5x^2)\right)}{d\mathbf{x}} = \frac{1}{g}\cdot\exp(5x^2)$$

and recognizing $g = \mathbf{x}\exp(5x^2)$,

$$\frac{d \ln\left(x \exp(5x^2)\right)}{dx} = \frac{\exp(5x^2)}{x \exp(5x^2)} = \frac{1}{x}$$

For the second instance of x, it helps to write the function as $f(x) = \ln\left(x\exp(5x^2)\right)$ Taking the "partial" with respect to $\mathbf{x}$ requires us to use Concept 1.

$$
\begin{aligned}
h(f) &= \ln(f) \\
f(g) &= x\exp(g) \text{ Recall in the second instance, this } x \text{ is a constant...} \\
g(x) &= 5x^2 \text{ and this } \mathbf{x} \text{ is the variable of interest.}
\end{aligned}
$$

Using Concept 1,

$$
\begin{aligned}
\frac{d\ln\left(x\exp(5x^2)\right)}{dx} &= \frac{dh(f)}{df}\frac{df(g)}{dg}\frac{dg(x)}{dx} \\
\frac{df(x) = \ln\left(x\exp(5x^2)\right)}{dx} &= \frac{d(\ln(f))}{df}\frac{dx\exp(g)}{dg}\frac{d5x^2}{dx} \\
\frac{df(x) = \ln\left(x\exp(5x^2)\right)}{dx} &= \frac{1}{f}\cdot x\exp(g)\cdot 10x = \frac{10x^2\exp(g)}{f}
\end{aligned}
$$

In the third step, recall the derivative of $\exp(g)$ times a constant with respect to g is $\exp(g)$ times the constant. Recognizing $g = 5x^2$ and $f(g) = x\exp(g) = x\exp(5x^2)$, we then determine

$$\frac{df(x) = \ln\left(x\exp(5x^2)\right)}{dx} = \frac{10x^2\exp(5x^2)}{x\exp(5x^2)} = 10x$$

Now that we know the "partial" of the second x term, we can once again refer to Concept 2, which states that once we have taken the partial derivative of each term, we must then add them to find the derivative of the original function. Adding up the two "partials", we have $f'(x) = \frac{1}{x} + 10x$.

2.2.9 Derivatives of a Quotient (The Quotient Rule)

$$\left[\frac{m(x)}{n(x)}\right]' = \frac{n(x)m'(x) - m(x)n'(x)}{n(x)^2}$$

The Quotient Rule "looks ugly", and is far from straight-forward. Luckily, there is absolutely no reason to memorize this equation. Like the Product Rule, Sum Rule, and Power Rule, we can use the Chain Rule to "back-out" the Quotient Rule. Specifically, we can recognize that $\frac{m(x)}{n(x)} = m(x)n(x)^{-1}$, then use the Chain Rule.

Example 2.24 († Derivatives of a Quotient):
Task: Using the Chain Rule, show that the derivative of $m(x)n(x)^{-1}$ is equivalent to $\frac{n(x)m'(x)-m(x)n'(x)}{n(x)^2}$, as given by the Quotient Rule.

Answer: There are two terms containing x, $m(x)$ and $n(x)^{-1}$. We need to take the partial with respect to each term, while keeping the other terms constant. For the first instance of x, it helps to write the function as $f(x) = \mathbf{m(x)}n(x)^{-1}$. Taking the partial of $\mathbf{m(x)}$ with respect to $\mathbf{x}$ while keeping $n(x)^{-1}$ constant gives us $m'(x)n(x)^{-1}$ (since the partial of $m(x)$ times a constant is just the constant times the derivative of $m(x)$, which is $m'(x)$). For the second instance of x, it helps to write the function as $f(x) = m(x)\mathbf{n(x)^{-1}}$. Taking the partial of $\mathbf{n(x)^{-1}}$ with respect to $\mathbf{x}$ while keeping $m(x)$ constant gives us $m(x)\frac{d\left(n(x)^{-1}\right)}{dx}$. To find $\frac{d\left(n(x)^{-1}\right)}{dx}$, we can use Concept 1 of the Chain Rule.

$$f(g) = g^{-1}$$
$$g(x) = n(x)$$

Using Concept 1,

$$\frac{d\left(\ln(n(x)^{-1})\right)}{dx} = \frac{df(g)}{dg}\frac{dg(x)}{dx}$$
$$\frac{d\left(\ln(n(x)^{-1})\right)}{dx} = \frac{d(g^{-1})}{dg}\frac{d(n(x))}{dx}$$
$$\frac{d\left(\ln(n(x)^{-1})\right)}{dx} = (-1)g^{-2}n'(x)$$

and recognizing $g(x) = n(x)$,

$$\frac{d\left(\ln(n(x)^{-1})\right)}{dx} = (-1)n(x)^{-2}\cdot n'(x)$$

Which means that the "partial" of the second x term is $m(x)(-1)n(x)^{-2}n'(x)$.

Concept 2 states that once we have taken the partial derivative of each term, we must then add them to find the derivative of the original function. Adding up the two "partials", we have

$$f'(x) = m'(x)n(x)^{-1} + m(x)(-1)n(x)^{-2}n'(x)$$

or, in fractional form,

$$f'(x) = \frac{m'(x)}{n(x)} - \frac{m(x)n'(x)}{n(x)^2}$$

or, combining terms via a common denominator,

$$f'(x) = \frac{m'(x)n(x) - m(x)n'(x)}{n(x)^2}$$

which is the Quotient Rule.

Note that while using the Chain Rule to solve for the Quotient Rule took a little bit of work, using it on specific functions is quite easy. This example also illustrates the fact that you can save time by using Derivative Rules in combination with other Rules. As all the Rules are based on the same Concepts, if applied correctly you will calculate a correct derivative.

Example 2.25 (Derivatives of a Quotient):
Task: What is the derivative of $\frac{x}{e^x}$ with respect to x? Do not use the Quotient Rule.

Answer: We will use the Product Rule with $f(x) = x$ and $g(x) = e^{-x}$ (recall this is a specific instance of the Chain Rule).

$f'(x) = 1$. Using the Chain Rule, we know $g'(x) = -e^{-x}$ (verify this for yourself). Plugging these values into the Product Rule,

$$
\begin{aligned}
[f(x)g(x)]' &= f'(x)g(x) + f(x)g'(x) \\
[xe^{-x}]' &= (1)(e^{-x}) + (x)(-e^{-x}) \\
&= \frac{1-x}{e^x}
\end{aligned}
$$

Note this is identical to the result predicted by the Quotient Rule.

2.2.10 Derivatives of Unspecified Functional Forms

The last two examples shows a very important point concerning taking derivatives. In particular, the Derivative Rules work whether functional forms are fully specified or not. When deriving the Quotient Rule, we were able to use the Chain Rule even though we did not know the specific form of $m(x)$ and $n(x)$. The next example does the same.

Example 2.26 († Derivatives of an Unspecified Function):
Task: Using the Chain Rule, find the derivative of $f(p) = pD(p) - C(D(p))$.

Answer: There are three terms containing p, but as the derivative of $pD(p)$ is easily determined using the Product Rule, we will focus on the two terms $pD(p)$ and $C(D(p))$. As before, we need to take the partial with respect to each term, while keeping the other terms constant. For the first instance of p, it helps to write the function as $f(p) = \mathbf{p}\mathbf{D}(\mathbf{p}) - C(D(p))$. Taking the partial of $\mathbf{p}\mathbf{D}(\mathbf{p})$ with respect to $\mathbf{p}$ while keeping $C(D(p))$ constant gives us $pD'(p) + D(p)$ (since the partial of $pD(p)$ minus a constant is just the derivative of $pD(p)$, which we calculated via the Product Rule). For the second instance of p, it helps to write the function as $f(p) = pD(p) - \mathbf{C}(\mathbf{D}(\mathbf{p}))$. Taking the partial of $-\mathbf{C}(\mathbf{D}(\mathbf{p}))$ with respect to $\mathbf{p}$ while keeping $pD(p)$ constant gives us $\dfrac{d\left(-C\left(D(p)\right)\right)}{dp}$. To find $\dfrac{d\left(-C\left(D(p)\right)\right)}{dp}$, we can Concept 1 of the Chain Rule.

$$f(g) = -C(g)$$
$$g(p) = D(p)$$

Using Concept 1,

$$\frac{d\left(-C(D(p))\right)}{dp} = \frac{df(g)}{dg}\frac{dg(p)}{dp}$$

$$\frac{d\left(-C(D(p))\right)}{dp} = \frac{d(-C(g))}{dg}\frac{d(D(p))}{dp}$$

$$\frac{d\left(-C(D(p))\right)}{dp} = -C'(g)D'(p)$$

and recognizing $g(p) = D(p)$,

$$\frac{d\left(-C\left(D(p)\right)\right)}{dp} = -C'\left((D(p))D'(p)\right)$$

Which means that the "partial" of the second p term is $-C'(D(p))D'(p)$.

Concept 2 states that once we have taken the partial derivative of each term, we must then add them to find the derivative of the original function. Adding up the two "partials", we have

$$f'(p) = pD'(p) + D(p) - C'(D(p))D'(p)$$

2.2.11 Additional Practice

Mastering the Derivative Rules, especially the Chain Rule, takes patience and practice. A fantastic resource to help you gain this practice is www.wolframalpha.com. To take derivatives using wolframalpha, Type in "derivative of " then the function of which you would like to take a derivative, as shown in Figure 2.3.

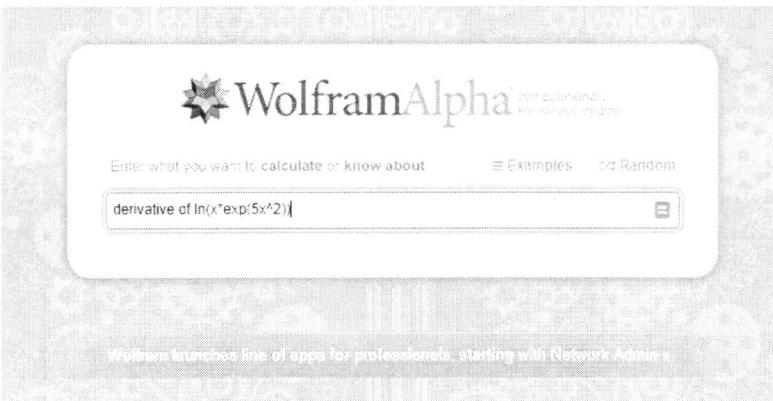

Figure 2.3: www.wolframalpha.com Entry Page

Once you hit "Return" or click the equal sign, www.wolframalpha.com will display the correct derivative as shown in Figure 2.4.

In addition, if you click the Show Steps button, it will give you an indication on how the derivative was calculated using the steps outlined in this Section, as

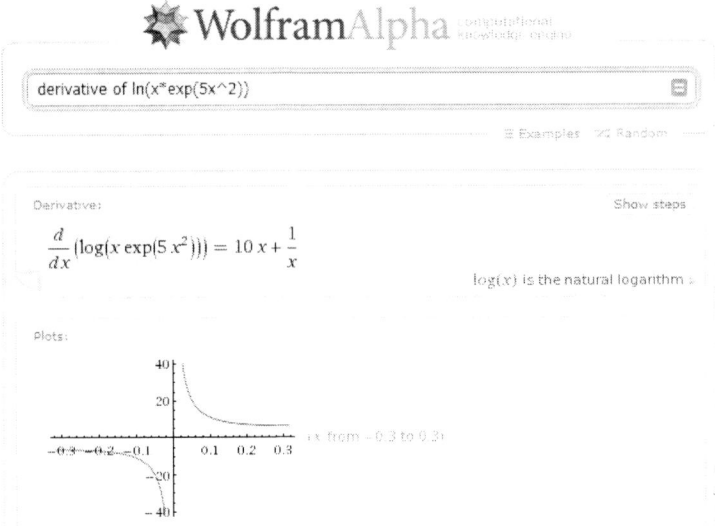

Figure 2.4: www.wolframalpha.com Solution Page

shown in Figure 2.5.

Note if you would like to calculate a partial derivative or if your function is not a function of x, then you need to type "derivative of *function* with respect to *variable*". For instance, "derivative of xy with respect to y" will give you the result $\frac{\partial(xy)}{\partial y} = x$.

Lastly, another great resource is http://khan-academy.appspot.com/. Besides having thousands of instructional videos covering virtually all subject areas, it also allows you to practice math problems at your own pace, while providing step-by-step hints as needed.

2.3 Maximization - Single Variable

The main reason economists place so much emphasis on derivatives lies in the derivative's ability to determine the value that maximizes a function. As an example, consider Microsoft's decision as to how many Xbox's to produce during the holiday season. Assume their profits follow the function shown in figure 2.6.

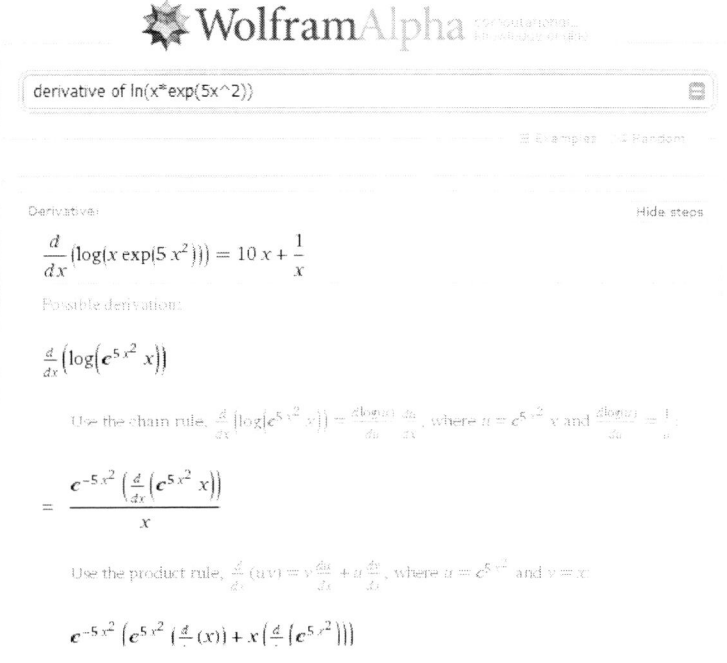

Figure 2.5: www.wolframalpha.com Show Steps

From the picture, it is obvious that profits will be maximized when 300,000 units are produced, resulting in a profit of 9 million dollars. However, what if we took a more realistic view of Microsoft, and recognized that Xbox profits will rely not only on the number of units produced, but also the advertising budget, the number of available Xbox games, the targeted demographics, etc. In addition, the effectiveness of each value depends crucially on the other values. For instance, targeting 15-24 year olds could be extremely effective, but only if the advertising budget is significantly high enough. In such a case, we cannot simply draw a picture and "eyeball" the answer since we can only draw pictures in three dimensions. However, we can use derivatives to perform the mathematical equivalent.

When determining the maximum in Figure 2.6, it should be obvious that we look for the location where the graph "flattens out". If the graph is not flat, we can increase or decrease our value, thereby increasing profits. For instance, consider the profits at 200,000 units. At that point, the profit function is not flat. Instead, it is increasing, implying more units will result in more profits. Thus, 200,000

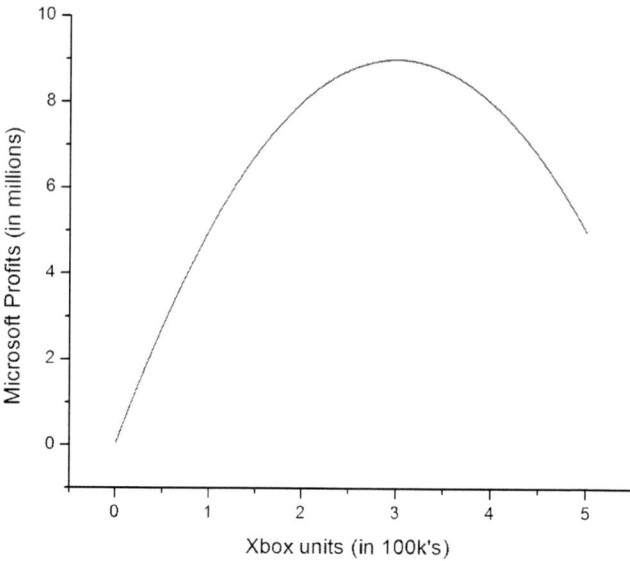

Figure 2.6: Hypothetical Xbox Profits

units cannot be the maximum. At 300,000 units, however, this is not the case.

The mathematical equivalent to looking for the location where the graph "flattens out" is finding the point at which the derivative equals zero. In particular, consider Figure 2.7. At 100,000 units, the derivative (or slope of the tangent line) is extremely steep. More specifically, the value $\frac{f(x)-f(a)}{x-a}$ is large since $f(x)-f(a)$ is large, as shown in the Figure. As we move the 200,000 units, $f(x)-f(a)$ gets considerably smaller, making $\frac{f(x)-f(a)}{x-a}$ considerably smaller. Finally, at 300,000 units, $f(x)-f(a)$ equals zero, making $\frac{f(x)-f(a)}{x-a} = 0$. In other words, the function achieves a maximum at the point where the derivative equals zero. If we performed this exercise starting from 500,000 units and working backwards, we would achieve the same result. In this case, the derivative would start extremely negative at 500,000 units, and become less negative as we move to 300,000 units. Again, at 300,000 units, the derivative would equal zero.

Because the condition where the derivative of a function equals zero is so valuable, it has been given a specific name.

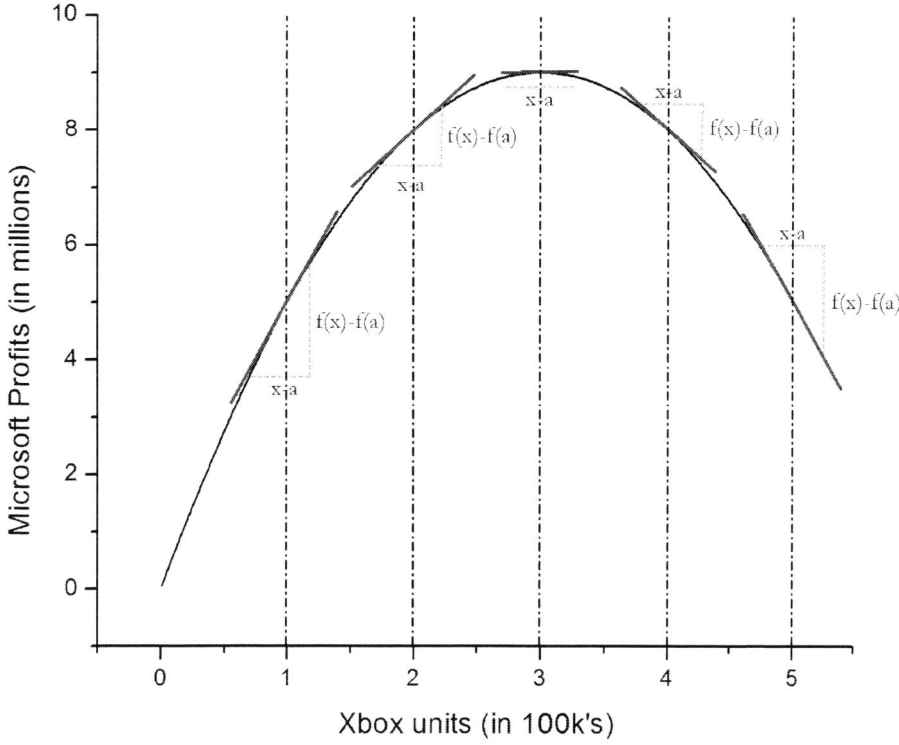

Figure 2.7: Hypothetical Xbox Profits

Definition 2.4 (First Order Condition):
The *first order condition* of a function, $f(x)$, is

1. The condition, $f'(x) = 0$.

2. **Informal:** The condition which holds at the point where $f(x)$ "flattens out".

If a maximum exists, solving the first order condition for x tells us the point at which the function achieves this maximum. Note a solution might not always exist, as in the case shown in Figure 2.8. In this Figure, there is no point where the first order condition holds. Instead, the function is always increasing, implying that Microsoft would always want to sell another Xbox. If, for instance, you claimed that selling 600,000 units would maximize Microsoft's profits, I would argue that selling 600,001 units would increase profits, contradicting you. If the first order condition holds, we call the point that satisfies it an *interior optimum*.

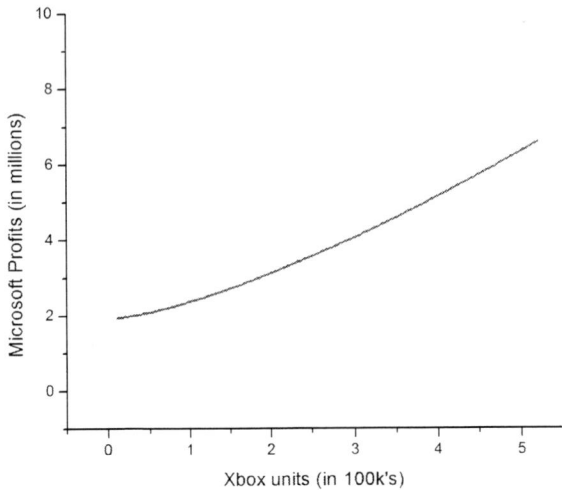

Figure 2.8: Function That Does Not "Flatten Out"

Definition 2.5 (Interior Optimum):
An *interior optimum* or *interior solution* of a function, $f(x)$, is a point, x^* at which $f'(x^*) = 0$.

Note also that an interior optimum does not ensure a maximum is reached, as in the case shown in Figure 2.9. This function "flattens out", but does not achieve a maximum. Instead, it achieves a minimum. If you were an analyst at Microsoft responsible for determining the optimal number of Xbox's to sell, your job security would be in question if you simply found the interior optimum. Instead, you need to verify that you do, in fact, have a maximum. Luckily, there is a mathematical equivalent to this, as well.

Note in Figure 2.7 that the slope of the tangent line at 100,000 units is very steep and positive. In other words, $\frac{f(x)-f(a)}{x-a}$ is very large. As we approach the maximum, the slopes become less steep: $\frac{f(x)-f(a)}{x-a}$ becomes smaller. As we pass the maximum, the slopes again become steep, but negative: $\frac{f(x)-f(a)}{x-a} < 0$. Ultimately,

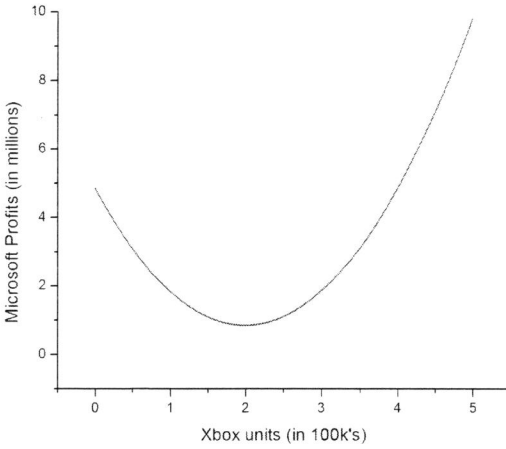

Figure 2.9: Function With An Interior Optimum That As Not A Maximum

this results in the visual effect that the tangent lines are "falling". Mathematically, this means the the slopes are decreasing, starting from extremely positive to extremely negative. Compare this to Figure 2.9. In this case, at 100,000 units, the slope of the tangent line is extremely negative (it is pointing downward very steeply). As we approach the minimum, the slopes become less negative, eventually becoming positive as we pass the minimum. In other words, the slopes are increasing.

We can use this property to determine if an interior optimum is a maximum or a minimum. If the slopes of the tangent lines of an interior optimum are decreasing, we have a maximum. Alternatively, if the slopes of the tangent lines of an interior optimum are increasing, we have a minimum. Recall the slopes of the tangent lines are equal to the derivative of the original function. Therefore, to determine if the slopes of the tangent lines are increasing or decreasing, we need to check the signs of the derivatives of the original function's derivatives.

Definition 2.6 (Second Order Conditions):
Given an interior optimum, x^*, of the function, $f(x)$,

1. If $f''(x^*) \leq 0$, x^* is a maximum.

2. If $f''(x^*) \geq$, x^* is a minimum.

These conditions are known as the *Second Order Conditions*.

Example 2.27 (Single Variable Maximization):
Task: At what value is the function $f(x) = -(x-3)^2$ maximized? What value does $f(x)$ take at this optimal value?

Answer: To determine the optimal value, we must check the first order conditions.

$$
\begin{aligned}
\text{FOC: } f'(x^*) &= 0 \\
-2(x^* - 3) &= 0 \\
\Rightarrow x^* - 3 &= 0 \\
\Rightarrow x^* &= 3
\end{aligned}
$$

Thus, an interior optimum exists at $x^* = 3$. To verify if this is, indeed, a maximum, we must check the second order conditions.

$$
\begin{aligned}
\text{SOC: } f''(x^*) &< 0 \Rightarrow \text{maximum} \\
f''(x) &= \frac{d}{dx}\left(-2(x-3)\right) \\
\Rightarrow f''(x) &= -2 \\
\Rightarrow f''(x^*) = f''(3) &= -2 < 0
\end{aligned}
$$

Since $f''(x)$ evaluated at $x^* = 3$ is less than 0, we have a maximum. Thus, $x^* = 3$ is a maximum. $f(x)$ takes on the value $-\left((0) - 3\right)^2 = 0$ at this maximum.

Example 2.28 (Single Variable Maximization):
Task: At what value is the function $f(x) = x - \frac{x^3}{3}$ maximized? What value does $f(x)$ take at this optimal value?

Answer: To determine the optimal value, we must check the first order conditions.

$$
\begin{aligned}
\text{FOC}: f'(x^*) &= 0 \\
1 - \frac{3(x^*)^2}{3} &= 0 \\
\Rightarrow 1 &= (x^*)^2 \\
\Rightarrow x^* &= (1, -1)
\end{aligned}
$$

Thus, an interior optimum exists at $x^* = 1$ and $x^* = -1$. To check if either is a maximum, we must check the second order conditions.

$$
\begin{aligned}
\text{SOC}: f''(x^*) &< 0 \Rightarrow \text{maximum} \\
f''(x) &= \frac{d}{dx}\left(1 - x^2\right) \\
\Rightarrow f''(x) &= -2x \\
\Rightarrow f''(x^*) = f''(1) &= -2(1) = -2 < 0 \\
\Rightarrow f''(x^*) = f''(-1) &= -2(-1) = 2 > 0
\end{aligned}
$$

Since $f''(x)$ evaluated at $x^* = 1$ is less than 0, we have a maximum. Thus, $x^* = 1$ is a maximum. $f(x)$ takes on the value $\left((1) - \frac{(1)^3}{3}\right) = \frac{2}{3}$ at this maximum. Since $f''(x)$ evaluated at $x^* = -1$ is greater than zero, we have a minimum at this point.

Example 2.29 (Single Variable Maximization):
Task: At what value is the function $f(x) = x$ maximized? What value does $f(x)$ take at this optimal value?

Answer: To determine the optimal value, we must check the first order conditions.

$$
\begin{aligned}
\text{FOC}: f'(x^*) &= 0 \\
1 &= 0
\end{aligned}
$$

We immediately see that for no value of x^* will the first order conditions hold, since $1 \neq 0$. Thus, no interior optimum exists. Intuitively, this should make sense, since $f(x)$ is the equation of the 45-degree line passing through the origin. This line is always increasing.

2.4 Derivative - Multiple Variables

2.4.1 Partial Derivative - Definition

As discussed in the Xbox example, in most situations a firm's profits (or a consumer's preferences) will be determined by multiple variables. We will not be able to graphically determine a function's maximum, and first order conditions will be crucial. Thus far, we have only dealt with functions containing one variable. Luckily, dealing with functions containing multiple variables is not significantly more difficult. It ultimately relies on the concept of a *partial derivative*.

Consider the function $f(x_1, x_2) = x_1 x_2$. f is obviously a function of multiple variables. It should also be obvious the definitions we have established for a derivative do not exactly apply. For instance, if we use the informal definition "The amount $f(x)$ increases as x increases by 1", we should immediately ask the question "is x_1 or x_2 increasing by 1?". Or, stated differently, "should we increase x in the x_1 direction or the x_2 direction?". The concept of a partial derivative exactly answers this question.

Definition 2.7 (Partial Derivative):
The *partial derivative* of a function, $f(x_1, x_2, \ldots)$, with respect to x_1 at a given point, P, is

1. The slope of the secant line between P and a point infinitely close to P in the x_1 direction.

2. The slope of the tangent line of $f(x_1, x_2, \ldots)$ at P in the x_1 direction.

3. The ratio $\frac{f(x_1, x_2, \ldots) - f(a, x_2, \ldots)}{x - a}$ where $P = ((x_1, x_2, \ldots), f(x_1, x_2, \ldots))$ and $((a, x_1, \ldots), f(a, x_2, \ldots))$ is a point infinitely close to P in the x_1 direction.

4. **(Informal)** The amount $f(x_1, x_2, \ldots)$ increases as x_1 increases by 1.

5. **(Informal)** The amount $f(x_1, x_2, \ldots)$ decreases as x_1 decreases by 1.

Like the regular derivative, the partial derivative can be written in a few ways.

Definition 2.8 (Partial Derivative Notation):
The partial derivative of a function, $f(x)$, is written

1. $\frac{\partial f}{\partial x_1}$

2. $f_{x_1}(x_1, x_2, \ldots)$

3. $f_1(x_1, x_2, \ldots)$

In other words, assume we are at the point $(x_1, x_2, x_3, \ldots)$. If we want to know the partial derivative with respect to x_i (x_4, for instance), then we keep all other variables the same and calculate the derivative of the variable in question per our normal techniques. The key is that the partial derivative tells us how the function changes as that particular variable changes.

2.4.2 Partial Derivative - Calculation

Calculating a partial derivative is essentially the same as calculating a normal derivative. The key is to remember while taking the partial derivative with respect to a specific variable, *you are assuming all other variables are constant.* This concept is most easily illustrated via. examples.

Example 2.30 (Partial Derivative):
Task: What is the partial derivative of $f(x_1, x_2) = x_2 x_1$ with respect to x_1? With respect to x_2?

Answer: To determine f_{x_1}, we must take the derivative of $x_2 x_1$ with respect to x_1. This means we must assume all other variables are constants. In this case, that means to assume x_2 is constant. It helps to write the function as $f(\mathbf{x}_1, x_2) = x_2 \mathbf{x}_1$ to illustrate the fact that x_2 should be viewed as a constant. How would we differentiate $x_2 \mathbf{x}_1$ if x_2 were a constant? For instance, how would we differentiate $3\mathbf{x}_1$? It should be clear that the derivative of a constant times a variable is simply the constant.

$$
\begin{aligned}
f_{x_1} &= \frac{d}{d\mathbf{x}_1}(x_2 \mathbf{x}_1) \text{ where } x_2 \text{ is a constant.} \\
&= x_2
\end{aligned}
$$

To determine $\frac{\partial}{\partial x_2}(x_2 x_1)$, we must now assume x_1 is constant and differentiate with respect to x_2. Again, it helps to write the function as $f(x_1, \mathbf{x}_2) = \mathbf{x}_2 x_1$. Using identical logic from above, it should be clear that $\frac{\partial}{\partial \mathbf{x}_2}(\mathbf{x}_2 x_1) = x_1$.

Example 2.31 (Partial Derivative):
Task: What is the partial derivative of $\frac{x_1}{x_2}$ with respect to x_1? With respect to x_2?

Answer: As always, we will replace $\frac{1}{x_2}$ with x_2^{-1}. To determine $\frac{d}{dx_1}(x_1 x_2^{-1})$, we will take the derivative with respect to x_1, while viewing x_2 as a constant. Again, to illustrate this it helps to write the function as $\frac{x_1}{x_2}$. It should be clear the partial derivative of $\mathbf{x_1} x_2^{-1} = x_2^{-1} = \frac{1}{x_2}$.

To determine f_{x_2}, we must view x_1 as a constant and take the derivative with respect to x_2. Writing the function as $\frac{x_1}{x_2}$ and using the Chain Rule, the partial derivative of $x_1 x_2^{-1}$ is $-x_1 x_2^{-2}$.

Example 2.32 (Partial Derivative):
Task: What is the partial derivative of $e^{x_1 x_2} + x_3$ with respect to x_1? With respect to x_2? With respect to x_3.

Answer: As always, to determine f_1 we must assume all other variables are constants. In this case, that means assuming x_2 and x_3 are constants. Writing the function as $e^{x_1 x_2} + x_3$ and using the Chain Rule, the partial derivative is

$$f_{x_1} = \frac{d}{d\mathbf{x_1}}(e^{x_1 x_2} + x_3) \text{ where } x_2 \text{ and } x_3 \text{ are constants.}$$
$$= x_2 e^{x_1 x_2}$$

Likewise,

$$f_{x_2} = \frac{d}{d\mathbf{x_2}}(e^{x_1 x_2} + x_3) \text{ where } x_1 \text{ and } x_3 \text{ are constants.}$$
$$= x_1 e^{x_1 x_2}$$

Finally, to calculate the partial derivative with respect to x_3, note that if x_1 and x_2 are constants, $e^{x_1 x_2}$ is also a constant, making

$$f_{x_3} = \frac{d}{d\mathbf{x_3}}(e^{x_1 x_2} + \mathbf{x_3}) \text{ where } x_1 \text{ and } x_2 \text{ are constants.}$$
$$= 1$$

2.5 Maximization - Multiple Variables

As we can use calculus to determine the maximum of a function with a single variable, we can also use it to determine the maximum of a function with multiple variables. Recall the mathematical condition for an internal maximum is that the function's slope equals zero. In other words, moving "a little to the left" or "a little to the right" will not increase the function's value. Determining the maximum for a function with multiple variables relies on identical logic. The only difference is that there are multiple variables we can move "a little to the left". If any of these variables can increase the function by moving them, we obviously do not have a maximum (increase that variable and you have a higher functional value). Thus, to maximize a multivariable function, the slope in each variable's direction must equal zero. In other words, the partial derivative with respect to each variable must equal zero.

Definition 2.9 (FOC for a Multivariate Function):
The *first order conditions* of a function, $f(x_1, x_2, \ldots)$, are the conditions,

$$f_1(x_1^*, x_2^*, \ldots) = 0$$
$$f_2(x_1^*, x_2^*, \ldots) = 0$$
$$f_3(x_1^*, x_2^*, \ldots) = 0$$
$$\vdots$$

As with a single-variable function, if an internal maximum exists, it will satisfy these first order conditions. Note that these conditions establish a system of equations, which must be solved as in Section 2.1.6.

Also note the same caveats for a single variable function exist for a multivariable function. In particular, a maximum might not exist, and an interior solution might be a minimum. To determine if an interior solution is a maximum or a minimum, analogous conditions to the Second Order Conditions exist, which are beyond the scope of this course. For our applications, we will assume these conditions are met, ensuring an interior optimum is a maximum.

Example 2.33 (Multiple Variable Maximization):
Task: At what value is the function $f(x_1, x_2) = 2x_1 + x_2 - x_1 x_2^2$ maximized? What value does $f(x_1, x_2)$ take at this optimal value?

Answer: To determine the optimal value, we must check the first order conditions.

$$
\begin{aligned}
\text{FOC: } f_1(x_1^*, x_2^*) &= 0 \\
\Rightarrow 2 - (x_2^*)^2 &= 0 \qquad (2.2) \\
f_2(x_1^*, x_2^*) &= 0 \\
\Rightarrow 1 - 2x_1^* x_2^* &= 0 \qquad (2.3)
\end{aligned}
$$

Solving Eqn. 2.2, we find $x_2^* = \sqrt{2}$. (Technically, $x_2^* = -\sqrt{2}$ is also a solution. However, we will only focus on the positive value.) Plugging this value into Eqn. 2.3 to solve for x_1^*,

$$
\begin{aligned}
1 - 2x_1^*(\sqrt{2}) &= 0 \\
\Rightarrow 1 &= 2x_1^*(\sqrt{2}) \\
\Rightarrow \frac{1}{2\sqrt{2}} &= x_1^*
\end{aligned}
$$

Thus, $(x_1^*, x_2^*) = (\frac{1}{2\sqrt{2}}, \sqrt{2})$ is the value that maximizes the function. At this point, $f(x_1^*, x_2^*) = 2(\frac{1}{2\sqrt{2}}) + (\sqrt{2}) - (\frac{1}{2\sqrt{2}})(\sqrt{2})^2 = \sqrt{2}$.

Example 2.34 (Multiple Variable Maximization):
Task: At what value is the function $f(x_1 + x_2) = x_1 + x_2 - x_2^2$ maximized? What value does $f(x)$ take at this optimal value?
Answer: To determine the optimal value, we must check the first order conditions.

$$
\begin{aligned}
\text{FOC: } f_1(x_1^*, x_2^*) &= 0 \\
\Rightarrow 1 &= 0 \\
f_2(x_1^*, x_2^*) &= 0 \\
\Rightarrow 1 - 2x_2^* &= 0
\end{aligned}
$$

We immediately see for no value of (x_1^*, x_2^*) will the first order conditions hold, since $1 \neq 0$. Thus, no interior optimum exists. Intuitively, this should make sense, since $f(x_1, x_2)$ is always increasing in x_1.

Chapter 3

Preferences

Our goal as Microeconomists is to make predictions/recommendations about individual behavior. Regardless of the type of question or the type of individual, we must form an analogy of human decision-making in order to develop new insights. With the complexities of humanity, this is clearly a daunting task. However, a framework has been developed that allows us to focus on those elements of choice-making that are relevant to the types of question we ask, while abstracting away from those that do not play a role.

Our first step in forming this mathematical analogy of the decision-making process is to consider the physiological processes involved as a "black-box". We will assume a decision is made, but we will not concern ourselves with the actual mechanics. By making this assumption, we allow ourselves to ignore the extremely complex task of modeling the human brain. As always, making a simplifying assumption requires us to trade off some level of "correctness". However, the types of questions Economists ask do not require us to know how a decision is being made. Instead, we need only know that decisions are being made according to some underlying pattern. In other words, we need only know that human behavior is not completely random.

3.1   Preference Relations

Assuming decisions are made in a "black-box", we can now focus on the specific characteristics of the choice itself. Specifically, we can use a mathematical comparison known as a *preference relation*.

Definition 3.1 (Preference Relation):
Given two bundles, *a* and *b*, define a *preference relation*, $\succsim$, as follows:

for an individual, $a \succsim b$ if and only if (iff) *a is at least as good as b*

Example 3.1 (Preference Relation):
  Question: State what each of the following means *in words*.

1. hot dog $\succsim$ hamburger
2. 2 cars $\succsim$ 1 car
3. 2 cars $\precsim$ 1 car (note the preference relation is reversed)
4. $4 \succsim 5$

Answer:

1. a hot dog is at least as good as a hamburger
2. 2 cars is at least as good as 1 car
3. 1 car is at least as good as 2 cars
4. the number 4 is at least as good as the number 5

In order to understand the concept of a preference relation, consider each of the previous scenarios and ask in what circumstances it might apply. In what conditions, for instance, is having 1 car (weakly) better than having 2 cars? Also, note that "$\succsim$" is very different than "$\geq$". While the symbols look the same, they have very different meanings. The fourth example above illustrates this fact.

Also note that a preference relation is specific to the individual making the decision. If I prefer cars to trucks and you prefer to opposite, our preference relations would be in the form:

Me: cars $\succsim$ trucks
You: trucks $\succsim$ cars

3.2 Strict Preference/Indifference Relations

As defined above, a bundle, *a*, is preferred to a bundle, *b*, if *a* is weakly preferred to *b*. However, what if *a* is strictly preferred to *b*? Alternatively, what if an individual is indifferent between a and b?

Definition 3.2 (Strict Preference Relation):
Given two bundles, a and b, define a *strict preference relation,* $\succ$, as follows:

for an individual, $a \succ b$ iff a *is better than* b

Definition 3.3 (Indifference Relation):
Given two bundles, a and b, define an *indifference relation,* $\sim$, as follows:

for an individual, $a \sim b$ iff a *is indifferent to* b

You should recognize the symbol for a preference relation, $\succsim$, is made up of the strict indifference relation, $\succ$, and the indifference relation, $\sim$. This should be intuitive, since a is at least as good as b only if it is better than b or indifferent to b.

Note at this point we have, to some degree, completed the first two steps of Quantitative Economic Thinking. We have Identified the Problem ("What choice will an individual make") and Created a Mathematical Analogy ("A preference relation is analogous to the choices an individual would make"). Our model is still extremely general and we do not have nearly enough structure to make significant predictions, but we have developed a mathematical framework in which we can operate. Let us now create a stronger analogy by placing structure on our mathematical representation of individual choice that is consistent with actual human choice.

3.3 Properties of Preference Relations

Having established a definition for what *represents* an individual's preference, we can now look to characterize specific preference behavior.

◇ Complete

Definition 3.4 (Complete):
A preference relation is *complete* if for each x and y, either $x \succsim y$ or $y \succsim x$ or both.

If an individual's preferences are complete, she will never find herself in a situation in which she is simply unable to compare two options. Note this is different than indifference, in which case she *is* comparing the two options, but finding them to be essentially equivalent.

Example 3.2 (Complete):
Question: The book, "Sophie's Choice", introduces a Polish woman in Nazi Germany who must decide which of her two children must die. In the movie version, Meryl Streep, playing the role of Sophie, declares "Don't make me choose. I can't choose!" Are Sophie's preferences over the lives of her children complete?

Answer: Sophie's preferences are *not* complete. She is unable to choose between her children. Note her inability to choose is very different from indifference, in which case Sophie would be indifferent as to which child she must give up.

◇ Symmetric

Definition 3.5 (Symmetric):
A preference relation is *symmetric* if for each x and y, if $x \succeq y$ then $y \succeq x$.

If an individual's preferences are symmetric, he will never strictly prefer one option to another. In other words, if an individual is able to compare two options, he will always find them indifferent.

Example 3.3 (Symmetric):
Question: A starving man walks into a Brazilian Steakhouse. He is told he can have any type of meat he would like (and Brazilian Steakhouses have all

different kinds). Would you expect his preferences over meat to be symmetric?

Answer: A starving man would likely be completely indifferent between any type of meat being offered to him. As such, his preferences would likely be symmetric.

⋄ **Local Nonsatiation**

> **Definition 3.6 (Local Nonsatiation):**
> A preference relation is *locally nonsatiated* if for each bundle, a, another bundle exists, b, such that $b \succ a$ and b has a little bit more of the good(s) in the bundle, a little bit less of the good(s) in the bundle, or a little bit more of some goods, and a little bit less of other goods.

Local nonsatiation rules out scenarios in which an individual possesses a "bliss point". Alternatively, it tells us that we either like or dislike having more (or less) of every good. As an example, assume we are looking at preferences over houses. An individual with a bliss point would make a claim such as "My perfect house has 2000 square feet and a grocery store 1.5 miles away". He would select this house over a house with 2010 square feet and a grocery store 1.5 miles away, a house with 1910 square feet and a grocery store 1 mile away, a house with 2010 square feet and a grocery store 1 mile away, etc.

⋄ **Monotonicity**

> **Definition 3.7 (Monotonicity):**
> A preference relation displays *monotonicity* if for each bundle, a, every bundle, b, with more of each good in the bundle is strictly preferred to a.

Monotonicity is a specific case of local nonsatiation. In particular, it tells us that for the goods in question, we always prefer more of the good. In general, we will assume monotonicity holds unless we can prove otherwise. To do so, we must explicity find a pair of bundles such that $a >> b$ but $b \succ a$.

> **Example 3.4 (Monotonicity):**
> **Question:** A CEO feels her "ideal" company has exactly 40 employees. When ranking possible sizes for her company, her preferences are such that
>
> - If two companies both have fewer than 40 employees, the one that is closer to 40 is preferred. Thus, $40 \succeq 39 \succeq 38 \succeq 37 \ldots$
> - If two companies both have more than 40 employees, the one that is closer to preferred. Thus, $40 \succeq 41 \succeq 42 \succeq 43 \ldots$.
>
> Are the CEO's preferences monotonic?
>
> **Answer:** In this example, bundles will be comprised of a single good. Specifically, the number of employees in a company. Note that a company with 41 employeees has more of each good (in this case, the only good) than a company with 40 employees. Since $41 > 40$, monotonicity would imply $41 \succ 40$. However, we are told $40 \succ 41$. Thus, monotonicity is violated.

Note we are assuming monotonicity holds unless we can find a counter-example in which $a >> b$, but $b \succ a$. It is important to realize when learning theory that if we change our assumptions, we could end up with different results, as the next example illustrates.

> **Example 3.5 (Monotonicity):**
> **Question:** An individual's preferences are such that he prefers more sleep and less work. Using only what we are given, are his preferences monotonic?
>
> **Answer:** In this example, bundles will be comprised of two goods, sleep and work. By assuming preferences are monotonic, we have a burden of proof to show that for some set of bundles, $a >> b$, but $b \succ a$. In this case, $a >> b$ is equivalent to having more sleep and more work. To have non-monotonic preferences, it must be the case that more sleep and more work is preferred to less sleep and less work. However, we only know that the individual prefers more sleep and less work. We do not know how the individual compares more of both. Thus, we are not able to find a non-monotonic set of bundles so we assume the preferences are monotonic.
>
> If we instead assumed that monotonicity does NOT hold unless we can explicity show that when $a >> b$, then $a \succ b$, then these identical preferences will result in us assuming that preferences are not monotonic. Specifically, we will not

be able to prove that when $a >> b$, $a \succ b$ since we do not have that information.

Clearly, if we had all the information concerning the individual's preferences we could precisely determine if they are monotonic, but it is important to realize that assumptions and formal definitions can play crucially important roles.

◇ Transitive

> **Definition 3.8 (Transitive):**
> A preference relation is *transitive* if for every x, y, and z; if $x \succeq y$ and $y \succeq z$ then $x \succeq z$

If an individual's preferences are transitive, he displays a certain level of consistency in his choices. In a simple experiment, Weinstein (1968) repeatedly asked individuals of different age groups to select their preferred bundle from pairs of the following items valued at $3 each in 1968 dollars

1. A brush-stroke print of El Greco's "View of Toledo."
2. A pair of white tennis shoes (low sneakers).
3. A 15-inch pizza pie with mushrooms and sausage plus two 8-ounce glasses of Coca Cola
4. The three latest "Beatles" 45-rpm phonograph records
5. A vanilla malted milk (two glasses) per day for ten days.
6. Three dollars in cash.
7. A Parker "T-ball" Jotter ball-point pen plus an extra refill for it.
8. Three men's clip-on bow ties, all with red polka dots, one brown, one blue, and one gray.
9. An 8-cup "Wearever" aluminum coffee percolator.
10. A free pass to the next four Saturday matinees at the subject's favorite motion picture theater

As the test was repeated with randomized pairs of items, Weinstein was able to observe whether intransitive cycles occurred. For instance, if an individual preferred three dollars to a vanilla malted milk, preferred a vanilla malted milk to a pair of white tennis shoes, but then preferred a pair of white tennis shoes to three dollars, she would display an intransitive cycle. Not surprisingly, Weinstein found that as individuals become older, their preferences become more transitive. Specifically, Table 3.1 shows the mean level of transitivity in each of the four age groups he studied

Age Group	% Transitivity
9-12	79%
14-16	83%
17-18	88%
18+ (mostly teachers)	94%

Table 3.1: Age Group and Transitivity

This coincides with the study of Bradbury and Ross (1990), in which individuals of different ages were asked to select between pairs of colors. Table 3.1 shows the percentage of individuals at each age whose preferences displayed transitivity. Once again, older individuals tend to have more stable preferences. It is interesting to note that at age 13, individuals display a lower level of transitivity than expected, which coincides with the notion that young teenagers are crazy.

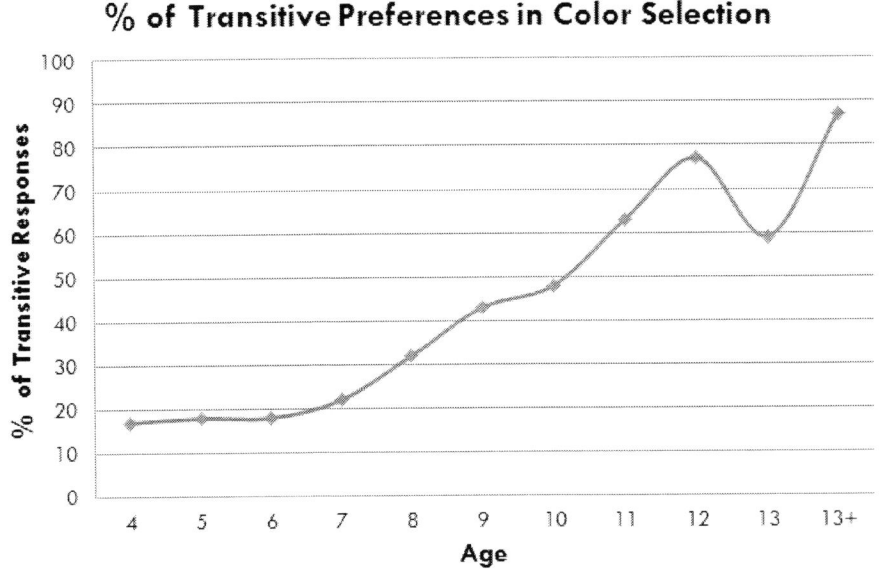

Figure 3.1: Bradbury and Ross (1990) Study

In general, we assume preferences are transitive unless we can explicitly prove otherwise. To do so, we must find an explicit reversal of preferences, which we call an intransitive cycle.

> **Definition 3.9 (Intransitive Cycle of the Preference Relation):**
> An *intransitive cycle* of the preference relation, $\succeq$, is a set of three bundles, x, y, and z, for which $x \succeq y$ and $y \succeq z$ are true, but $x \succeq z$ is not. In other words, $x \succeq y$, $y \succeq z$, but $z \succ x$.

Note that a single intransitive cycle implies that preferences are not transitive.

> **Example 3.6 (Intransitive Cycle):**
> **Question:** An individual's preferences are as follows. $x \succeq y$, $a \succeq b$, $d \succeq f$, $y \succeq a$, $f \succeq x$, $a \succ x$, and $y \succ b$. Are the individual's preferences transitive?
>
> **Answer:** No. To prove an individual's preferences are not transitive, we must demonstrate an intransitive cycle. In this case, the intransitive cycle is $x \succeq y$, $y \succeq a$, but $a \succ x$. The individual's preferences "reversed".

> **Example 3.7 (Intransitive Cycle):**
> **Question:** A CEO feels her "ideal" company has exactly 40 employees. When ranking possible sizes for her company, her preferences are such that
>
> - If two companies both have fewer than 40 employees, the one that is closer to 40 is preferred. Thus, $40 \succeq 39 \succeq 38 \succeq 37\ldots$
> - If two companies both have more than 40 employees, the one that is closer to preferred. Thus, $40 \succeq 41 \succeq 42 \succeq 43\ldots$.
> - If one company has more than 40 employees and one has less, we have limited information concerning her preferences. Specifically, we know that $39 \succeq 37$ and $37 \succeq 41$.
> - For all company comparisons for which we do not have explicit information, the CEO's preferences are transitive.
>
> Is it possible that the CEO has transitive preferences? Under what conditions would this be the case?
>
> **Answer:** Let us first determine if the CEO's preferences are transitive when we consider companies that have less than 40 employees. Note the CEO's

preferences will maintain their order based on the size of the company. For instance, if $x \succeq y$ and $y \succeq z$, it must be the case that $x \geq y$ and $y \geq z$ since larger companies are preferred. Based on the properties of numbers, this must imply that $x \geq z$, which finally implies that $x \succeq z$. Thus, no intransitive cycle exists.

If we consider bundles all greater than or equal to 40, we get an equivalent result, with smaller numbers of employees being preferred to larger numbers.

Thus, the only way in which the CEO would have intransitive preferences are if an intransitive cycle exists when comparing employees of size 37, 39, and 41. We know that $39 \succeq 37$ and $37 \succeq 41$. An intransitive cycle will then exist if $41 \succ 39$. Therefore, if $39 \succeq 41$, the CEO's preferences will be transitive.

Note that if a consumer's preferences ($\succeq$) are transitive per Definition 3.8, then her strict and indifference preference relations must also be transitive. This leads to two important Corollaries.

Corollary 3.1 (Transitive - Strict Preference Relation):
If an individual's strict preferences ($\succ$) are not transitive, then her preferences ($\succeq$) are also not transitive. To show a strict preference relation is intransitive, we must show an intransitive cycle. Specifically, an intransitive cycle of the strict preference relation, $\succ$, is a set of three bundles, x, y, and z, for which $x \succ y$ and $y \succ z$ are true, but $x \succ z$ is not. In other words, $x \succ y$, $y \succ z$, but $z \succ x$ or $z \sim x$.

Corollary 3.2 (Transitive - Indifference Relation):
If an individual's indifference relation ($\sim$) is not transitive, then her preferences ($\succeq$) are also not transitive. To show an indifference relation is intransitive, we must show an intransitive cycle. Specifically, an intransitive cycle of the indifference relation, $\sim$, is a set of three bundles, x, y, and z, for which $x \sim y$ and $y \sim z$ are true, but $x \sim z$ is not. In other words, $x \sim y$, $y \sim z$, but $x \succ z$ or $z \succ x$.

Example 3.8 (Transitive):

Question: Bob is on a diet and is faced with three options:

1. Go to Vespa, where he can get a cannoli for dessert.
2. Go to Noodles & Company, which does not have any dessert that tempts him.
3. Stay home and eat healthy.

On Monday, his wife asks him if he would prefer to go to Vespa or Noodles & Company. Bob figures since he is going out to eat anyway, he might as well go to the restaurant with the dessert since his diet is wrecked anyway. Therefore, Bob selects Vespa. On Tuesday, his wife asks him if he wants to go to Noodles & Company or stay home and eat healthy. Since Bob knows that Noodles & Company is reasonably healthy and he enjoys going out, Bob selects Noodles & Company. On Wednesday, Bob's wife asks him if he would prefer to go to Vespa or stay home and eat healthy. Bob knows that if he goes to Vespa, he will end up eating a cannoli. Since Bob enjoys living a healthy lifestyle, he decides to stay home.

Do Bob's choices display transitivity?

Answer: No. Bob's preferences can be represented as "Vespa" $\succ$ "Noodles & Company" $\succ$ "staying home and eating healthy". Transitivity would then require "Vespa" $\succ$ "staying at home and eating healthy". However, we found "staying at home and eating healthy" $\succ$ "Vespa", forming an intransitive cycle.

Example 3.9 (Transitive - Strict Preferences):

Question: Britney Spears's manager is trying to determine the ideal length of a pop song. After extensive surveys, he has determined the average consumer has the following preferences:

- 3 minutes $\succ$ 2 minutes
- 3 minutes $\prec$ 5 minutes
- 2 minutes $\succ$ 5 minutes

Does the average consumer's preferences ($\succeq$) display transitivity?

Answer: No. It is immediately clear that the consumer's strict preferences do not display transitivity since 5 minutes $\succ$ 3 minutes $\succ$ 2 minutes $\succ$ 5 minutes, forming an intransitive cycle. Corollary 3.1 then tells us the average consumer's preferences are also not transitive.

◇ † **Strict Convexity**

> **Definition 3.10 (Strict Convexity):**
> A preference relation displays *strict convexity* if for every x, y, and z such that $x \succeq z, y \succeq z$, then $\alpha x + (1 - \alpha)y \succ z$, where $0 \leq \alpha \leq 1$.

In other words, if two bundles are both weakly preferred to a third bundle, then any mixture of those bundles that sums to 1 (1/2 of the first bundle + 1/2 of the second bundle, 1/4 of the first bundle + 3/4 of the second bundle, etc.) will be strictly preferred to the third bundle.

Strict convexity is essentially a preference for diversity. To see this, assume $y \succeq x$. Also note that $x \succeq x$ (is x at least as good as itself? Of course! It is the same). Combining these two results with strict convexity implies $\alpha x + (1 - \alpha)y \succ x$. In other words, given any bundle, mixing it with another bundle you like (weakly) more will make you better off.

> **Example 3.10 (Strict Convexity):**
> **Question:** Varsity Theater generally only has two movies showing. Would you expect your preferences over these movies to be strictly convex?
>
> **Answer:** Your preferences over the two movies will likely not be strictly convex. In particular, assume your options are:
>
> 1. Watch the movie, Kung-Fu Panda 2 (KFP)
> 2. Watch the movie, The Hangover, Part 2 (H)
>
> and you prefer "watching KFP" to "watching H". Note "watching KFP" $\succeq$ "watching KFP" and "watching KFP" $\succeq$ "watching H". Strict Convexity would then imply "watching 1/2 of KFP + watching 1/2 of H" $\succ$ "watching H". Assuming that you do not absolutely hate The Hangover series, you would likely prefer to watch all of H than watch the first half of KFP then the first half of H.

◇ † **Continuity**

Definition 3.11 (Continuity):
Loosely, preferences are *continuous* if, whenever $a \succeq b$ and a is "close" to the bundle c, then $c \succeq b$.

In other words, if you prefer one bundle to another, then all bundles "near" the first bundle will still be preferred to the second bundle. As an example, assume you prefer eating at Top of the Stairs to Cosmic Cantina. Now assume a restaurant opens up that is almost identical to Top of the Stairs, except it has one less appetizer on the menu. Continuity of preferences would imply you still prefer this restaurant to Cosmic Cantina since it is so "close" (not physical proximity, but similarity) to Top of the Stairs.

3.4 Rational Preferences

We see that our mathematical representation of individual choice can be structured according to specific properties, but the question remains, "which properties would make a good analogy of an actual human decision-maker?" Looking at the properties listed above, for each we ask "is this property realistic for most set of choices?". If the answer is "yes", then it seems reasonable to model human choice with this property.

Economists have determined that two of the above properties are necessary to accurately reflect "rational" choice behavior.

Definition 3.12 (Rational Preferences):
Preferences are *rational* if they are *complete* and *transitive*

In modeling human choice behavior, completeness is a reasonably innocuous assumption. It is hard to conjure examples in which completeness does not hold. Even in Sophie's Choice, the example we used to motivate completeness, when a young Nazi is told to take both children away, in the movie version Meryl Streep releases her daughter, shouting "Take my little girl!".

Transitivity, however, is a much less universally accepted assumption on individual decision-making. Even in the simple decision of selecting a favorite color, Figure 3.1 shows that 13% of adults displayed intransitive preferences. Despite this fact, economists assume transitivity holds for two major reasons:

1. A species who developed transitive preferences would have an evolutionary advantage over a species that did not.

2. As we will see, assuming transitivity allows us to fully utilize the language of calculus in modeling choice behavior.

To understand the first point, consider the following scenario

Mr. G. Ray Tape has intransitive preferences. Specifically, bananas ≻ apples ≻ oranges ≻ bananas. Dr. Hugh Mann is a passing acquaintance of Mr. Tape's and over time learns these preferences. Being a shrewd businessman, Dr. Hugh comes up with the following plan. He goes to the store one evening and purchases an apple and a banana. The next morning, he sneaks a glance into Mr. Tape's lunch bag and notices he brought an orange to eat at lunch. Dr. Hugh says "What a fine morning, Mr. Tape! I see you have an orange, but I'd like to offer you this generous proposition! For $.01, I'll trade you this apple for your orange." Mr. Tape considers the offer and grunts yes, since his preferences are such that the apple is preferred to the orange. He passes over his orange and $.01 and gets himself a fine apple.

Ten minutes later, Dr. Hugh approaches Mr. Tape again and says "Mr. Tape, I was thinking about our previous offer, and I think I can make you another offer you will like even more. For $.01, I'll trade you this banana for the apple you bought from me earlier." Mr. Tape thinks about it, and since he prefers bananas to apples, he grunts yes, forks over the $.01 and apple and receives a banana.

Ten minutes later, Dr. Hugh approaches Mr. Tape and says "Mr. Tape, I feel we have been making some trades today that are really benefiting both of us. As you are a valued business partner, I would like to offer you another trade that I think you will like. For $.01, I'll trade you this orange for your banana." As Mr. Tape is not the cleverest fellow, he does not notice that the orange he is being offered is the exact orange he originally brought to eat at lunch. As his preferences are such that he prefers oranges to bananas, he grunts yes, forks over the $.01 and banana and receives an orange.

A gleam in his eye, ten minutes later Dr. Hugh approaches Mr. Tape again and says "Mr. Tape...

This scenario illustrates the concept of a "money pump". If an individual has systematically intransitive preferences, an individual with transitive preferences can devise a mechanism to take all his resources, while the victim is blissfully unaware. If a species develops a brain with intransitive preferences, a species with transitive preferences has the potential to develop an evolutionary advantage by exploiting this property.

As we expand our analysis, we will include other properties of preference relations. Note that whenever we make an assumption on preferences, we are limiting the cases for which our model is relevant. For instance, if we assume the monotonicity property, then we are explicitly ignoring choices over things we do not like. In studying pollution or traffic congestion, this assumption would be problematic.

3.5   Indifference Curves/Maps

Having established the concept of a preference relation and defined specific properties a preference relation should have to accurately reflect human behavior, we can now begin Step 3 of Quantitative Economic Thought, "Solve the Mathematical Model". We will first approach the issue graphically, then introduce calculus to further expand our predictions.

To graphically analyze choice behavior, we beginning by introducing the concept of an indifference cure.

> **Definition 3.13 (Indifference Curve):**
> An *indifference curve* is the graphical set of all bundles of goods
> that a consumer views as equally desirable.

As an example, assume there are only two goods in the world, pizza and beer. Assume you currently have 1 pizza and 5 beers, written as (1 pizza, 5 beers). What combinations of pizza and beer would make you equally well off? Assuming you cannot eat an entire pizza by yourself and you would like an extra beer, you might be just as well off with 1/2 a pizza and 6 beers (1/2 pizza, 6 beers). Alternatively, if you had more pizza you might be able to avoid buying lunch tomorrow. Assuming you would be willing to give up a beer for this luxury, you also might be just as well off with 1.5 pizzas and 4 beers (1.5 pizza, 4 beers).

Pizza	Beers
1	5
0.5	6
1.5	4
2	3.5
.3	10

Table 3.2: Combinations of Pizza and Beer to which a consumer is indifferent.

Continuing in this manner, assume you develop the following table of pizza/beer combinations that make you just as well off as 1 pizza and 5 beers.

As shown in Figure 3.2, plotting Table 3.2 generates an indifference curve. Specifically, when drawing an indifference curve, each axis represents a good and we plot all points that make the consumer equally well off.

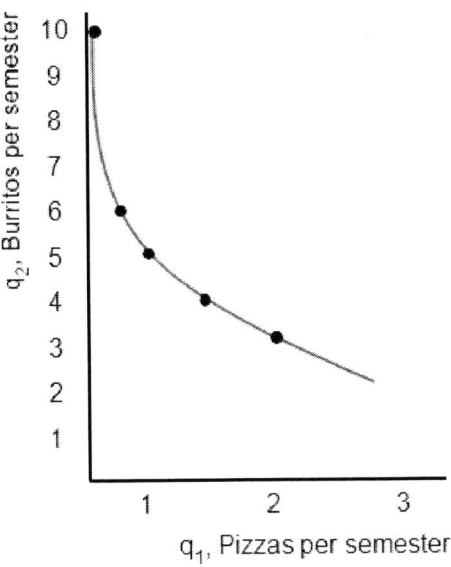

Figure 3.2: Indifference Curve for pizza/beer combinations equivalent to (1 pizza, 5 beers)

Note that an indifference curve is particular to a specific individual. If, for instance, an individual does not like beer, she would not be willing to give up much pizza to gain an extra beer.

In our example, if we plot the indifference curve related to each possible starting combination of pizza and beer, we will generate an indifference map as shown in Figure 3.3.

Definition 3.14 (Indifference Map):
An *indifference map* is a complete set of indifference curves that summarize a consumer's tastes.

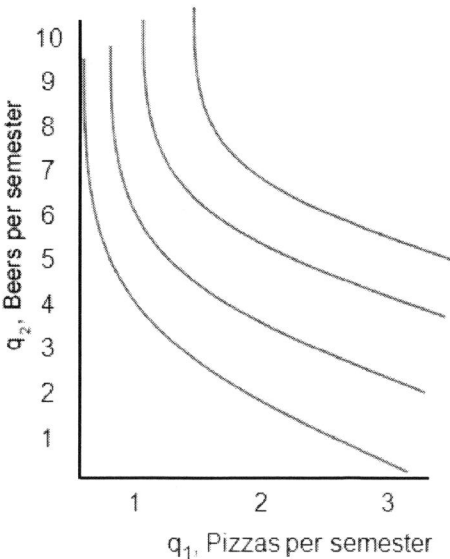

Figure 3.3: Indifference Map for pizza/beer

Note one indifference curve is specific to one level of "happiness". In Figure 3.2, for instance, the indifference curve is specific to the "happiness" gained by having 1 pizza and 5 beers. An indifference map is not specific to a particular level of "happiness". Instead, it shows you the full range of preferences over the goods on the axes.

3.6 Graphical Analysis of Consumer Behavior

Having established the concept of an indifference curve, we can now begin to ask what types of consumer behavior are analogous to specific preference relation traits. As always, we will assume preferences are *rational* (complete and transitive). In addition, we will assume the monotonicity property holds. Thus, our analysis is specific to goods consumers "like". With these three traits, we are able to predict the following:

1. **Indifference Curves Cannot Cross:** To prove this, first assume that indifference curves DO cross as in Figure 3.4a below. From the graph we know $e \sim b$ and $e \sim a$. Transitivity then tells us $a \sim b$. However, this violates the monotonicity property.

2. **Indifference Curves are Downward Sloping:** Assume an indifference curve IS upward sloping as in Figure 3.4b below. Since a and b are on the same indifference curve, that means $a \sim b$. However, the monotonicity property says $b \succ a$, a contradiction.

3. **Indifference Curves Cannot be Thick:** Assume an indifference curve IS thick as in Figure 3.4c below. Since a and b are on the same indifference curve, that means $a \sim b$. However, the monotonicity property says $b \succ a$, a contradiction.

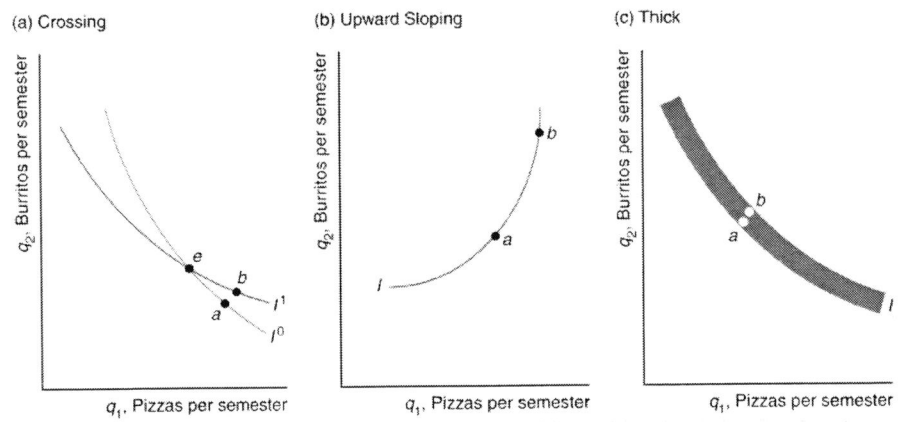

Figure 3.4: Impossible Indifference Curves

4. **Bundles on Indifference Curves Farther from the Origin are Preferred to Those on Curves Closer to the Origin:** Consider Figure 3.5. We know from the monotonicity property that $b \succ a$. We also know that indifference curves cannot cross, so all points on I^2 must be higher than I^1.

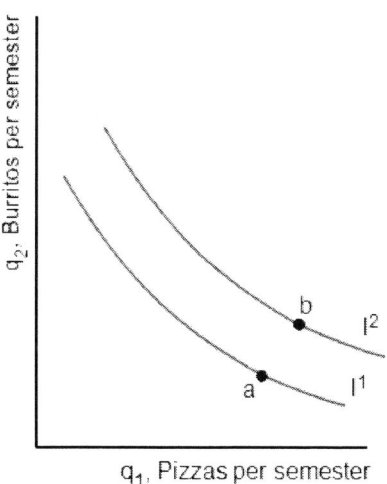

Figure 3.5: Bundles on Indifference Curves Farther from the Origin are Preferred to Those on Curves Closer to the Origin

5. **An Indifference Curve Exists Through Every Possible Bundle:** While we will not show the formal proof, it should be obvious from Figure 3.6 that given two indifference curves, another can be drawn between them.

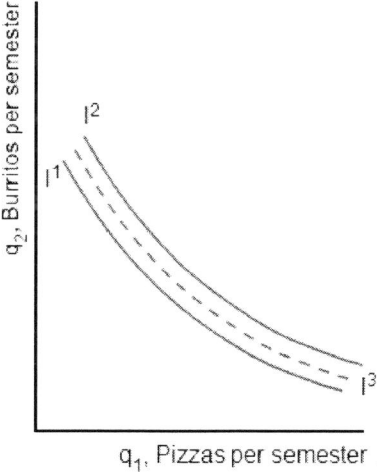

Figure 3.6: An Indifference Curve Exists Through Every Possible Bundle

3.7   Curvature of Indifference Curves

Having derived the basic "rules" of indifference curves, we can now look at more specific properties. For example, we know that indifference curves are downward sloping and do not cross. However, what shape do they take? Do particular shapes relate to specific preferences?

3.7.1   Perfect Complements

Definition 3.15 (Perfect Complements):
Perfect Complements are goods that a consumer is interested in consuming *only* in fixed proportions.

In other words, two goods are perfect complements if you want good *x only* if you also get good *y*. Examples include left & right shoes, peanut butter & jelly, and cigarettes & lighters.

Example 3.11 (Perfect Complements):
Task: Draw the indifference map for left and right shoes, assuming you only care about owning *pairs* of shoes.

Answer: Assume you have one left and one right shoe. If you had zero left shoes and one right shoe would you be indifferent? You would not, as you would no longer have a pair of shoes. If you had two left shoes and two right shoes you should also not be indifferent, as you would now have two pairs of shoes and you like pairs of shoes. However, imagine if you had one left shoe and two right shoes. Assuming you do not mind an extra shoe lying around your apartment, you still have one pair of shoes you can use. As that is all you care about, you are indifferent between this and having just one of each kind of shoe. Likewise, imagine you have three left shoes and one right shoe. Again, since you only care about *pairs* of shoes, you are indifferent between this and only having one of each shoe. If we continue with this logic and graphed all the combinations of shoes that make you indifferent to 1 pair of shoes, we would end up with the indifference curve illustrated in Figure (3.7).

To draw the "full" map, we need to represent other possible indifferent curves. For instance, what combinations of shoes will make you indifferent to having two pairs of shoes? Using the same logic, the combinations would be (2,3), (2,4), (2,5), (3,2), (4,2), (5,2), etc. If we continue with this logic and draw the different indifference curves, we will create the indifference map shown in Figure (3.8). Note the "kink's" in the indifference curves are the points where you have evenly matched pairs of shoes (no extra shoes). These are graphically represented by (1,1), (2,2), (3,3), etc. Consider for yourself where the kinks would be if you graphed the indifference map of bread and ham, where you only care about eating *sandwiches* which have two pieces of bread and one piece of ham.

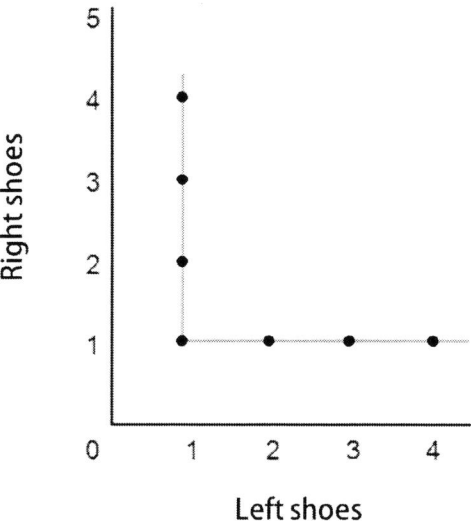

Figure 3.7: Example (3.11) Indifference Curve Containing (1,1)

3.7.2 Perfect Substitutes

Definition 3.16 (Perfect Substitutes):
Perfect Substitutes are goods that a consumer is indifferent as to which to consume. She only cares about the *total* amount consumed.

In other words, two goods are perfect substitutes if you do not care which you are given. Examples include pepsi & coke, salt shakers & packets of salt, and Cheerios & Toastie-O's.

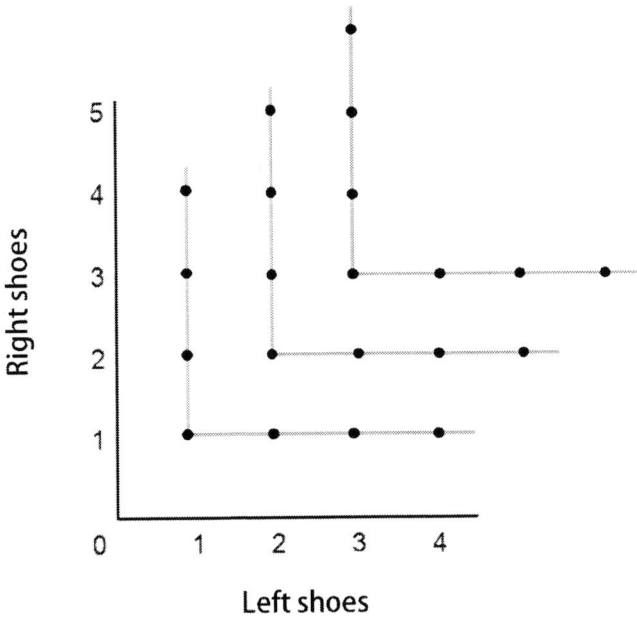

Figure 3.8: Example (3.11) Indifference Map for Shoes

Example 3.12 (Perfect Substitutes):

Task: Draw the indifference map for salt shakers and packets of salt. Assume that there is the same amount of salt in 1 salt shaker and 10 packets of salt.

Answer: Assume you have 3 salt shakers. Any combination of salt shakers and packets of salt that give you an identical amount of salt would make you indifferent. Thus, if you had 30 packets of salt, you would indifferent to 3 salt shakers. Likewise, you would be indifferent between that and 2 shakers plus 10 packets of salt. If we graphed all the combinations of salt shakers and salt packets that would make us indifferent to 3 salt shakers, we would end up with the indifference curve illustrated in Figure (3.9).

To draw the "full" map, we need to represent other possible indifferent curves. For instance, what combinations of shakers and packets will make you indifferent to having 2 salt shakers? Using the same logic, the combinations would be (1, 10), (0, 20), (.5, 15), etc. If we draw the different indifference curves, we will create the indifference map shown in Figure (3.10). Note the slope of the indifference curves says something very specific about the tradeoffs between the two goods.

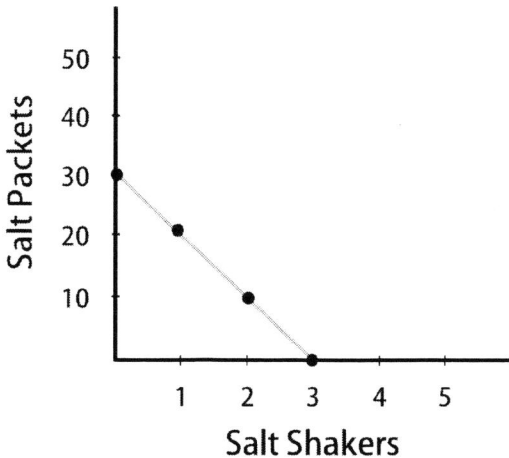

Figure 3.9: Example (3.12) Indifference Curve Containing (3,0)

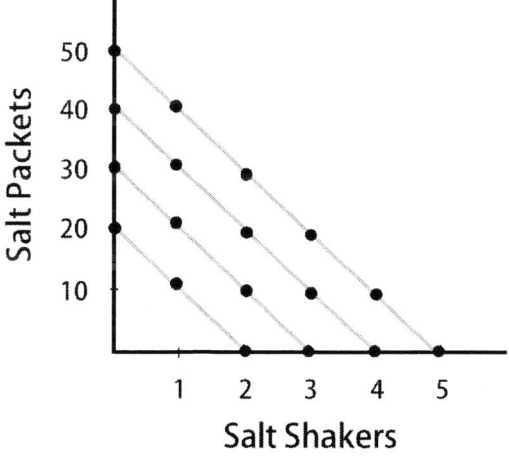

Figure 3.10: Example (3.12) Indifference Map for Salt

3.7.3 Imperfect Substitutes/Complements

Definition 3.17 (Imperfect Substitutes/Complements):
Imperfect Substitutes/Complements are goods that are not perfect substitutes and not perfect complements.

Most goods are imperfect substitutes/complements. Consider pizza and Coke. Both provide some caloric content, so to some degree an individual could substitute one for the other. However, it is certainly not a perfect substitution, in that pizza provides protein, while Coke does not. Likewise, you could eat a pizza by itself and still be partially satisfied. However, generally food is more enjoyable with a tasty beverage.

Example 3.13 (Imperfect Substitutes/Complements):
Task: Draw an indifference curve with Doritos on the x-axis and Cheetos on the y-axis, recognizing that these two goods are very similar, but not exact substitutes.

Answer: Let's ask what combinations of Doritos and Cheetos would make us indifferent to 10 Doritos and 10 Cheetos. Would having 20 Doritos make us just as happy? Maybe, but probably not. Assuming we like some variety, we would prefer 10 Doritos and 10 Cheetos. However, what if we were offered 30 Doritos and 0 Cheetos? The sheer volume of Doritos might us indifferent between this and the smaller-portioned 10 Dorito, 10 Cheeto option. We will assume this is the case. Likewise, would 20 Cheetos make us just as happy? Again, assuming we like some variety, we will need some extra Cheetos to offset the loss in variety 20 Cheetos gives us. Let's assume 25 Cheetos is enough to make us indifferent. If we graphed all the combinations of Doritos and Cheetos that would make us indifferent to 10 Doritos and 10 Cheetos, we would end up with the indifference curve illustrated in Figure (3.11).

Example 3.14 (Imperfect Substitutes/Complements):
Task: Now draw an indifference curve with Honda Civics on the x-axis and Bentley Continental GT on the y-axis, recognizing that these two cars are very different. More importantly, there is a certain status to owning a Bentley that owning the monetarily equivalent number of Civics does not capture. Consider, for instance, an episode of MTV's Cribs where your favorite artist finishes showing you "where the magic happens" then says "now let's look at

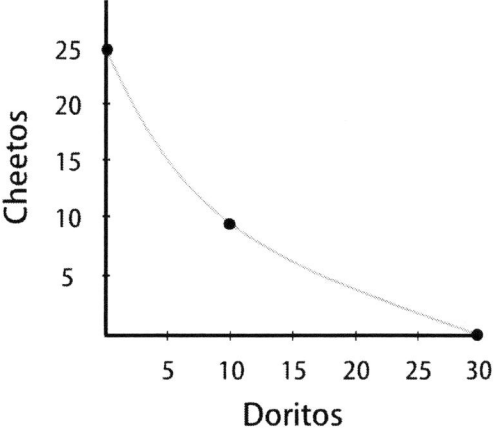

Figure 3.11: Example (3.13) Indifference Curve Containing (10,10)

my whips". He then walks to his driveway where 15 Honda Civics are parked...

Answer: This is similar to the above example, but now ask what combinations of cars would make you indifferent between 2 Bentleys and 0 Civics. Theoretically, it is possible that no amount of Civics could offset the loss in prestige you would get from losing a Bentley. However, we will assume that having a large amount of money can substitute the prestige, but it has to be a very large amount of money. Let us assume that 50 Civics could offset the loss of 1 Bentley and 300 Civics could offset the loss of both Bentleys. If we graphed all the combinations of Civics and Bentleys that would make us indifferent to 2 Bentleys and 0 Civics, we would end up with the indifference curve illustrated in Figure (3.12).

Example 3.15 (Imperfect Substitutes/Complements):
Task: Now draw an indifference curve with Bentley Continental GT on the y-axis and high-performance tires on the x-axis, recognizing that high-performance tires enhance the performance of a high-performance car but you do not *have* to have high-performance tires for a Bentley to perform extremely well.

Answer: Let's ask what combinations of cars would make you indifferent between 2 Bentleys and 8 high-performance tires. In theory, you would like 4 high-performance tires per Bentley, but it is not absolutely required. Thus, you

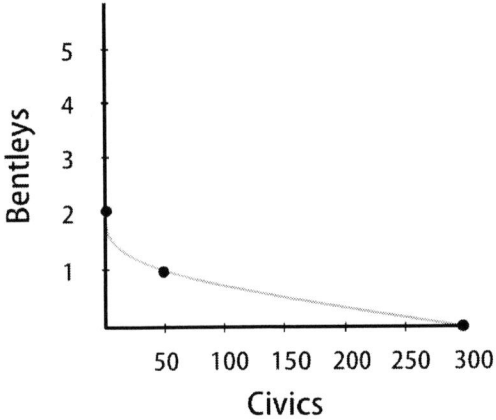

Figure 3.12: Example (3.14) Indifference Curve Containing (0,2)

might be just as happy if you only had 4 high-performance tires but had 3 Bentleys. Likewise, you might be willing to give up 0.5 Bentleys (assume that you are renting a Bentley and 0.5 Bentleys equates to renting the Bentley for 12 hours during a day) if you received 30 high-performance tires (probably not, but let's just assume for the sake of argument). If we graphed all the combinations of tires and Bentleys that would make us indifferent to 2 Bentleys and 8 tires, we would end up with the indifference curve illustrated in Figure (3.13).

Note how the shape of the indifference curves in the last few examples changed. In general, the more alike two goods are, the more their indifference curves "look like" lines (i.e. they "look more like" perfect substitutes). The more two goods require each other to be useful, the more L-shaped their indifference curves (i.e. they "look more like" perfect complements).

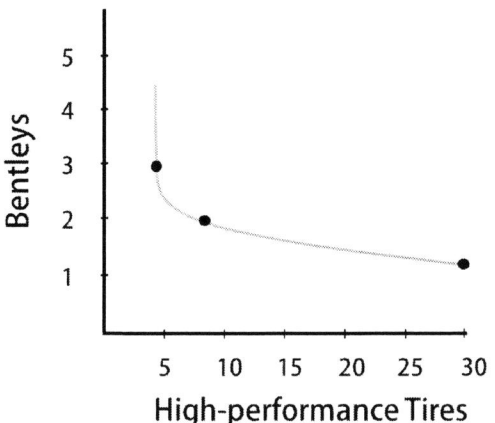

Figure 3.13: Example (3.15) Indifference Curve Containing (8,2)

Chapter 4

Utility

4.1 Utility Function Fundamentals

We now have a basic mathematical framework to model decision-making. Having only used three properties of preference relations (completeness, transitivity, and the monotonicity property) and the concept of an indifference curve, we have been able to make predictions that can be related to real-world choices. For instance, we have discovered that an individual's preferences will not result in indifference curves that cross, which can be interpreted to mean that as we receive more of two goods, we do not experience a major shift in their relative importance to each other.[1] While these findings are not trivial, they are still fundamentally basic. In order to gain a deeper insight into the behavior of individuals, we need to expand our mathematical analogy of decision-making. In particular, we must introduce the concept of a utility function.

> **Definition 4.1 (Utility Function):**
> A utility function is a mathematical function that *represents an individual's preferences*. In particular, $x \succeq y$ if and only if $u(x) \geq u(y)$.

In other words, a utility function gives a numerical value to every bundle. This numerical value can often be interpreted as the level of happiness a particular

---

[1] As this and our other current findings are not central to our final goals, we have excluded a lengthy exposition.

bundle brings an individual. It is important to recognize that this is only an interpretation. There is no "absolute" measure of happiness. To say "2 slices of bread and some lunch meat" gives me "4 utils" (where a util is the unit we put on utility) has no inherent meaning. However, to say "2 slices of bread and some lunch meat gives me 4 utils. 2 slices of bread and some cheese gives me 3 utils" tells us something very important. In particular, it tells us that the individual prefers a turkey club to a cheese sandwich.

In not all instances does a utility function exist. For instance, assume an individual's preferences violate transitivity and she has an ordering such that $x \succ y \succ z \succ x$. In order for a utility function to exist, it would have to be the case that $u(x) > u(y) > u(z) > u(x)$. However, this implies that $u(x) > u(x)$, which is impossible. Luckily, economists have determined in what situations utility functions exist.

Theorem 4.1 (Utility Function Existence):
A utility function that gives each bundle a numerical value that represents an individual's preferences exists if and only if that individual's preferences are complete and transitive.

In other words, a utility function exists that represents an individual's preferences if and only if those preferences are rational.

Besides existence, economists have determined when utility functions exist that have useful mathematical properties.

Theorem 4.2 (Continuous Utility Function Existence):
A continuous utility function that gives each bundle a numerical value that represents an individual's preferences exists if and only if that individual's preferences are complete, transitive, and continuous.

Theorem 4.3 (Increasing Utility Function Existence):
An increasing (more of a good gives a higher utility) utility function that gives each bundle a numerical value that represents an individual's preferences exists if and only if that individual's preferences are complete, transitive, and have the monotonicity property.

Example 4.1 (Existence of a Utility Function):

Question: An HR Manager is investigating a shortened work week. He believes that reducing the number of hours worked might allow the company to offer a significantly reduced salary. To validate his theory, he asks a worker to rank different combinations of weekly hours worked and salary. The worker returns with the following:

(40 hours worked, $45,000) $\succ$ (35 hours worked, $30,000)

(40 hours worked, $45,000) $\prec$ (30 hours worked, $30,000)

(40 hours worked, $45,000) $\succ$ (50 hours worked, $46,000)

Could the HR Manager represent the worker's preferences with an increasing utility function?

Answer: We know that in order for an increasing utility function to exist, preferences must be complete, transitive, and satisfy the monotonicity property. We have no reason to believe that preferences would not be complete, so we will assume they are. In addition, the worker rankings display no intransitive cycles.[2] However, note that monotonicity is violated. In particular, (40 hours worked, $45,000) $\succ$ (50 hours worked, $46,000), but the second bundle clearly has more of each good. Since monotonicity is required for the existence of a monotonic utility function, we know that one does not exist. Intuitively, this occurs because one of the items in the bundle is a "bad". Individuals want smaller work weeks, not larger work weeks.

4.2 Ordinal vs. Cardinal Utility

Assume you have the following preferences over potential careers: actor $\succeq$ consultant $\succeq$ economist. Also assume your preferences are such that a utility func-

---

[2]Although without knowing the full rankings, such as how (35 hours worked, $30,000) compares to (30 hours worked, $30,000), we cannot technically be sure.

tion exists with u(actor)=5, u(consultant)=3, u(economist)=1. Note this utility function represents preferences per our definition. Now consider the question "How much happier does being an actor make you compared to being an economist?". At first glance, you might say "4 utils". However, we have already established that a util is not a real concept. As such, from our utility function, we can not determine the difference in happiness between being an actor and being an economist. We can only determine that being an actor *is preferred* to being an economist. Because utility functions display this property, we call them ordinal.

Definition 4.2 (Ordinal):
An *ordinal* measure is one that tells us the relative ranking of two things, but does not tell us how much more one rank is than the other.

This is in contrast to a *cardinal* measure, which does tell us how much more one rank is than the other.

Example 4.2 (Cardinal vs. Ordinal):
Question: Is height a cardinal or ordinal measure?

Answer: Height is a cardinal measure. In particular, knowing the heights of two different individuals also tells you their difference in height. If, for instance, Katie is 5 feet tall and Pete is 6 feet tall, you can immediately infer that Pete is 1 foot taller.

Example 4.3 (Cardinal vs. Ordinal):
Question: Is "being taller" a cardinal or ordinal measure?

Answer: "Being taller" is an ordinal measure. In particular, knowing that one individual "is taller" than another individual does not tell you how much taller.

Once again consider your career preferences. Instead of u(actor)=5, u(consultant)=3, u(economist)=1, assume that u(actor)=10, u(consultant)=6, u(economist)=2. Has anything changed? Because utility is ordinal, the only thing that matters is the ranking of the choices. Because we have simply doubled each utility, the rankings have not changed. This demonstrates an important property of utility functions:

Theorem 4.4:
A utility function that is a monotonic transformation of another utility function represents the same preferences.

Monotonic transformations are functions that have the property if $x > y$ then $f(x) > f(y)$.

Examples of positive monotonic transformations are:

1. Adding a constant to each utility.

2. Multiplying a positive constant to each utility.

3. Assuming each utility is always positive, raising each utility to a positive power.

Even if they look extremely different, if two utility functions rank all bundles in the same manner, *they represent the same preferences!*

4.3 Examples of Utility Functions

4.3.1 Perfect Complements

Definition 3.15 tells us that complements are goods that "need" each other to be useful. Example 3.11 shows us the corresponding indifference curves are L-shaped. A utility function that captures this "shape" is

$$U(x_1, x_2) = \min(a x_1, b x_2) \tag{4.1}$$

where a and b are constants. To solve for a and b given a preference specification, we perform the following steps.

1. Assume you are told that i units of x_1 and j units of x_2 are required to be useful. For instance, for a pair of shoes to be useful, you need $i = 1$ unit of x_1 (left shoes) and $j = 1$ unit of x_2 (right shoes). In our sandwich example, $i = 2$ units of x_1 (bread) and $j = 3$ units of x_2 (meat) are required to have a sandwich.

2. Set $a = 1$.

3. Solve the following equation for b:

$$i = jb$$

In other words, once you have established the values of i and j given a set of preferences, a utility function that represents these preferences is

$$U(x_1, x_2) = \min(x_1, \frac{i}{j}x_2) \qquad (4.2)$$

Since a monotonic transformation maintains the representation, another utility function that represents these preferences is

$$U(x_1, x_2) = \min(jx_1, ix_2) \qquad (4.3)$$

Note the monotonic transformation we used is $f(x) = jx$. When constructing a utility function for perfect complements, be very careful when determining which value is i and which is j.

Example 4.4 (Perfect Complements):
Question: Find the utility function that represents preferences for automobile frames and tires. Note it requires 1 automobile frame and 4 tires for a "car" to have any value.

Answer: Since the goods are perfect complements, we know the utility function will be in the form $U(x_1, x_2) = \min(ax_1, bx_2)$ where x_1 is the number of automobile frames and x_2 is the number of tires. To solve for a and b,

1. **Assume you are told that i units of x_1 and...**
   We are told that 1 auto frame and 4 tires are required to be useful. Thus $i = 1$ and $j = 4$.

2. **Set a=1.**
   $a = 1$

3. **Solve the following equation for b: $i = jb$.**
   Plugging in $i = 1$ and $j = 4$,

   $$1 = 4b$$

   or

   $$b = \frac{1}{4}$$

Plugging $a = 1$ and $b = 1/4$ into our original utility function, $U(x_1, x_2) = \min(x_1, \frac{1}{4}x_2)$. Note the same preferences are represented by $U(x_1, x_2) = \min(4x_1, x_2)$, which is $U(x_1, x_2) = \min(x_1, \frac{1}{4}x_2)$ multiplied by 4, a monotonic transformation.

4.3.2 Perfect Substitutes

Definition 3.16 tells us that substitutes are goods that are interchangeable. Example 3.12 shows us that indifference curves are shaped like lines. A utility function that captures this "shape" is

$$U(x_1, x_2) = ax_1 + bx_2 \tag{4.4}$$

where a and b are constants. To solve for a and b given a preference specification, we perform the following steps.

1. Assume you are told that i units of x_1 are indifferent to j units of x_2. For instance, $i = 10$ units of salt packets (x_1) are indifferent to $j = 1$ units of salt shakers (x_2).

2. Set $a = 1$.

3. Solve the following equation for b:

$$i = jb$$

In other words, once you have established the values of i and j given a set of preferences, a utility function that represents these preferences is

$$U(x_1, x_2) = x_1 + \frac{i}{j}x_2 \tag{4.5}$$

Since a monotonic transformation maintains the representation, another utility function that represents these preferences is

$$U(x_1, x_2) = jx_1 + ix_2 \tag{4.6}$$

Note the monotonic transformation we used is $f(x) = jx$. When constructing a utility function for perfect substitutes, be very careful when determining which value is i and which is j.

Example 4.5 (Perfect Substitutes):
Question: Find the utility function that represents preferences for single cans of sodas and 6-packs of sodas, where the consumer only cares about the total amount of soda purchased.

Answer: Since the goods are perfect substitutes, we know the utility function will be in the form $U(x_1, x_2) = ax_1 + bx_2$) where x_1 is the number of cans and x_2 is the number of 6-packs. To solve for a and b,

1. **Assume you are told that i units of x_1 and...**
   We are told that 6 cans of soda are equivalent to 1 6-pack of soda. Thus, $i = 6$ and $j = 1$.

2. **Set a=1.**
   $a = 1$

3. **Solve the following equation for b: $i = jb$.**
   Plugging in $i = 6$ and $j = 1$,

   $$6 = b$$

   Plugging $a = 1$ and $b = 6$ into our original utility function, $U(x_1, x_2) = x_1 + 6x_2$.

4.3.3 Cobb-Douglas

A specific kind of utility function is the Cobb-Douglas utility function, which satisfies the equation:

$$U(x_1, x_2) = x_1^\alpha x_2^{1-\alpha} \tag{4.7}$$

where $0 < \alpha < 1$. Cobb-Douglas utility functions represent a specific type of imperfect substitutes/complements and have "nice" properties we will utilize as we extend our analysis. Figure 4.1 shows a typical indifference map of a Cobb-Douglas utility function.

4.4 Recovering Indifference Curves

Because indifference curves and utility functions are both representations of the same underlying preferences, it is natural that we can recover the indifference curves relating to a specific set of preferences by using its utility function. In particular, all points on an indifference curve must have an identical utility level.

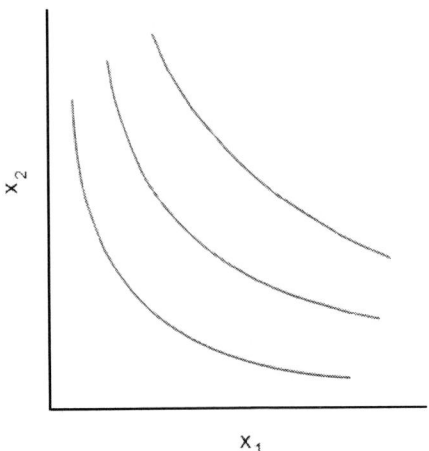

Figure 4.1: Cobb-Douglas Indifference Map

4.4.1 Imperfect Complement Utility Functions

We will demonstrate the technique to recover the indifference curves relating to the preferences of a utility function using Perfect Substitutes, but the steps are the same for any utility function other than Perfect Complements. For instance, assume $U(x_1, x_2) = ax_1 + bx_2$.

1. Replace $U(x_1, x_2)$ with $\overline{U}$ in the utility function equation. i.e. $\overline{U} = ax_1 + bx_2$.

2. Solve for x_2 in terms of x_1 and $\overline{U}$. In this example, $x_2 = \frac{\overline{U} - ax_1}{b}$

3. Select a value of $\overline{U}$ and and arbitrarily select an x_1 point. Solve for x_2 using these values and plot this combination of (x_1, x_2).

4. Keeping the same $\overline{U}$, plot a few more (x_1, x_2) combinations. Connect the dots and you have the indifference curve for $U(x_1, x_2) = \overline{U}$.

5. If you need another indifference curve, simply select a different $\overline{U}$ and repeat the process.

Example 4.6 (Perfect Substitutes):
  Question: $U(x_1, x_2) = 2x_1 + 3x_2$. Draw some indifference curves.

Answer:

1. **Replace $U(x_1, x_2)$ with $\overline{U}$ in the utility function equation.**
   $\overline{U} = 2x_1 + 3x_2$.

2. **Solve for x_2 in terms of x_1 and $\overline{U}$.**
   $x_2 = \frac{\overline{U} - 2x_1}{3}$

3. **Select a value of $\overline{U}$ and and arbitrarily select an x_1 point. Solve for x_2 using these values and plot this combination of (x_1, x_2).**
   Set $\overline{U} = 5$ (we could have used any value). Select $x_1 = 1$ (we again could have used any value).
   $$x_2 = \frac{(5) - 2(1)}{3} = 1$$

   Thus, (1,1) is a point on this indifference curve.

4. **Keeping the same $\overline{U}$, plot a few more (x_1, x_2) combinations. Connect the dots and you have the indifference curve for $U(x_1, x_2) = \overline{U}$.**
   Selecting a few more points for x_1 and solving for x_2, we find the following points are also on the indifference curve for $U(x_1, x_2) = 5$: (2, 1/3), (0,5/3), (5/2,0), (3/2, 2/3). Plotting these points gives us the indifference curve for $U(x_1, x_2) = 5$ as shown in Figure 4.2.

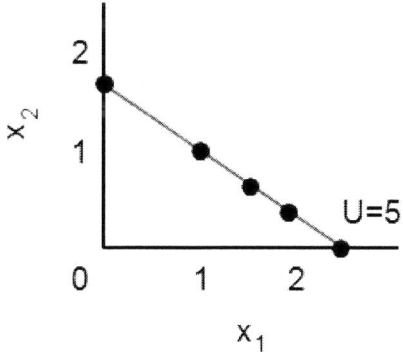

Figure 4.2: Indifference Curve for U=5

4.4.2 Perfect Complement Utility Functions

To recover the indifferent curves relating to the preferences of a perfect complement utility function, we must use a different approach. Assume you are given preferences of the form $U(x_1, x_2) = \min(ax_1, bx_2)$, which we know is the standard utility representation of perfect complements.

1. Select an integer, n.

2. Draw the point, (nb, na).

3. Draw a horizontal line to the right of that point and a vertical line above that point. In other words, make (nb, na) the "kink" in an "L".

4. The "L" you just drew is the indifference curve corresponding to a utility of $U(x_1, x_2) = nab$.

5. If you need another indifference curve, simply select a different n and repeat the process.

> **Example 4.7 (Perfect Complements):**
> **Question:** $U(x_1, x_2) = \min(2x_1, x_2)$. Draw some indifference curves.
>
> **Answer:**
>
> 1. **Select an integer, n. $n = 1$**
> 2. **Draw the point, (nb, na).** Since $a = 2$, $b = 1$, $(1, 2)$ is a point on an indifference curve.
> 3. **Draw a horizontal line to the right of that point and a vertical line above that point. In other words, make (nb, na) the "kink" in an "L".** With $(1,2)$ at the "kink", points that make up the "L" include $(2,2)$, $(3,2)$, $(1,3)$, $(1,4)$, etc.
> 4. **The "L" you just drew is the indifference curve corresponding to a utility of $U(x_1, x_2) = nab$.** Plotting these points gives us the indifference curve for $U(x_1, x_2) = nab = (1)(2)(1) = 2$ as shown in Figure 4.3.

4.5   Marginal Rate of Substitution

As we are still in the process of building up an Economic Model of decision-making, it is worthwhile to place our findings into the context of our Steps of Quantitative Economic Thinking outlined in Definition (1.4).

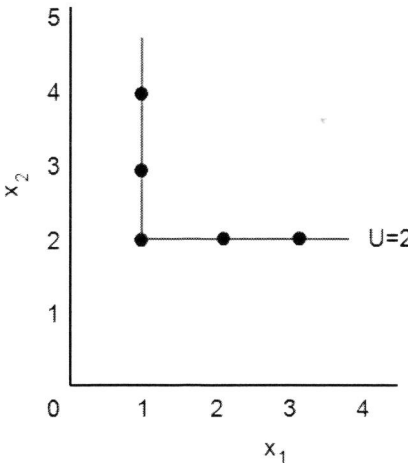

Figure 4.3: Indifference Curve for U=2

Definition 4.3 (Steps of Quantitative Economic Thinking):

1. Identify the Problem The problem we are currently addressing is "How will an individual choose when given the choice between options?"

2. Create a Mathematical Model We have mathematically modeled individual decision-makers as being analogous to rational preference relations.

3. Solve the Mathematical Model This is the step in which we currently find ourselves. We have made significant progress in Solving the Mathematical Model, as we have determined that a rational set of preference relations can be represented by a well-behaved Utility Function.

4. Relate the Results Back to Reality For the most part, we have not reached this step, yet.

This section will extend Step 3, by expanding on some of the benefits and intuition that a Utility representation offers. Specifically, we will introduce the concept of the Marginal Rate of Substitution, which has a very intuitive definition and can be directly calculated from a Utility function.

Example 4.8 (Maybe We Can?):
Question: Assume you are a policy wonk advising Barack Obama on optimal environmental policy. In particular, Mr. Obama has asked you the following question: "I would like to increase fuel efficiency standards but keep our average automobile consumer as happy as they are today. I have an estimated utility function for the average consumer, and I have been told the performance/fuel efficiency the average consumer currently obtains. I recognize that making a consumer's car more fuel efficient will result in decreased performance, so the fuel efficiency gains need to offset this performance loss. For a reduction of 1 horsepower (HP) of vehicle performance, how much efficiency gain must I deliver so the average consumer feels the tradeoff is worthwhile?"

Answer: ?

4.5.1 Definitions

To answer this question, we need to introduce the concept of the marginal rate of substitution.

Definition 4.4 (Marginal Rate of Substitution - Verbal):
- The *marginal rate of substitution* is the maximum amount of one good that a consumer will sacrifice to obtain one more unit of another good.

- Assume one unit of a good is taken away. The *marginal rate of substitution* is the number of units of the other good the consumer must be given to keep him just as well off (i.e. at the same utility level).

In other words, the marginal rate of substitution tells us how much we are willing to trade one good for the other. From the second definition, it should be clear that a marginal rate of substitution relates to a single indifference curve. Because we are dealing with a single curve, we can think of this curve as a function relating x_1 (the first good) to x_2, as demonstrated in Figure 4.4.

Thinking of the indifference curve as a function allows us to use the mathematical tools we developed in Calculus. First, consider the concept of the slope of a tangent line.

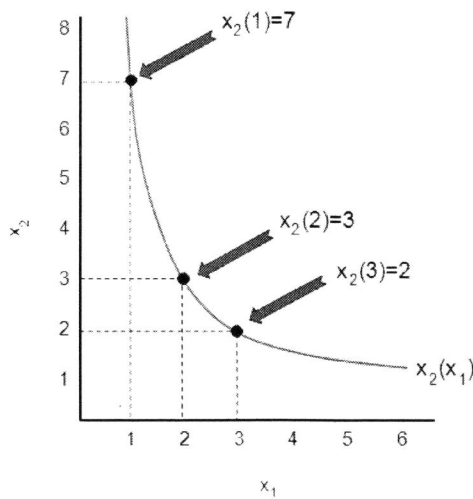

Figure 4.4: A Single Indifference Curve as a Function, $x_2(x_1)$

Definition 4.5 (Very Informal Slope of a Tangent Line):
When negative, the *slope of a tangent line* to the function, $f(x)$, tells us how much $f(x)$ must increase if 1 unit of x is taken away.

Note this definition is essentially identical to the second definition in Definition 4.4. In particular, using the indifference "function", $x_2(x_1)$, Definition 4.4 is the same as Definition 4.5 with:

- $f(x) = x_2(x_1)$

- $x = x_1$

We therefore see that the marginal rate of substitution at a given point is nothing more than the slope of the tangent line to the indifference curve at that point.

Definition 4.6 (Marginal Rate of Substitution - Graphical):
The *marginal rate of substitution* at a given point is the slope of the tangent line to the indifference curve at that point.

Figure 4.5 reflects this interpretation.

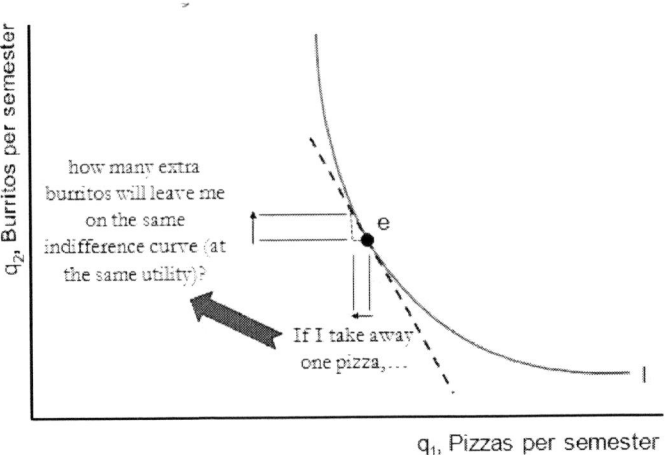

Figure 4.5: Marginal Rate of Substitution as Slope of the Tangent Line to the Indifference Curve

Note we have graphically established that the marginal rate of substitution is nothing more than the slope of the tangent line of the indifference curve at a particular point. Note from Definition 2.1 this is exactly the definition of the derivative of the indifference curve.

> **Definition 4.7 (Marginal Rate of Substitution - Calculus):**
> The *marginal rate of substitution* at a given point is the slope of the indifference curve, $x_2(x_1)$. Thus, $\text{MRS}_{x_1,x_2} = \frac{dx_2}{dx_1}$.

Note MRS_{x_1,x_2} is the amount of x_2 needed to compensate for 1 unit of x_1. The units are $\frac{x_2 \text{ units}}{x_1 \text{ units}}$. MRS_{x_2,x_1}, however, is the amount of x_1 needed to compensate for 1 unit of x_2. The units are $\frac{x_1 \text{ units}}{x_2 \text{ units}}$. Not surprisingly, $\text{MRS}_{x_1,x_2} = \frac{1}{\text{MRS}_{x_2,x_1}}$.

4.5.2 Marginal Utility

We can now revisit Barack Obama's assignment. From what we have just learned, we know that if we can determine the slope of the indifference curve, we will have exactly the information our President requires. Unfortunately, if we reexamine the information given to us, we are not given the slope of the indifference curve.

We are only given the utility function itself. Luckily, we can use the utility function to give us exactly what we need. In particular, we will introduce the concept of marginal utility.

> **Definition 4.8 (Marginal Utility - Verbal):**
> The *marginal utility* of a good is the extra amount of utility a consumer receives by receiving an extra unit of the good.

Alternatively, recalling the definition of a derivative, it should be clear that

> **Definition 4.9 (Marginal Utility - Calculus):**
> The *marginal utility* of good, x_1, is $\text{MU}_{x_1} = \frac{\partial U}{\partial x_1}$.

It is important to recognize that total utility is generally calculated from multiple goods. In our examples so far, for instance, we have always focused on 2 goods at a time. Notice that Definition 4.9 is specific to a *single* good at a time. As such, to solve for the marginal utility of a *specific* good, we need to calculate the *partial* derivative of U with respect to that good.

> **Example 4.9 (Marginal Utility):**
> **Question:** Given the utility function, $U(x_1, x_2) = x_1^{1/2} x_2^{1/2}$, what is the marginal utility with respect to x_1? What is the marginal utility with respect to x_2?
>
> **Answer:** To solve for the marginal utility of a particular good, we need only take the partial derivate of the utility function with respect to that good. Therefore:
>
> $$\begin{aligned} \text{MU}_{x_1} &= \frac{\partial U}{\partial x_1} \\ &= \frac{1}{2} x_1^{-1/2} x_2^{1/2} \end{aligned}$$
>
> and
>
> $$\begin{aligned} \text{MU}_{x_2} &= \frac{\partial U}{\partial x_2} \\ &= \frac{1}{2} x_1^{1/2} x_2^{-1/2} \end{aligned}$$

4.5.3 Marginal Rate of Substitution and Marginal Utility

To make the connection between a utility function and the slope of its indifference curve (its MRS), we need one additional step. In particular, recall that an indifference curve can be interpreted as a function, $x_2(x_1)$. Also, recall that a particular indifference curve is specific to a fixed level of utility, $\overline{U}$.

$$\overline{U} \equiv U\big(x_1, x_2(x_1)\big) \tag{4.8}$$

Note this equation always holds by definition. In particular, $x_2(x_1)$ is the value of x_2 that ensures the utility function remains at $\overline{U}$. Since this equation always holds, we can take its derivative with respect to x_1. Using the Chain Rule,

$$\frac{d\overline{U}}{dx_1} = 0 = \frac{\partial U\big((x_1, x_2(x_1))\big)}{\partial x_1} + \frac{\partial U\big((x_1, x_2(x_1))\big)}{\partial x_2}\frac{dx_2}{dx_1} \tag{4.9}$$

or, using simpler notation,

$$\frac{d\overline{U}}{dx_1} = 0 = U_1 + U_2\frac{dx_2}{dx_1} \tag{4.10}$$

Note $\frac{d\overline{U}}{dx_1} = 0$ because $\overline{U}$ is a constant and the derivative of a constant is 0. If we further simplify Eqn. 4.10, we find

$$\frac{dx_2}{dx_1} = -\frac{U_1}{U_2} = -\frac{\frac{\partial U}{\partial x_1}}{\frac{\partial U}{\partial x_2}} \tag{4.11}$$

Note that $\frac{dx_2}{dx_1}$ is exactly the definition of MRS_{x_1,x_2}. We can now combine all our results into one theorem.

Theorem 4.5 (Marginal Rate of Substitution):
The following are all characterizations of the marginal rate of substitution between goods x_1 and x_2

---

1. MRS_{x_1,x_2} *is the maximum amount of x_2 that a consumer will sacrifice to obtain one more unit of x_1.*

2. MRS_{x_1,x_2} *is the slope of the indifference curve, $x_2(x_1)$.*

3. $MRS_{x_1,x_2} = -\dfrac{U_1}{U_2}$

Example 4.10 (Yes We Can):

Question: Assume you are a policy wonk advising Barack Obama on optimal environmental policy. In particular, Mr. Obama has asked you the following question: "I would like to increase fuel efficiency standards but keep our average automobile consumer as happy as they are today. I have an estimated utility function for the average consumer and it is $U(x_1, x_2) = x_1 x_2$ where $x_1 = $ performance and $x_2 = $ fuel efficiency. I have also been told the average consumer vehicle currently has 150 horsepower (HP), and has a fuel efficiency of 20mpg. I recognize that making a consumer's car more fuel efficient will result in decreased performance, so the fuel efficiency gains need to offset this performance loss. For a reduction of 1 HP, how much efficiency gain must I deliver so the average consumer feels the tradeoff is worthwhile?"

Answer: The question is asking how much fuel efficiency is needed to offset 1 unit of performance. Thus we are looking for MRS_{x_1,x_2}. Using Theorem 4.5,

$$MRS_{x_1,x_2} = -\frac{U_1}{U_2} \tag{4.12}$$

Solving for U_1 and U_2,

$$U_1 = x_2 \tag{4.13}$$
$$U_2 = x_1 \tag{4.14}$$

Plugging Eqns. 4.13 and 4.14 into Eqn. 4.12, we find that

$$MRS_{x_1,x_2} = \frac{x_2}{x_1}$$

and at our current performance/fuel efficiency levels:

$$MRS_{x_1,x_2} = \frac{20}{150} = \frac{2}{15} \text{ mpg /HP}$$

In other words, the average consumer will require an extra $\frac{2}{15}$ mpg to offset a 1 HP reduction in their car's performance.

Note in this example, the final results seem plausible. You should always check to see if your results "make sense". What if we had found that the average consumer requires an extra 250 mpg to offset a 1 HP reduction in their car's performance? Given the recent trend toward fuel-efficient cars, does this make sense? In situations where the results are nonsensical, your first step should be to check your math. If you are sure of your steps, question your assumptions. In particular, did Mr. Obama give you the correct utility function? Are the current estimates of fuel efficiency correct? Are consumer preferences rational?

Example 4.11 (Perfect Substitutes):
Question: Consider the preferences for 6-inch meatball subs and 12-inch meatball subs. An individual is indifferent between receiving 2 6-inch meatball subs or 1 12-inch meatball sub. We have previously determined these preferences can be represented via. the utility function, $U(x_1, x_2) = x_1 + .5x_2$ where x_1 is a 12-inch sub and x_2 is a 6-inch sub. What are the slopes of the indifference curves?.

Answer: Using Theorem 4.5,

$$MRS_{x_1, x_2} = -\frac{U_1}{U_2} \qquad (4.15)$$

Solving for U_1 and U_2,

$$U_1 = 1 \qquad (4.16)$$
$$U_2 = 0.5 \qquad (4.17)$$

Plugging Eqns. 4.16 and 4.17 into Eqn. 4.15, we find that

$$MRS_{x_1, x_2} = -2$$

Note this finding corresponds to Example 3.12, which showed us the indifference curves of perfect substitutes are lines. A key property of lines is that their slope stays the same regardless of the point at which the slope is measured. This is the case here, where $MRS_{x_1, x_2} = -2$ at every x_1 and x_2. Compare this to Example 4.10, where the slope of the indifference curve changes with x_1 and x_2.

Example 4.12 (Cobb-Douglas):
Question: What is the marginal rate of substitution between goods x_1 and x_2 for a consumer having a Cobb-Douglas utility function, $U = x_1^\alpha x_2^{1-\alpha}$?
Answer: Using Theorem 4.5,

$$MRS_{x_1, x_2} = -\frac{U_1}{U_2} \qquad (4.18)$$

Solving for U_1 and U_2,

$$U_1 = \alpha x_1^{\alpha-1} x_2^{1-\alpha} \tag{4.19}$$

$$U_2 = (1-\alpha) x_1^{\alpha} x_2^{-\alpha} \tag{4.20}$$

Plugging Eqns. 4.19 and 4.20 into Eqn. 4.18, we find that

$$
\begin{aligned}
MRS_{x_1,x_2} &= -\frac{\alpha x_1^{\alpha-1} x_2^{1-\alpha}}{(1-\alpha) x_1^{\alpha} x_2^{-\alpha}} \\
&= -\frac{\alpha}{1-\alpha} x_1^{\alpha-1-\alpha} x_2^{1-\alpha-(-\alpha)} \\
&= -\frac{\alpha}{1-\alpha} \frac{x_2}{x_1}
\end{aligned}
$$

Chapter 5

Constrained Optimization

We have made considerable strides in modeling human choice. We have gone from the concept that "a person has a preference between two bundles" to "that preference can be mathematically modeled using a utility function". While this is a fundamental step in economics, it still does not give us insight into how consumers will act on a daily basis. The reason is demonstrated in the following example.

> **Example 5.1 (Unconstrained Optimization):**
> **Question:** An individual views chocolate chip cookies and milk as perfect complements. She would like as many cookies and glasses of milk as possible. What bundle would make her most happy?
>
> **Answer:** If, as stated, this individual would really like as many cookies and glasses of milk as possible, then this consumer would like all the cookies in the world and all the glasses of milk in the world.

Obviously, this scenario is unrealistic. As long as cookies cost money, even Bill Gates could not afford all the cookies in the world. The concept we have ignored up to this point is that individuals cannot select any bundle they desire. They can only select a bundle *they can afford*. This selection process is called *constrained optimization*.

> **Definition 5.1 (Constrained Optimization):**
> When faced with a constraint such as a limited budget or a limited supply of a product, *constrained optimization* is the process of selecting the most preferred bundle subject to the constraint.

5.1 Budget Constraint

The constraint we will focus on is the *budget constraint*.

> **Definition 5.2 (Budget Constraint):**
> A consumer's *budget constraint* is the amount of income they have available to purchase goods.

The budget constraint limits the bundles the consumer can afford. Because we assume all goods have a price, there is a limited number of goods an individual can buy given his income. The bundles that an individual can purchase are referred to as the *budget set* (or opportunity set).

> **Definition 5.3 (Budget Set - Verbal):**
> A consumer's *budget set* (or opportunity set) is the set of bundles he can afford.

To further utilize the tools we have developed so far, it would be useful to develop a graphical representation of the budget set.

> **Example 5.2 (Budget Set):**
> **Question:** Assume the price of a pencil is $2.00 and the price of a notebook is $3.00. You have $12 budgeted for purchasing your writing materials. Graphically, with pencils on the x-axis and notebooks on the y-axis, what does your budget set look like?
>
> **Answer:** Your budget set is all combinations of pencils and notebooks that will cost you less than or equal to $12. For instance, if you spent all your money on notebooks, you could purchase 4 notebooks. Thus, (0 pencils, 4 notebooks) is a point in your budget set. Note if you could afford (0 pencils, 4 notebooks), then you can also afford (0 pencils, 3 notebooks) since that costs less money. Thus, (0 pencils, 3 notebooks) is also in your budget set. Likewise, if you spent all your money on pencils, you could purchase (6 pencils, 0 notebooks) and since that is affordable, so is (5 pencils, 0 notebooks), (4 pencils, 0 notebooks), etc.. You could also afford a combination of the two products, such as (3 pencils, 2 notebooks), which implies (3 pencils, 1 notebook) is also affordable as well as (2 pencils, 2 notebooks), etc. If we plot all possible affordable bundles, we obtain the budget set illustrated in Figure (5.2)

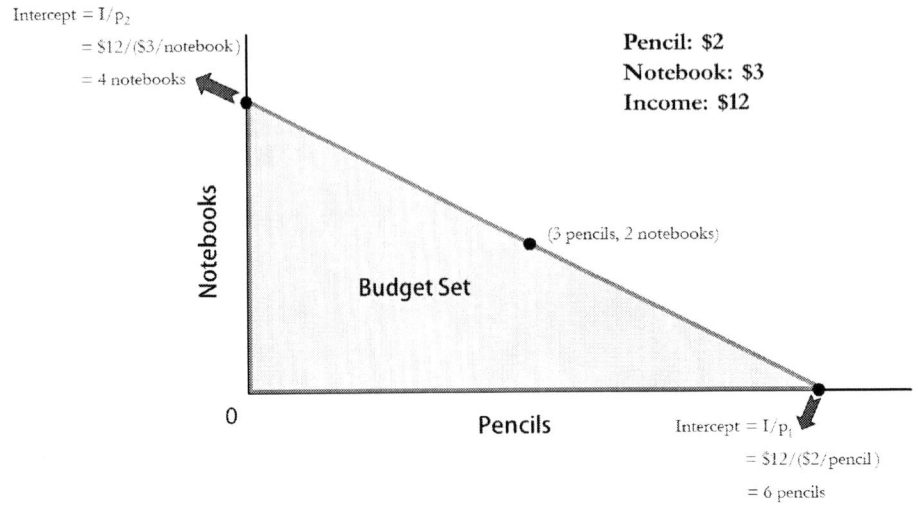

Figure 5.1: Example (5.2) - Graphical Representation of the Budget Set

5.1.1 Budget Line

From Figure 5.1, it can be seen that the sets of goods that cause the consumer to spend all their income make up a downward sloping line. Specifically, note that these points satisfy the equation

$$p_1 x_1 + p_2 x_2 = I \tag{5.1}$$

where

p_1: the price of good 1

p_2: the price of good 2

x_1: the number of units of good 1 the consumer purchases

x_2: the number of units of good 2 the consumer purchases

I: the consumer's income

If we rearrange this equation, we find

$$x_2 = -\frac{p_1}{p_2}x_1 + \frac{I}{p_2} \tag{5.2}$$

Compare Eqn. 5.2 with the standard "slope-intercept" form of a line with x_1 on the x-axis and x_2 on the y-axis: $x_2 = mx_1 + b$. You should note it is identical with $m = -\frac{p_1}{p_2}$ and $b = \frac{I}{p_2}$.

Example 5.3 (Budget Line):

Question: Assume the price of a pencil is $2.00 and the price of a notebook is $3.00. You have $12 budgeted for purchasing your writing materials. Graphically, with pencils on the x-axis and notebooks on the y-axis, what does your budget line look like?

Answer: As shown in Figure (5.2), the budget line is just the upper limit of the entire budget set. i.e. it is the combination of products that fully exhausts the consumer's income.

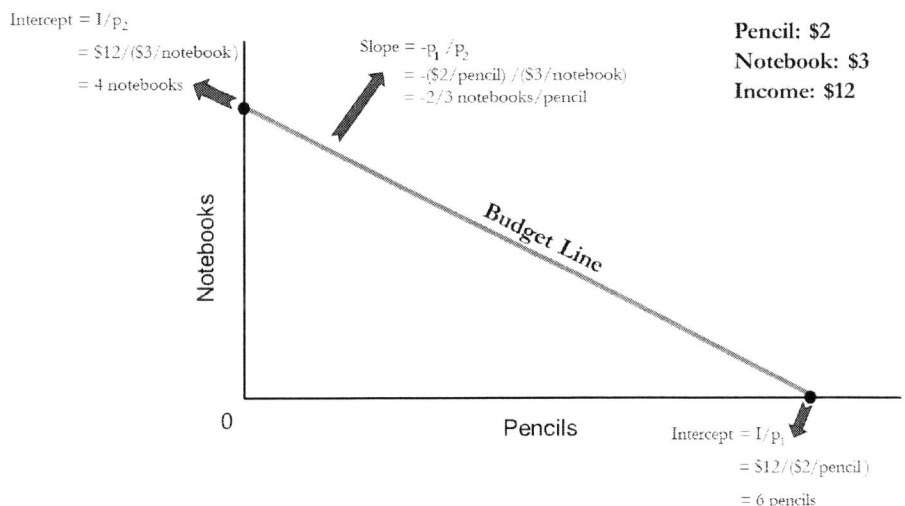

Figure 5.2: Example (5.3) - Graphical Representation of the Budget Line

The budget line has several extremely important properties.

- The *budget set* consists of all points on or below the *budget line*. Naturally, if you can afford a bundle on the budget line, you can afford a bundle below the budget line, in which you buy less of good x_2.

- As shown in Eqn. 5.2, the y-axis intercept is equal to $\frac{I}{p_2}$. This should make intuitive sense, since the y-axis intercept of the budget line tells us how many units of x_2 we can purchase if we spent all our income on it. Naturally, this will be your income divided by the price of the good. As an example, ask yourself how many cars you could buy if you have $100,000, a car costs $20,000, and you spend all your money on cars.

- The x-axis intercept is equal to $\frac{I}{p_1}$. This can be solved from Eqn. 5.2, or can be intuitively found using the same logic as the y-axis intercept.

5.2 Marginal Rate of Transformation

The final property of the budget line, and perhaps the most important, concerns its slope. As shown in Eqn. 5.2, the slope of the budget line is $-\frac{p_1}{p_2}$. As discussed in Definition 4.5, this slope (because it is negative) can be interpreted as how much x_2 can increase if 1 unit of x_1 is taken away.

> **Example 5.4 (Budget Line Slope):**
> **Question:** Assume the price of a pencil is $2.00 and the price of a notebook is $3.00. If 1 pencil is given up, how many additional notebooks can be purchased?
>
> **Answer:** If 1 pencil is given up, the consumer can gain $2.00 (since that is the price of pencils). He can then purchase $2.00/($3/notebook) = 2/3 notebook. Note this is identical to the statement "the slope of the budget line is $-\frac{p_1}{p_2} = -\frac{2}{3}$".

It should be clear that this tradeoff if very similar to the tradeoff made when studying the marginal rate of substitution. The marginal rate of substitution tells us how much additional x_2 *is required* to offset a 1 unit reduction of x_1 for the consumer. The slope of the budget line tells us how much additional x_2 *can be purchased* given a 1 unit reduction of x_1. Because of the similarities, the slope of the budget line has been given a specific name.

> **Definition 5.4 (Marginal Rate of Transformation):**
> The slope of the budget line is also called the *Marginal Rate of Transformation*, or MRT_{x_1,x_2}.

Combining our results,

Theorem 5.1 (Marginal Rate of Transformation):
The following are all characterizations of the marginal rate of transformation between goods x_1 and x_2

1. MRT_{x_1,x_2} *is the maximum additional amount of x_2 that a consumer can purchase given a 1-unit reduction of x_1.*

2. MRT_{x_1,x_2} *is the slope of the budget line.*

3. $MRT_{x_1,x_2} = -\frac{p_1}{p_2}$

The fundamental difference between the MRS and MRT is that the MRS is specific to one individual. It relates to their specific preferences and their specific willingness to exchange the goods. The MRT, on the other hand, is specific to the market. Any consumer trading two goods faces the same MRT, in that it is simply related to the market prices.

While these two terms measure drastically different concepts, we will soon find they are crucially related in a consumer's budget-constrained optimization problem.

5.3 Constrained Optimization - Graphical

Example 5.5 (Constrained Optimization):
Question: Consider a student selecting the optimal number of burritos and pizza slices she would like to consume for a given week. The price of a slice of pizza is $1.00 and the price of a burrito is $2.00. She has $25.00 to spend on food, making her budget set as shown in Figure 5.3(a). Her preferences are such that pizza and burritos are neither perfect substitutes nor perfect complements, as demonstrated in Figure 5.3(b). Assuming this student selects bundles according to her preferences (which we will always assume), what affordable bundle will she select?

Answer: ?

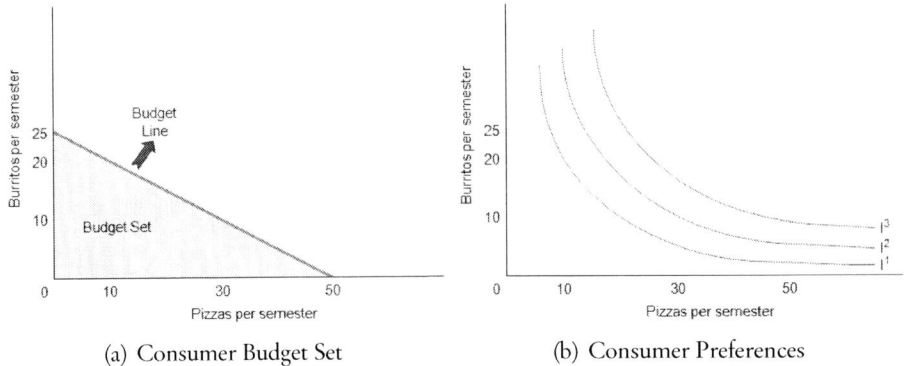

(a) Consumer Budget Set   (b) Consumer Preferences

Figure 5.3: Constrained Optimization Problem

To answer this question, we will examine different possible bundles. First, we look at a point below the budget line, as shown in Figure 5.4(a).

Example 5.6 (Constrained Optimization - Point Below the Budget Line):
Question: Will the student in Example 5.5 select point d, as shown in Figure 5.4(a)?

Answer: Assuming the monotonicity property holds, then we know from section 3.6 that bundles on indifference curves farther from the origin are preferred to those on curves closer to the origin. Consider a point with slightly more pizza and burritos that is still affordable. It will be on an indifference curve farther from the origin than D, and therefore preferred to D. If selecting according to her preferences, the student will then select this bundle instead of D.

From this example, it is clear that as long as the monotonicity property holds (which we will generally assume is the case), the optimal constrained bundle will be on the budget line. In other words, all the individual's income will be spent on the goods.[1] To determine if all points on the budget line will be optimal, let us look at another example.

Example 5.7 (Constrained Optimization - Point On the Budget Line):
Question: Will the student in Example 5.5 select point c, as shown in Figure 5.4(b)?

---

[1]It is worth noting in these examples that we are assuming only two goods exist, and there is no benefit to saving money for future consumption. Richer models incorporate these concepts.

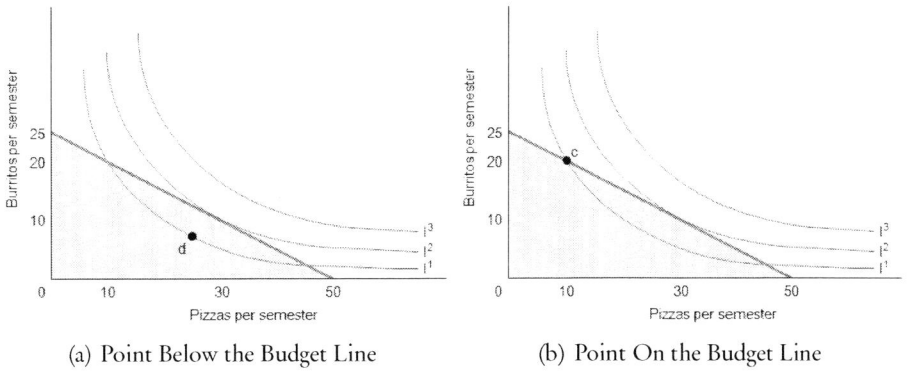

(a) Point Below the Budget Line   (b) Point On the Budget Line

Figure 5.4: Constrained Optimization Problem

Answer: Move slightly down the budget line from point C. Due to the shape of the indifference curves, this point will be on a higher indifference curve than point C, and therefore preferred. Therefore, if selecting according to her preferences, the student will not select C.

Continuing with this logic, we find that the student will prefer point E, as shown in Figure 5.5.

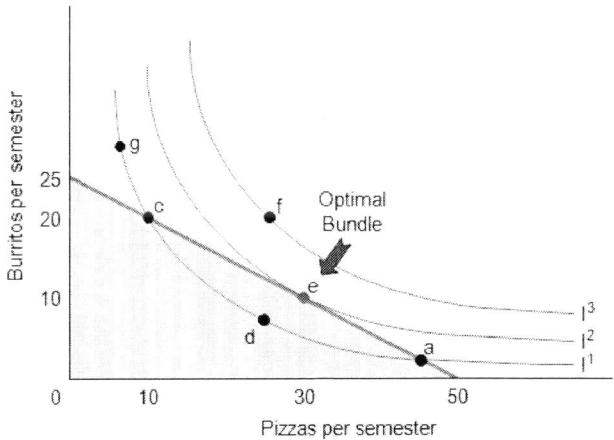

Figure 5.5: Constrained Optimization - Optimal Bundle

From Figure 5.5, we see a very important property concerning the optimal bundle. In particular, when the optimal bundle contains positive amounts of each good, the budget line is tangent to the indifference curve containing the ideal point. In other words, the slope of the budget line is identical to the slope of the indifference curve at the ideal point. Using Theorem 4.5 and Definition 5.4, this is identical to recognizing that at the ideal bundle the marginal rate of substitution equals the marginal rate of transformation. Or, intuitively, the rate at which the consumer is willing to exchange the goods is equal to the rate at which the market is willing to exchange the goods.

Note these characterizations are for situations in which the optimal bundle contains positive amounts of each good. We call bundles such as these *interior solutions*, per Definition 2.5.

Definition 5.5 (Interior Solution):
Consider a consumer's budget-constrained optimization problem. An *interior solution* or *interior optimum* is an optimal bundle such that a positive amount of both goods is consumed.

Combining our findings,

Theorem 5.2 (Interior Solution to the Consumer Problem):
An interior solution to the budget-constrained optimization problem of a consumer having the monotonicity property has the following properties

1. *All income is spent on the goods. i.e.* $I = p_1 x_1^* + p_2 x_2^*$.

2. *The budget line is tangent to the indifference curve at the interior optimum.*

3. *The slope of the budget line is identical to the slope of the indifference curve at the interior optimum.*

4. $MRS_{x_1,x_2}(x_1^*, x_2^*) = MRT_{x_1,x_2}(x_1^*, x_2^*)$ *where* (x_1^*, x_2^*) *is the interior optimum.*

5. $-\frac{U_1(x_1^*, x_2^*)}{U_2(x_1^*, x_2^*)} = -\frac{p_1}{p_2}$ *where* (x_1^*, x_2^*) *is the interior optimum.*

It is important to note that not all solutions to a consumer's constrained optimization problem are interior. Recall solutions that are not interior are called *corner solutions*

> **Definition 5.6 (Corner Solution):**
> Consider a consumer's budget-constrained optimization problem. A *corner solution* is an optimal bundle such that at least one good is not consumed.

Consider the following example.

> **Example 5.8 (Constrained Optimization (Noninterior)):**
> **Question:** Consider a student selecting the optimal number of burritos and pizza slices she would like to consume for a given week. The price of a slice of pizza is $1.00 and the price of a burrito is $2.00. She has $25.00 to spend on food, making her budget set as shown in Figure 5.3(a). Her preferences are quasilinear, as demonstrated in Figure 5.6(b). Assuming this student selects bundles according to her preferences (which we will always assume), what affordable bundle will she select?
>
> **Answer:** The solution is shown in Figure 5.6(c).

Note that Theorem 5.2 only says that *if* the solution is interior, then the stated conditions will hold. For corner solutions, these conditions do not necessarily have to hold. In Figure 5.6(c), the tangency condition does hold, but this is abnormal. Generally, corner solutions will look like Figure 5.7, in which none of the conditions in Theorem 5.2 apply.

5.3.1 Interior vs. Corner

Mathematical methods exist to determine if an interior solution exists. Because we are only dealing with two goods, we will take an easier approach. In particular:

1. Assume an interior solution exists and solve per Theorem 5.2 to determine (x_1^*, x_2^*). If no solution exists with $x_1^* \geq 0$ and $x_2^* \geq 0$, you have a corner solution. Alternatively, it might be the case that your objective function is not differentiable, such as the case of Perfect Complements. In such a situation, draw the budget line and indifference curves, and take a strictly graphical approach using intuition.

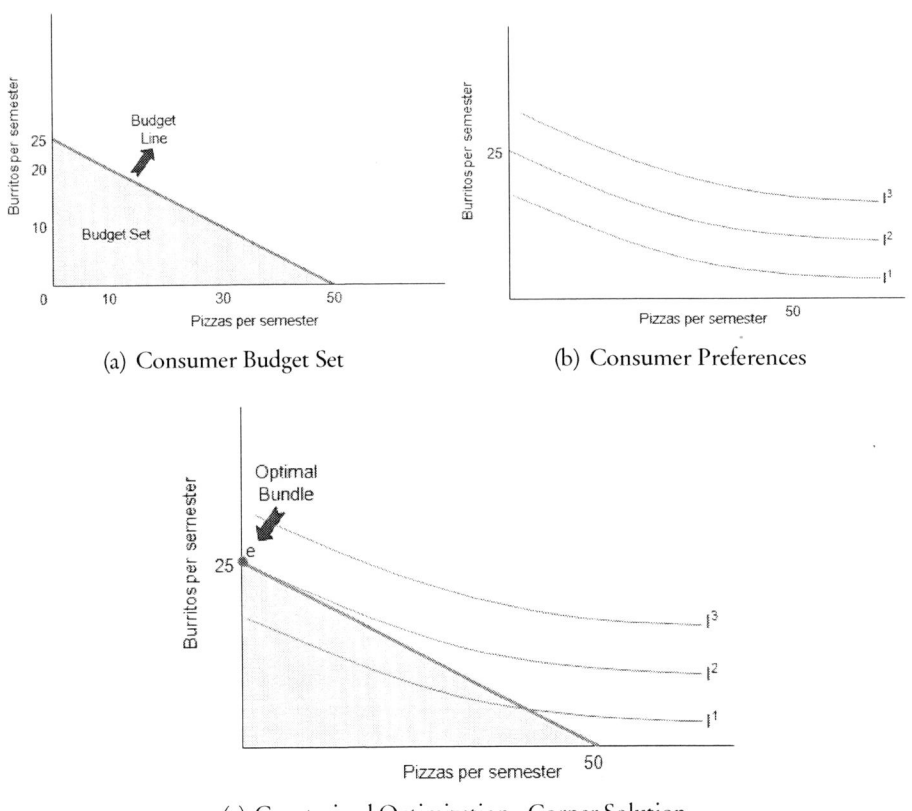

(a) Consumer Budget Set

(b) Consumer Preferences

(c) Constrained Optimization - Corner Solution

Figure 5.6: Example (5.8) - Constrained Optimization Problem

$160 = 4x_1 + 10x_2 \qquad 25x_1 \qquad 10x_2 \qquad 10$

$96 = 3x_1 + 10x_2 \qquad 30x_1 \qquad 9x_2 \quad y_2$

$x_1 \qquad 15 \qquad 25$

$y_1 = 10 - \frac{2}{5}x$

$y_2 = 9 - \frac{3}{10}x$

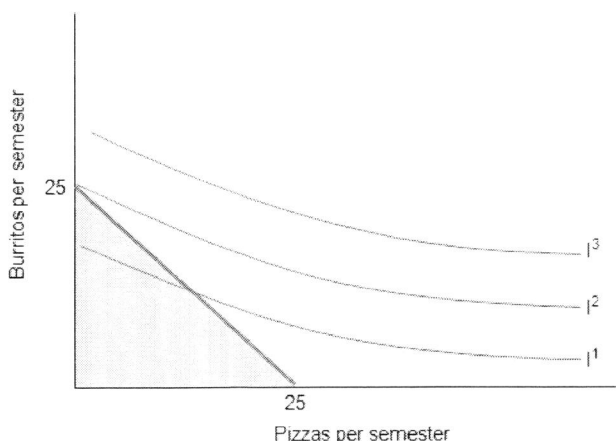

Figure 5.7: Constrained Optimization - Corner Solution

2. Determine the utility at the two corner solutions. In particular, solve for $U(\frac{I}{p_1},0)$ and $U(0,\frac{I}{p_2})$. Compare $U(x_1^*,x_2^*)$, $U(\frac{I}{p_1},0)$, and $U(0,\frac{I}{p_2})$. If $U(x_1^*,x_2^*)$ is the largest, you have an interior solution and (x_1^*,x_2^*) is your optimal bundle. If $U(\frac{I}{p_1},0)$ is the largest, you have a corner solution and $(\frac{I}{p_1},0)$ is your optimal bundle. If $U(0,\frac{I}{p_2})$ is the largest, you have a corner solution and $(0,\frac{I}{p_2})$ is your optimal bundle.

5.4 Constrained Optimization - Calculus

While the graphical approach to constrained optimization generates correct results, it is extremely limited in its applications. Consider, for instance, the scenario in which there are more than 2 goods. Drawing the budget "line" and indifference curves would prove difficult. For more than 3 goods, it is impossible. By using calculus and the utility representation of preferences, we are able to bypass this problem and develop significant insights. We will focus on the 2-good case, but all results can be extended using normal calculus techniques.

As always, we assume that consumers are rational. We also continue to assume the monotonicity property holds. Using Theorem 4.1, we then know that an increasing utility function exists which represents the consumer's preferences. Therefore, the "most preferred" bundle will have the highest utility value. The problem of maximizing the utility function subject to the budget constraint is called the *utility maximization problem (UMP)* or the *consumer's problem*.

> **Definition 5.7 (Utility Maximization Problem):**
> The *utility maximization problem* (or *consumer's problem*) is the constrained optimization problem:
>
> $$\max_{x_1,x_2} U(x_1, x_2) \text{ such that (s.t.) } I = p_1 x_1 + p_2 x_2 \qquad (5.3)$$

In words, the UMP states "find the optimal bundle, (x_1^*, x_2^*), that makes the utility function as large as possible such that all the available income is spent". To find the interior optimal bundle in a constrained optimization problem, two approaches can be used. Note these approaches, like Theorem 5.2, are not valid for corner solutions.

5.4.1 UMP - Substitution Approach

The first approach to solving for an interior solution to a constrained optimization is:

1. Using the constraint, solve for one variable, a, in terms of the other, b. This will result in an equation for a in terms of b, $a(b)$.

2. Plug $a(b)$ into the utility function wherever a is found.

3. Remove a from the list of variables to be maximized.

4. Maximize this utility function with respect to the remaining variables (b) using standard calculus techniques.

5. Plug the optimal values of b solved in the last step into $a(b)$ to solve for the optimal value of a.

Using this technique on the UMP,

> **Example 5.9 (UMP - Substitution Approach):**
> **Question:** Solve the UMP using the substitution approach
>
> **Answer:** Following the steps above,

1. **Using the constraint, solve for x_2 in terms of x_1:**

$$
\begin{aligned}
I &= p_1 x_1 + p_2 x_2 \\
\Rightarrow p_2 x_2 &= I - p_1 x_1 \\
\Rightarrow x_2 &= \frac{I - p_1 x_1}{p_2}
\end{aligned}
$$

2. **Plug this equation into the utility function wherever x_2 is found:**

$$
U(x_1, x_2) \Rightarrow U(x_1, \frac{I - p_1 x_1}{p_2})
$$

3. **Remove x_2 from the list of variables to be maximized:**

$$
\max_{x_1, x_2} U(x_1, \frac{I - p_1 x_1}{p_2}) \Rightarrow \max_{x_1} U(x_1, \frac{I - p_1 x_1}{p_2})
$$

4. **Maximize this utility function with respect to the remaining variables using standard calculus techniques:**

To maximize the above equation, we use its first order conditions. In particular, find the derivative of $U(x_1, \frac{I - p_1 x_1}{p_2})$ with respect to x_1, set this equal to zero, then solve for the optimal x_1^*. Using the Chain Rule,

$$
\frac{dU}{dx_1} = U_1(x_1, \frac{I - p_1 x_1}{p_2}) + -\frac{p_1}{p_2} x_1 U_2(x_1, \frac{I - p_1 x_1}{p_2})
$$

The optimal amount of x_1 will cause the above equation to equal zero at an interior solution.

$$
U_1(x_1^*, \frac{I - p_1 x_1^*}{p_2}) + -\frac{p_1}{p_2} x_1^* U_2(x_1^*, \frac{I - p_1 x_1^*}{p_2}) = 0 \tag{5.4}
$$

$$
\Rightarrow -\frac{U_1(x_1^*, \frac{I - p_1 x_1^*}{p_2})}{U_2(x_1^*, \frac{I - p_1 x_1^*}{p_2})} = -\frac{p_1}{p_2} \tag{5.5}
$$

At this point, because we do not have an explicit form for $U(x_1, x_2)$, we cannot solve for explicit values of x_1^*. However, look closely at Eqn. 5.4. Specifically, recall $x_2^* = \frac{I - p_1 x_1^*}{p_2}$. Plugging this back into Eqn. 5.5,

$$-\frac{U_1(x_1^*, x_2^*)}{U_2(x_1^*, x_2^*)} = -\frac{p_1}{p_2}$$

This is identical to the condition we derived using graphical methods in Theorem 5.2!

5.4.2 UMP - Lagrangian Approach

An alternative approach to substitution is the Lagrangian Approach. This approach utilizes a mathematical result that states the interior solution to the first order conditions of a specific "modified" equation (called the Lagrangian equation) is the same as the solution to the original constrained optimization problem. This mathematical result holds under very general conditions on well-behaved functions, and is widely used throughout the Economics literature. To use this technique on the UMP:

1. **Create the Lagrangian equation:**

$$\mathcal{L} \equiv U(x_1, x_2) + \lambda(I - p_1 x_1 - p_2 x_2)$$

2. **Take the first order conditions of $\mathcal{L}$ with respect to the original choice variables (x_1 and x_2 in this case) *and* the Lagrangian multiplier, λ:**

$$\frac{\partial \mathcal{L}}{\partial x_1} = 0 : U_1(x_1^*, x_2^*) - \lambda^* p_1 = 0$$

$$\frac{\partial \mathcal{L}}{\partial x_2} = 0 : U_2(x_1^*, x_2^*) - \lambda^* p_2 = 0$$

$$\frac{\partial \mathcal{L}}{\partial \lambda} = 0 : I - p_1 x_1 - p_2 x_2 = 0$$

3. **Solve for the optimal x_1^*, x_2^*, λ^*:**

As with the substitution approach, we cannot solve for explicit values of x_1^*, x_2^*, and λ^* without explicit utility functions. However, we can simplify the first order conditions:

$$U_1(x_1^*, x_2^*) - \lambda^* p_1 = 0 \quad \Rightarrow \quad \lambda^* = \frac{U_1(x_1^*, x_2^*)}{p_1}$$

$$U_2(x_1^*, x_2^*) - \lambda^* p_2 = 0 \quad \Rightarrow \quad \lambda^* = \frac{U_2(x_1^*, x_2^*)}{p_2}$$

Note that since $\frac{U_1(x_1^*, x_2^*)}{p_1}$ and $\frac{U_2(x_1^*, x_2^*)}{p_2}$ both equal λ, they must equal each other as well. Therefore, these equations further reduce to

$$\frac{U_1(x_1^*, x_2^*)}{p_1} = \frac{U_2(x_1^*, x_2^*)}{p_2}$$

$$\Rightarrow -\frac{U_1(x_1^*, x_2^*)}{U_2(x_1^*, x_2^*)} = -\frac{p_1}{p_2}$$

Once again, we have derived the same condition we derived using graphical methods in Theorem 5.2!

As a final note on the Lagrangian method, note that our construction of the Lagrangian function was specific to the UMP problem. If the problem is changed slightly (consider a different budget constraint, for instance, in which bargain discounts are offered), the exact form of the Lagrangian will be different. Please refer to Sundaram (1996) for a general treatment of the Lagrangian function. In addition, note that if the utility function or budget constraint are not differentiable, neither the Lagrangian technique, the substitution method, nor the graphical shortcut, $-\frac{U_1(x_1^*, x_2^*)}{U_2(x_1^*, x_2^*)} = -\frac{p_1}{p_2}$ can be used.

5.5   Examples

5.5.1   Cobb-Douglas Utility

Question: Assume a consumer has $10.00 to spend on beer and pizza. A beer at the Deep End costs $.50 and a slice of pizza at I Love N.Y. Pizza costs $2.00. The consumer's preferences are represented with the Cobb-Douglas utility function, $U(x_1, x_2) = 3x_1^{2/3} x_2^{1/3}$ with $x_1 =$ glasses of beer and $x_2 =$ slices of pizza. How many slices of pizza and glasses of beer will the consumer purchase? Use all three methods to solve the problem.

Answer:

1. **Graphical Solution:** If an interior optimum exists, we know from Theorem 5.2 that at the optimum $-\frac{U_1(x_1^*, x_2^*)}{U_2(x_1^*, x_2^*)} = -\frac{p_1}{p_2}$. To use this property, we must first solve for U_1 and U_2.

$$
\begin{aligned}
U_1 &= (2/3)3x_1^{-1/3}x_2^{1/3} \\
U_2 &= (1/3)3x_1^{2/3}x_2^{-2/3}
\end{aligned}
$$

Plugging these equations into our optimality condition,

$$
\begin{aligned}
-\frac{(2/3)3x_1^{*-1/3}x_2^{*1/3}}{(1/3)3x_1^{*2/3}x_2^{*-2/3}} &= -\frac{0.5}{2} \\
\Rightarrow -\frac{2x_1^{*-1/3}x_2^{*1/3}}{x_1^{*2/3}x_2^{*-2/3}} &= -\frac{1}{4} \\
\Rightarrow \frac{8x_1^{*-1/3}x_2^{*1/3}}{x_1^{*2/3}x_2^{*-2/3}} &= 1 \qquad (5.6) \\
\Rightarrow \frac{8x_2^*}{x_1^*} &= 1 \\
\Rightarrow x_1^* &= 8x_2^* \qquad (5.7)
\end{aligned}
$$

We can now plug this equation back into our budget constraint to determine the optimal (x_2^*):

$$
\begin{aligned}
10 &= 0.5x_1^* + 2x_2^* \\
\Rightarrow 10 &= 0.5(8x_2^*) + 2x_2^* \\
\Rightarrow 10 &= 6x_2^* \\
\Rightarrow x_2^* = 5/3 & \qquad (5.8)
\end{aligned}
$$

Finally, we can plug Eqn. 5.8 into Eqn. 5.7 to solve for x_1^*.

$$
\begin{aligned}
x_1^* &= 8x_2^* \\
x_1^* &= 8(5/3) \\
x_1^* &= 40/3
\end{aligned}
$$

Thus, our optimal interior bundle is (40/3, 5/3). To ensure we have an interior solution, we must now compare the utility from this bundle to the utility from the corner solutions, (10/(0.5), 0)=(20,0) and (0, 10/2)=(0,5).

$$
\begin{aligned}
U(40/3,5/3) &= 3(40/3)^{2/3}(5/3)^{1/3} = 20 \\
U(20,0) &= 3(20)^{2/3}(0)^{1/3} = 0 \\
U(0,5) &= 3(0)^{2/3}(5)^{1/3} = 0
\end{aligned}
$$

Thus, we have an interior solution and our optimal bundle is (40/3,5/3).

2. **Substitution Solution:** We are attempting to solve the maximization problem,

$$
\max_{x_1,x_2} 3x_1^{2/3}x_2^{1/3} \text{ s.t. } 10 = 0.5x_1 + 2x_2
$$

We will first solve the constraint for x_1 then substitute it into the utility function. Note we could instead solve for x_2 then substitute it into the utility function. It makes no difference.

$$
\begin{aligned}
10 &= 0.5x_1 + 2x_2 \\
\Rightarrow 0.5x_1 &= 10 - 2x_2 \\
\Rightarrow x_1 &= 20 - 4x_2
\end{aligned}
\tag{5.9}
$$

Thus we have a function, $x_1(x_2)$, which tells us x_1 in terms of x_2. Plugging this into the original utility function and removing x_1 from the list of variables to maximize, we have the maximization problem

$$
\max_{x_2} 3(20 - 4x_2)^{2/3}x_2^{1/3}
$$

Per standard techniques, we will solve the first order condition with respect to x_2.

$$U_2 = 0 : (2/3)3(-4)(20 - 4x_2^*)^{-1/3}x_2^{*1/3} + (1/3)3(20 - 4x_2^*)^{2/3}x_2^{*-2/3} = 0$$

$$\Rightarrow -8(20 - 4x_2^*)^{-1/3}x_2^{*1/3} + (20 - 4x_2^*)^{2/3}x_2^{*-2/3} = 0$$

$$\Rightarrow -8x_2^{*1/3} + (20 - 4x_2^*)x_2^{*-2/3} = 0$$

$$\Rightarrow -8x_2^* + 20 - 4x_2^* = 0$$

$$\Rightarrow 12x_2^* = 20$$

$$\Rightarrow x_2^* = 5/3$$

We can now solve for x_1^* using Eqn. 5.9.

$$x_1^* = 20 - 4x_2^*$$

$$\Rightarrow x_1^* = 20 - 4(5/3)$$

$$\Rightarrow x_1^* = 40/3$$

Thus, our optimal interior bundle is (40/3, 5/3). To ensure we have an interior solution, we must now compare the utility from this bundle to the utility from the corner solutions, (10/(0.5), 0)=(20,0) and (0, 10/2)=(0,5). We already performed this step in the Graphical Solution, showing that we have an interior solution and our optimal bundle is (40/3,5/3).

3. **Lagrangian Solution:** We are attempting to solve the maximization problem,

$$\max_{x_1, x_2} 3x_1^{2/3}x_2^{1/3} \text{ s.t. } 10 = 0.5x_1 + 2x_2$$

We must first set up the Lagrangian function:

$$\mathcal{L} = 3x_1^{2/3}x_2^{1/3} + \lambda(10 - 0.5x_1 - 2x_2) \tag{5.10}$$

Next, we must set up the first order conditions.

$$\frac{\partial \mathcal{L}}{\partial x_1} = 0 : (2/3)3x_1^{*^{-1/3}}x_2^{*^{1/3}} - 0.5\lambda^* = 0$$

$$\frac{\partial \mathcal{L}}{\partial x_2} = 0 : (1/3)3x_1^{*^{2/3}}x_2^{*^{-2/3}} - 2\lambda^* = 0$$

$$\frac{\partial \mathcal{L}}{\partial \lambda} = 0 : 10 - 0.5x_1^* - 2x_2^* = 0 \tag{5.11}$$

Solving these first order conditions will give us the optimal (x_1^*, x_2^*).

$$(2/3)3x_1^{*^{-1/3}}x_2^{*^{1/3}} - 0.5\lambda^* = 0 \Rightarrow 2x_1^{*^{-1/3}}x_2^{*^{1/3}} - 0.5\lambda^* = 0$$

$$\Rightarrow \lambda^* = 4x_1^{*^{-1/3}}x_2^{*^{1/3}} \tag{5.12}$$

$$(1/3)3x_1^{*^{2/3}}x_2^{*^{-2/3}} - 2\lambda^* = 0 \Rightarrow x_1^{*^{2/3}}x_2^{*^{-2/3}} - 2\lambda^* = 0$$

$$\Rightarrow \lambda^* = 0.5x_1^{*^{2/3}}x_2^{*^{-2/3}} \tag{5.13}$$

Noting that Eqns. 5.12 and 5.13 both equal λ^*, they must also equal each other:

$$4x_1^{*^{-1/3}}x_2^{*^{1/3}} = 0.5x_1^{*^{2/3}}x_2^{*^{-2/3}}$$

$$\Rightarrow 4x_2^{*^{1/3}} = 0.5x_1^* x_2^{*^{-2/3}}$$

$$\Rightarrow 4x_2^* = 0.5x_1^*$$

$$\Rightarrow x_1^* = 8x_2^* \tag{5.14}$$

We can now plug this result into Eqn. 5.11 (our third first order condition) to solve for x_2^*:

$$10 - 0.5x_1^* - 2x_2^* = 0$$

$$\Rightarrow 10 - 0.5(8x_2^*) - 2x_2^* = 0$$

$$\Rightarrow 10 - 6x_2^* = 0$$

$$\Rightarrow 6x_2^* = 10$$

$$\Rightarrow x_2^* = \frac{5}{3}$$

To solve for x_1^*, we plug x_2^* back into Eqn. 5.14.

$$
\begin{aligned}
x_1^* &= 8x_2^* \\
\Rightarrow x_1^* &= 8(5/3) \\
\Rightarrow x_1^* &= 40/3
\end{aligned}
$$

Thus, our optimal interior bundle is (40/3, 5/3). To ensure we have an interior solution, we must now compare the utility from this bundle to the utility from the corner solutions, (10/(0.5), 0)=(20,0) and (0, 10/2)=(0,5). We already performed this step in the Graphical Solution, showing that we have an interior solution and our optimal bundle is (40/3,5/3).

5.5.2 Perfect Substitutes

Question: I view Pepsi and Faygo brand cola as perfect substitutes. As such, my preferences are represented with the utility function, $U(x_1, x_2) = x_1 + x_2$ where x_1 is Pepsi and x_2 is Faygo . I am not a big soda drinker, so in any month I am only willing to spend \$5.00 on either. A 2-liter bottle of Pepsi costs \$1.29, while a 2-liter bottle of Faygo brand cola costs \$0.99. How many 2-liter bottles of Pepsi will I purchase in a given month? How many bottles of Faygo will I purchase? Assume it is possible to purchase a fraction of a 2-liter bottles. Use all three methods to solve the problem.

Answer:

1. **Graphical Solution:** If an interior optimum exists, we know from Theorem 5.2 that at the optimum $-\frac{U_1(x_1^*, x_2^*)}{U_2(x_1^*, x_2^*)} = -\frac{p_1}{p_2}$. To use this property, we must first solve for U_1 and U_2.

$$
\begin{aligned}
U_1 &= 1 \\
U_2 &= 1
\end{aligned}
$$

Plugging these equations into our optimality condition,

$$
-\frac{1}{1} = -\frac{1.29}{.99}
$$

We immediately see there is a problem. In particular, -1 does not equal $-\frac{1.29}{.99}$. This tells us that an interior solution must not exist. To further illustrate this point, let us draw the indifference curves and the budget line and graphically show that an interior solution cannot exist.

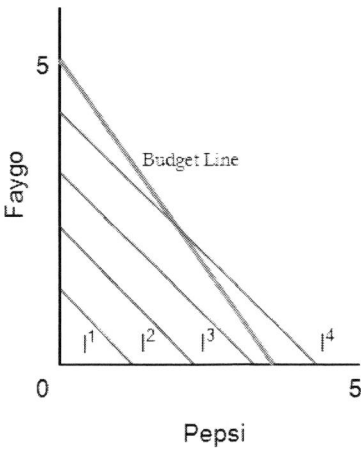

Figure 5.8: Perfect Substitutes Example

It should be clear from Figure 5.8 that there will be no point at which the slope of the budget line equals the slope of an indifference curve. In particular, the slope of the indifference curves are always the same, and this slope is different than the slope of the budget line.

Since no interior solution exists, we must therefore check the corner solutions. Consider the two possible corner solutions in Figure 5.9, A and B. It should be clear that the indifference curve passing through point A, I^A, is lower than the indifference curve passing through point B, I^B. Thus, point B must be the preferred point.

To mathematically determine which corner solution is preferred, we need to compare the utilities of the two possible corner solutions, $(5/(.99), 0) = (5.05, 0)$ and $(0, 5/1.29) = (0, 3.9)$.

$$
\begin{aligned}
U(5.05, 0) &= 5.05 + 0 = 5.05 \\
U(0, 3.9) &= 0 + 3.9 = 3.9
\end{aligned}
$$

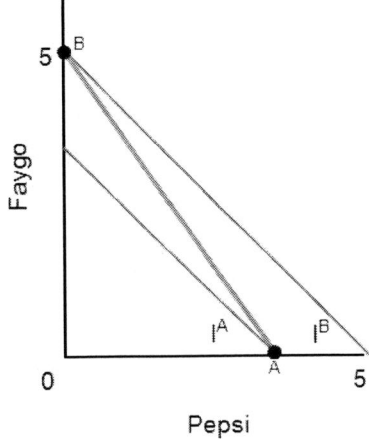

Figure 5.9: Perfect Substitutes Corner Solutions

It is clear the bundle (5.05,0) is the most preferred bundle, which corresponds to point B in Figure 5.9.

Chapter 6

Demand

With the tools we have developed up to this point, we now have the ability to answer the very general question, "with a defined set of preferences and a constrained set of choices, what will an individual choose?". This is a very powerful question to be able to answer, and we do so throughout the economics literature to make predictions on human behavior in a variety of scenarios. However, we oftentimes want to expand the question to ask "with a defined set of preferences, how will an individual's choice change as the world changes?". For instance, will a government mandate on ethanol fuel-blends cause the price of corn (a common ingredient used to create ethanol) to increase? If so, how will that affect the decisions of lower-income individuals? Could we potentially see a decrease in college education for lower-income individuals due to the fact their increased food budget makes paying for college more difficult?[1]

6.1 Demand Curve - Graphical Derivation

Consider the preferences represented by Figure 6.1(a). Given an income of $20, a Good 1 price of $5 and a Good 2 price of $4, we can determine the individual's optimal choice. Using the graphical tools presented in the previous chapters, we know the individual will choose a bundle of (1,4), as shown in Figure 6.1(b).

If the price of Good 1 decreases to $p_1 = 4$, Figure 6.2(a) shows us the individual's optimal bundle will change to (2,3). If the price of Good 1 decreases to $p_1 = 2$, Figure 6.2(b) shows us the individual's optimal bundle will change to (4,3).

---

[1] Anderson and Coble (2010), Hayes (2009), Pimentel (2003), and others discuss the many policy impacts of ethanol usage.

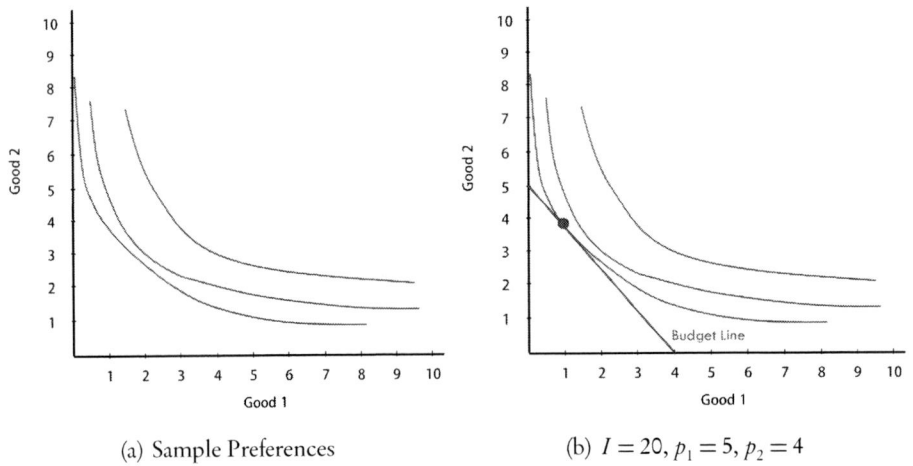

(a) Sample Preferences   (b) $I = 20, p_1 = 5, p_2 = 4$

Figure 6.1: Constrained Optimization Problem

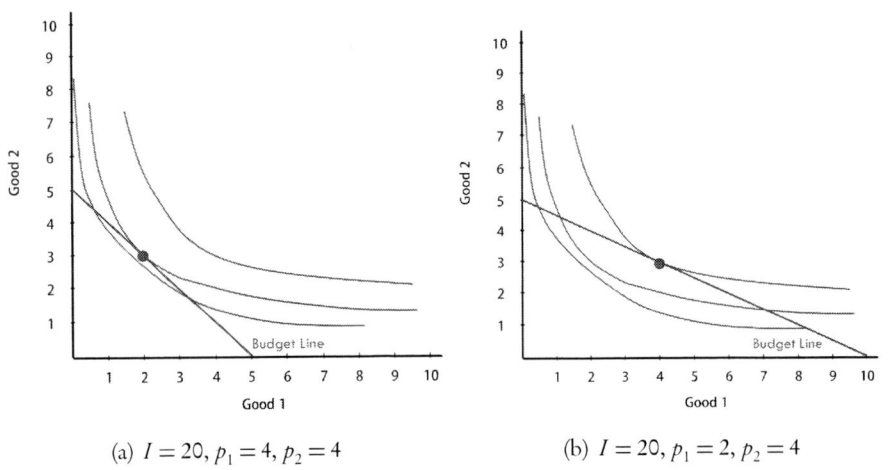

(a) $I = 20, p_1 = 4, p_2 = 4$ (b) $I = 20, p_1 = 2, p_2 = 4$

Figure 6.2: Constrained Optimization Problem

If we repeated this process for all possible Good 1 prices and plotted the amount of Good 1 selected on the x-axis and the price of Good 1 on the y-axis, we would obtain Figure 6.3, which we call the individual's Demand Curve.

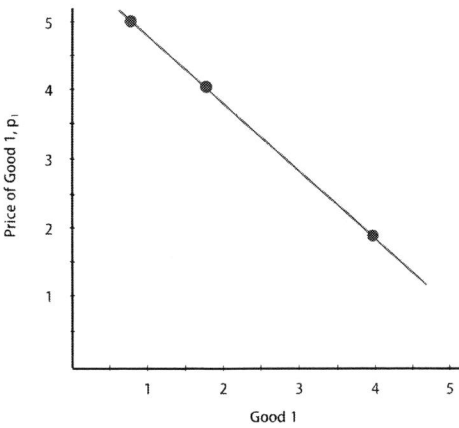

Figure 6.3: Individual Demand Curve

Definition 6.1 (Individual Demand Curve):
An *Individual Demand Curve* is the graphical relationship between a Good's price and the amount of the Good an individual will select when optimizing over her changing budget set.

It is important to note the axes on the demand curve. Specifically, up until now our graphical analysis has consisted of looking at combinations of two goods. With the demand curve, we are looking at one specific good and the effect a price change will have on the quantity demanded of that good. While Good 2 does not explicitly appear on the Good 1 demand curve, note that it plays a fundamental role, as the individual's optimal bundle crucially depends on the tradeoff the individual is willing to make between the two goods. In addition, the individual's income also affects the quantity of Good 1 demanded. This is consistent with Principles of Economics, in which an individual's demand curve for a specific good is affected by the individual's income and the price of other goods.

6.2 Demand Curve - Mathematical Derivation

Not surprisingly, in many cases we can solve for an individual's demand function using a mathematical approach instead of a graphical approach. The steps we take are:

1. Set up a constrained optimization problem using the specified utility function and a general budget line of the form $I - p_1 x_1 - p_2 x_2$. Note I, p_1, and p_2 are left as constants.

2. Solve the constrained optimization problem for the optimal x_1^* and x_2^* using one of the mathematical techniques we have established. Your results will be in terms of I, p_1, and p_2 and are called your *Demand Functions*.

3. (Optional) To more easily plot your Good 1 *Demand Curve*, solve your optimal x_1 solution for p_1. Plug in points for x_1 and plot the corresponding values of p_1. To more easily plot your Good 2 *Demand Curve*, solve your optimal x_2 solution for p_2. Plug in points for x_2 and plot the corresponding values of p_2.

> **Example 6.1 (Demand Curve Derivation):**
> **Question:** Assume an individual's preferences can be represented by the Cobb-Douglas utility function, $U(x_1, x_2) = x_1^{1/2} x_2^{1/2}$. Solve for her x_1 and x_2 demand functions then plot her Good 1 demand curve.
>
> **Answer:** Following the steps above,
>
> 1. **Set up a constrained optimization problem using the specified utility function and a general budget line of the form $I - p_1 x_1 - p_2 x_2$:**
>
> $$\mathscr{L} \equiv x_1^{1/2} x_2^{1/2} + \lambda(I - p_1 x_1 - p_2 x_2)$$
>
> 2. **Solve the constrained optimization problem for the optimal x_1^* and x_2^* using one of the mathematical techniques we have established.**
>
> Taking the first order conditions,
>
> $$\frac{1}{2} x_1^{*-\frac{1}{2}} x_2^{*\frac{1}{2}} - \lambda p_1 = 0 \tag{6.1}$$
>
> $$\frac{1}{2} x_1^{*\frac{1}{2}} x_2^{*-\frac{1}{2}} - \lambda p_2 = 0 \tag{6.2}$$
>
> $$I - p_1 x_1 - p_2 x_2 = 0 \tag{6.3}$$

Solving for λ in Eqn. (6.1),

$$\lambda = \frac{\frac{1}{2}x_1^{*-\frac{1}{2}}x_2^{*\frac{1}{2}}}{p_1} \tag{6.4}$$

Solving for λ in Eqn. (6.2),

$$\lambda = \frac{\frac{1}{2}x_1^{*\frac{1}{2}}x_2^{*-\frac{1}{2}}}{p_2} \tag{6.5}$$

Setting λ from Eqn. (6.4) equal to λ from Eqn. (6.5),

$$\frac{\frac{1}{2}x_1^{*-\frac{1}{2}}x_2^{*\frac{1}{2}}}{p_1} = \frac{\frac{1}{2}x_1^{*\frac{1}{2}}x_2^{*-\frac{1}{2}}}{p_2} \tag{6.6}$$

Solving Eqn. (6.6), we find

$$x_1^* = \frac{p_2 x_2^*}{p_1} \tag{6.7}$$

Plugging Eqn. (6.7) into Eqn. (6.3),

$$
\begin{aligned}
I - p_1\left(\frac{p_2 x_2^*}{p_1}\right) - p_2 x_2^* &= 0 \\
\Rightarrow I - 2p_2 x_2^* &= 0 \\
\Rightarrow x_2^* &= \frac{I}{2p_2} \tag{6.8}
\end{aligned}
$$

which is the individual's demand function for Good 2. Plugging Eqn. (6.8) into Eqn. (6.7),

$$
\begin{aligned}
x_1^* &= \frac{p_2}{p_1}\left(\frac{I}{2p_2}\right) \\
\Rightarrow x_1^* &= \frac{I}{2p_1} \tag{6.9}
\end{aligned}
$$

which is the individual's demand function for Good 1.

3. **(Optional) To more easily plot your Good 1 *Demand Curve*, solve your optimal x_1 solution for p_1. Plug in points for x_1 and plot the corresponding values of p_1.**

For a given income level, I, we could directly plug in p_1 values into Eqn. (6.9), solve for the corresponding x_1^*, then plot our (x_1^*, p_1) values to graph our Demand Curve. We will take our optional approach and solve for p_1 then plug in our x_1^* values.

Solving Eqn. (6.9) for p_1,

$$p_1 = \frac{I}{2x_1^*} \tag{6.10}$$

For a given income level, I, we can now graph our demand curves by plugging in values of x_1^* and plotting our corresponding values of p_1. For instance, if $I = \$2$, when $x_1^* = 1/2$, $p_1 = \frac{2}{2(1/2)} = 2$. When $x_1^* = 1$, $p_1 = \frac{2}{2(1)} = 1$. When $x_1^* = 2$, $p_1 = \frac{2}{2(2)} = 1/2$. If we plot these and other points, we generate the demand curve shown in Figure 6.4 that is specific to $I = 2$.

Note if we wanted to plot the demand curve for Good 2, we would solve Eqn. (6.8) for p_2 and plot (x_2^*, p_2) points.

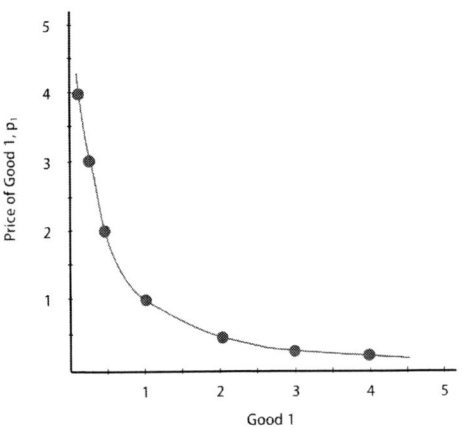

Figure 6.4: Example 6.1 Demand Curve

Note the mathematical approach will not work in all cases. For instance, in the case of perfect substitutes, we cannot use the Lagrangian approach. In these cases, the demand curve can be generated using the graphical approach.

6.2.1 Law of Demand

With our demand function, it is straight-forward to verify that the Law of Demand holds. Recall the Law of Demand states that demand curves should be downward sloping. In other words, if we are consuming our optimal constrained bundles, if the price of a good goes down we will purchase more of the good. We can directly check this by calculating the derivative of a good's demand function with respect to the price of the good.

> **Example 6.2 (Law of Demand):**
> **Question:** Show the Law of Demand holds for Good 1 and Good 2 in Example 6.1.
>
> **Answer:** Taking the derivative of Eqn. (6.9),
>
> $$\frac{\partial x_1^*}{\partial p_1} = -\frac{I}{2p_1^2} < 0$$
>
> Thus, when the price of Good 1 (p_1) decreases, the consumption of Good 1 (x_1) will increase.
>
> Taking the derivative of Eqn. (6.8),
>
> $$\frac{\partial x_2^*}{\partial p_2} = -\frac{I}{2p_2^2} < 0$$
>
> Thus, when the price of Good 2 (p_2) decreases, the consumption of Good 2 (x_2) will increase.

6.3 Income and Substitution Effects

As the Law of Demand generally holds for most goods, we would expect that dropping the price of a good will result in an individual consuming more of that good. However, is it the case that the "savings" resulting from the lower price will always be spent on that good? Could you possibly take your "savings" and purchase more of other goods? Could it even be the case that the Law of Demand does not hold, and a price decrease will encourage you to purchase *less* of the good since you can now afford more of another good you prefer? To answer these questions, we introduce the concepts of Income and Substitution Effects.

Definition 6.2 (Substitution Effect):
Assume a Good's price changes. The *Substitution Effect* is the change in an individual's consumption of the Good due to the fact that the relative prices between the goods have changed.

The substitution effect captures the idea that if the price of a good decreases, it is now relatively cheaper compared to other goods, making you more likely to purchase the good. If you were previously indifferent between where you spent your last dollar (which is what the MRS=MRT condition implies), if one good suddenly becomes cheaper, it will become more attractive.

Definition 6.3 (Income Effect):
Assume a Good's price changes. The *Income Effect* is the change in an individual's consumption of the Good due to the fact that the individual's budget set has changed, controlling for the Substitution Effect.

The income effect captures the idea that if the price of a good decreases, you might be able to purchase bundles that you previously were not able to purchase.

6.3.1 Graphical Derivation

To determine the Income and Substitution Effects graphically, we use the following steps.[2]

1. Using graphical techniques, find the optimal bundle *before* the price change. Label the amount of Good 1 "x_{orig}". Identify the Indifference Curve passing through this optimal point and label it "IC_{orig}".

2. Label the Budget Line corresponding to the new prices as "BL_{new}".

3. Using graphical techniques, find the optimal bundle *after* the price change. Label the amount of Good 1 "x_{new}".

4. Shift BL_{new} until it is tangent to IC_{orig}. Label this shifted line "$BL_{compensated}$" and the amount of Good 1 in the tangency point "x_{subs}".

---

[2]Note this is specific to finding the effects in a change of Good 1's price. Equivalent steps can be used to determine the effects in a change of Good 2's price.

5. The Substitution Effect is $x_{subs} - x_{orig}$. The Income Effect is $x_{new} - x_{subs}$.

Example 6.3 (Income and Substitution Effects):
Question: Given the preferences represented by the Indifference Curves in Figure 6.5, find the Income and Substitution Effects if I=\$20, p_2=\$4, and p_1 changes from \$5 to \$2.

Answer: To find the Income and Substitution Effects, we follow the steps outlined above.

1. **Using graphical techniques, find the optimal bundle *before* the price change. Label the amount of Good 1 "x_{orig}". Identify the Indifference Curve passing through this optimal point and label it "IC_{orig}".**
   Initially, $I = \$20$, $p_1 = \$5$, and $p_2 = \$4$. Per the graphical techniques developed in the previous chapters and demonstrated in Figure 6.6, we find the Budget Line before the price change has intercepts at (0,5) and (4,0). Finding the point on this budget line that is tangent to an indifference curve, we observe the optimal bundle is (1,4). Thus, $x_{orig} = 1$ and we label the indifference curve through which the optimal bundle passes IC_{orig}.

2. **Label the Budget Line corresponding to the new prices as "BL_{new}".**
   After the price change, prices are $p_1 = \$2$ and $p_2 = \$4$. As demonstrated in Figure 6.7, BL_{new} has intercepts at (10,0) and (0,5).

3. **Using graphical techniques, find the optimal bundle *after* the price change. Label the amount of Good 1 "x_{new}".**
   As demonstrated in Figure 6.8, finding the point on the new budget line that is tangent to an indifference curve, we observe the optimal bundle after the price change is (4, 3.2). Thus, $x_{new} = 4$.

4. **Shift BL_{new} until it is tangent to IC_{orig}. Label this shifted line "$BL_{compensated}$" and the amount of Good 1 in the tangency point "x_{subs}".**
   As demonstrated in Figure 6.9, when we shift BL_{new} inward until the shifted line is tangent to IC_{orig}, the point at which the tangency occurs is (3.5, 1.8). Thus, $x_{subs} = 3.5$.

5. **The Substitution Effect is $x_{subs} - x_{orig}$. The Income Effect is $x_{new} - x_{subs}$.**
   Using our results from above, the Substitution Effect is 3.5-1=2.5. In other words, because Good 1 became relatively cheaper, the individual consumed 2.5 more units. The Income Effect is 4-3.5=0.5. Thus, because the individual's budget set changed, the individual consumed 0.5 more units of Good 1.

To more fully understand the income and substitution effects, consider the compensated budget line, $BL_{compensated}$. Note from Figure 6.9 that it allows the in-

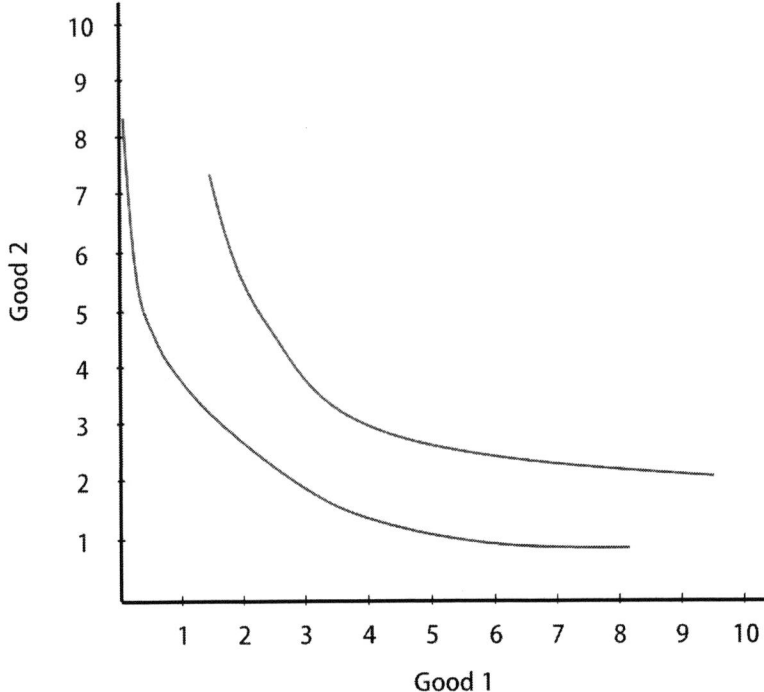

Figure 6.5: Example 6.3 Preferences

dividual to purchase a bundle that makes her indifferent to the original bundle. Specifically, since $BL_{compensated}$ is tangent to IC_{orig}, they share a point in common. Since all points on IC_{orig} are indifferent to the original bundle, this point of tangency makes the individual indifferent to the original bundle. Where $BL_{compensated}$ differs from the original budget line is that it reflects the new price ratio, as reflected by its slope. As such, determining what bundle the individual would select constrained by the budget set defined by $BL_{compensated}$ tells us how the individual's choices would change given different relative prices of the goods, while still being able to afford their original "level of happiness". In other words, it shows us the change in an individual's consumption of the good due to the fact that the relative prices between the goods have changed, which is exactly the Substitution Effect. Any other effects must then be the Income Effect.

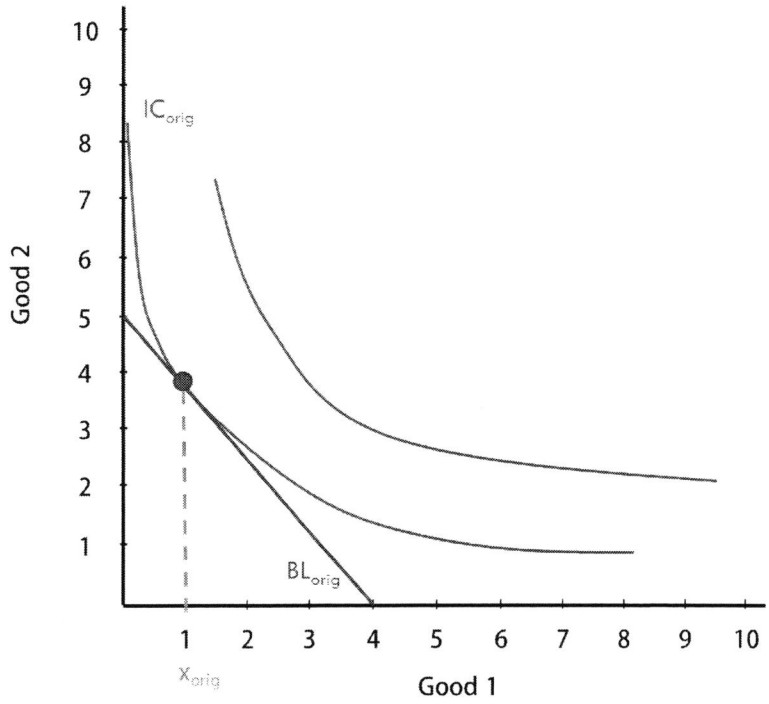

Figure 6.6: Example 6.3 Step 1

6.3.2 Normal and Inferior Goods

Note in Example 6.3, the Income Effect moved in the same direction as the Sub-stitution Effect. However, this is not necessarily the case. Consider, for instance, the scenario in which your food bundles consist of ramen noodles and meat. If the prices of ramen noodles and meat are such that you could afford a large amount of ramen noodles and a very small amount of meat or a very small amount of ramen noodles and a small (but slightly larger) amount of meat, you might choose to spend most of your money on ramen noodles just so you have enough food to live. If the price of ramen noodles goes down, it might be the case that you can now afford a small amount of ramen noodles and a larger amount of meat, which might be enough to sustain you. If so, and if you prefer meat to ramen noodles, you might actually consume less ramen noodles given the price drop, violating the Law of Demand. This decision would be entirely driven by the Income Effect, specifically your ability to consume a bundle you were not previously able to consume.

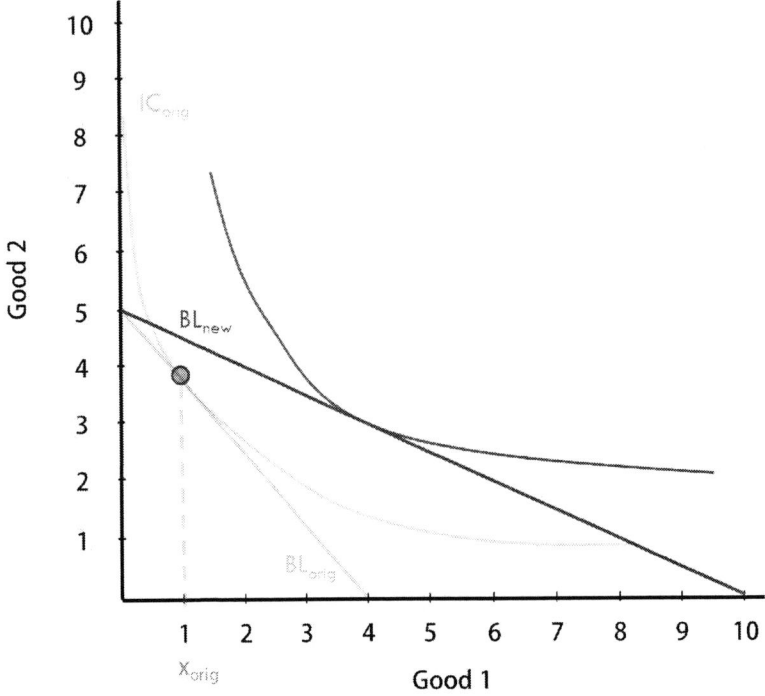

Figure 6.7: Example 6.3 Step 2

Example 6.4 (Negative Income Effects):

Question: Given the preferences represented by the Indifference Curves in Figure 6.10, find the Income and Substitution Effects if I=\$20, p_2=\$4, and p_1 changes from \$4 to \$2.

Answer: To find the Income and Substitution Effects, we follow the steps outlined above.

1. **Using graphical techniques, find the optimal bundle *before* the price change. Label the amount of Good 1 "x_{orig}". Identify the Indifference Curve passing through this optimal point and label it "IC_{orig}".**

   Initially, $I = \$20$, $p_1 = \$4$, and $p_2 = \$4$. Per the graphical techniques developed in the previous chapters and demonstrated in Figure 6.11, we find the Budget Line before the price change has intercepts at (0,5) and (5,0). Finding the point on this budget line that is tangent to an indifference curve, we observe the optimal bundle is (2.9, 2.3). Thus, $x_{orig} = 2.9$ and we label the indifference curve through which the optimal bundle passes IC_{orig}.

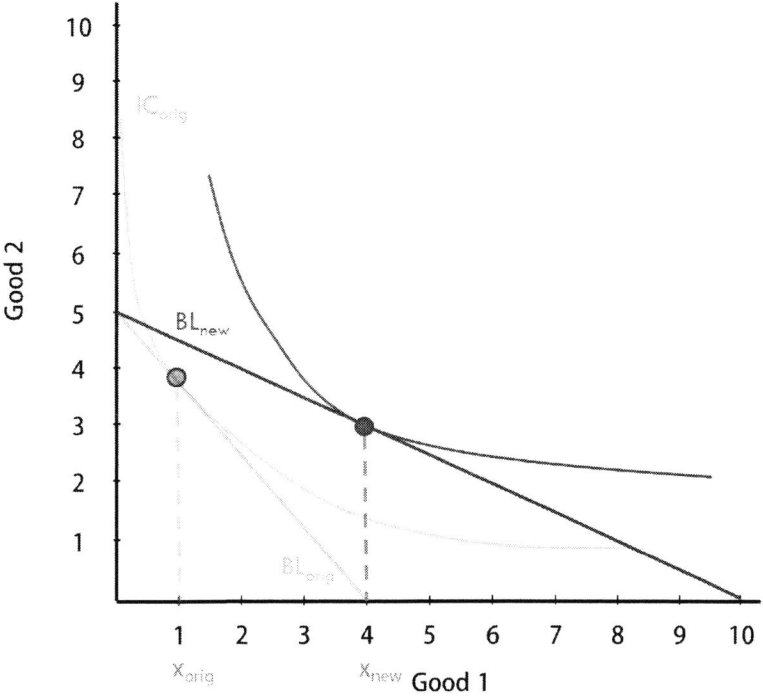

Figure 6.8: Example 6.3 Step 3

2. **Label the Budget Line corresponding to the new prices as "BL$_{\text{new}}$".**
   After the price change, prices are $p_1 = \$2$ and $p_2 = \$4$. As demonstrated in Figure 6.11, BL$_{\text{new}}$ has intercepts at (10,0) and (0,5).

3. **Using graphical techniques, find the optimal bundle *after* the price change. Label the amount of Good 1 "x_{new}".**
   As demonstrated in Figure 6.11, finding the point on the new budget line that is tangent to an indifference curve, we observe the optimal bundle after the price change is (2.3, 3.9). Thus, $x_{\text{new}} = 2.3$.

4. **Shift BL$_{\text{new}}$ until it is tangent to IC$_{\text{orig}}$. Label this shifted line BL$_{\text{compensated}}$ and the amount of Good 1 in the tangency point "x_{subs}".**
   As demonstrated in Figure 6.11, when we shift BL$_{\text{new}}$ inward until the shifted line is tangent to IC$_{\text{orig}}$, the point at which the tangency occurs is (4.6, 1). Thus, $x_{\text{subs}} = 4.6$.

5. **The Substitution Effect is $x_{\text{subs}} - x_{\text{orig}}$. The Income Effect is $x_{\text{new}} - x_{\text{subs}}$.**
   Using our results from above, the Substitution Effect is 4.6-2.9=1.7. In other words, because Good 1 became relatively cheaper, the individual

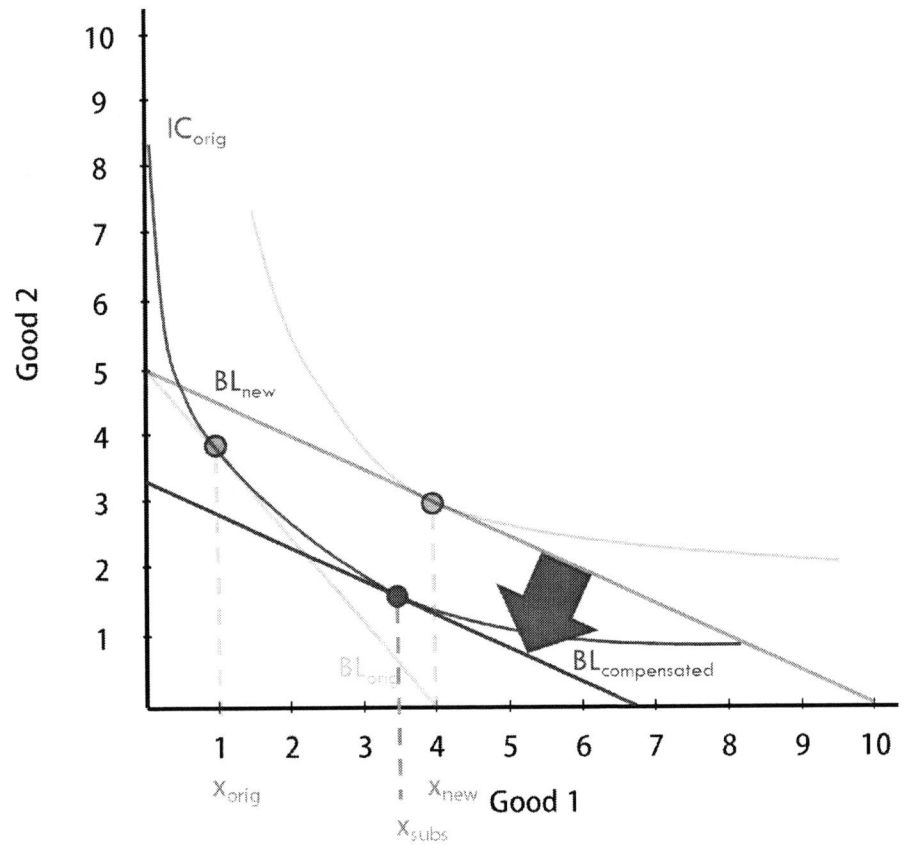

Figure 6.9: Example 6.3 Step 4

consumed 1.7 more units. The Income Effect is 2.3-4.6=-2.3. Thus, because the individual's budget set changed, the individual consumed 2.3 *fewer* units of Good 1.

Depending on the direction of the Income Effect in relation to the Substitution Effect, we define two types of goods.

Definition 6.4 (Normal Good):
A *Normal Good* is a good whose Income Effect is in the same direction of the Substitution Effect.

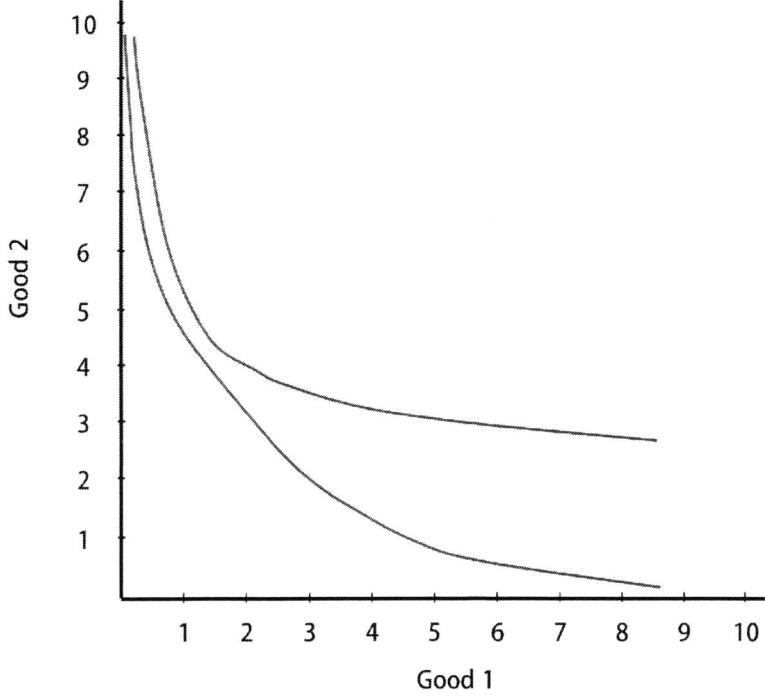

Figure 6.10: Example 6.4 Preferences

Definition 6.5 (Inferior Good):
An *Inferior Good* is a good whose Income Effect is in the opposite direction of the Substitution Effect.

Inferior goods can be thought of those goods we purchase because we cannot afford a better alternative. As such, as our budget set expands, we consume less of these goods and more of the goods we desire. Examples include ramen noodles, canned meat, potatoes, etc.

If an inferior good's income effect is severe, as in Example 6.4, it can even be the case the the Law of Demand does not hold, and a decrease in price will lead to a decrease in consumption. We call these types of goods Giffen Goods.

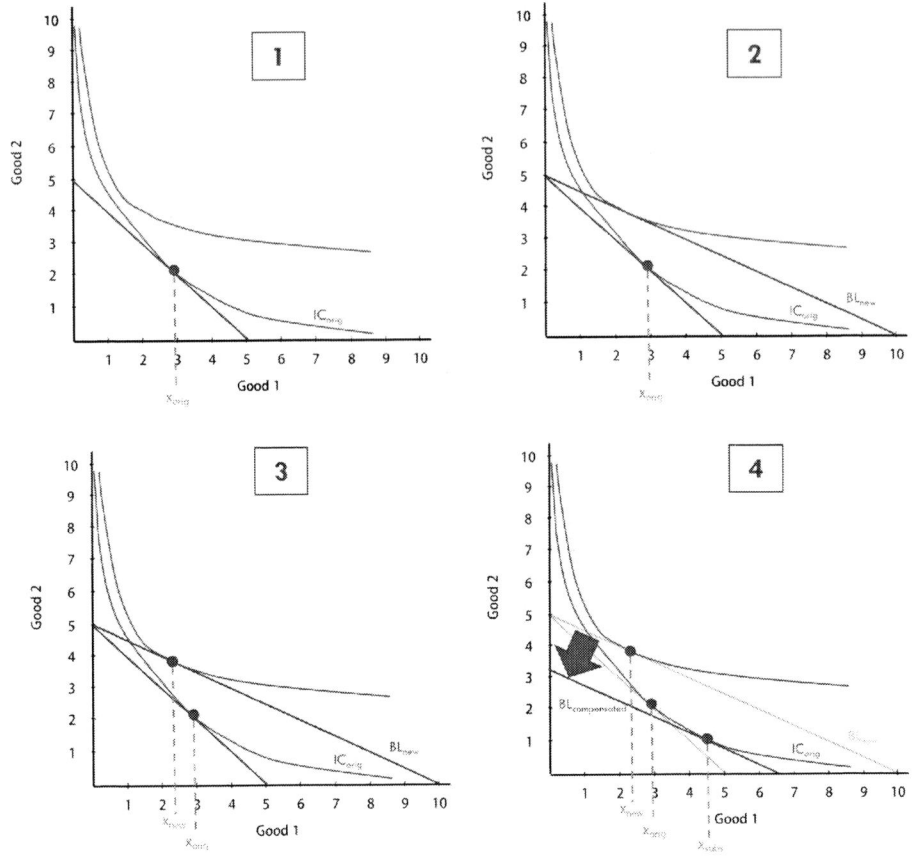

Figure 6.11: Example 6.4 Solution

Definition 6.6 (Giffen Good):
A *Giffen Good* is a specific type of Inferior good whose Income Effect

1. Is in the opposite direction of the Substitution Effect

2. Exceeds the Substitution Effect in magnitude.

Thus, the Law of Demand does not hold.

In general, very few goods are Giffen Goods, as verified through econometric techniques.

6.4 Income Effects - Graphical Derivation

In the same manner that we can derive an individual's Demand Curve for a good, we can also determine how a change in the individual's income will affect her consumption. Plotting this relationship generates an *Engel Curve*.

Definition 6.7 (Engel Curve):
An *Engel Curve* is the graphical relationship between an individual's income and the amount of a Good an individual will select when optimizing over her changing budget set.

Graphically, we need only find the optimal bundles at different income levels, then plot the optimal quantity of the good versus income, as demonstrated in Example 6.5

Example 6.5 (Generating an Engel Curve):
Question: Assume the price of Good 1 is $5 and the price of Good 2 is $4. Given the preferences represented by the Indifference Curves in Figure 6.12(a), graph the Engel Curve with respect to Good 1.

Answer: To graph the full Engel Curve, we would need the entire preference map. Instead, we will plot the points specific to Income levels of $20, $24, and $28 and use these three points to infer the shape of the Engel Curve.

Figures 6.12(b), 6.12(c), and 6.12(d) show the optimal consumption bundles when $I =$20$, $24, and $28. Note the slopes of the budget lines do not change, as the price levels stay the same. When $I = 20, we see that the optimal bundle contains 1 unit of Good 1. When $I = 24, the optimal bundle contains 1.8 units of Good 1. When $I = 28, the optimal bundle contains 2.7 units of Good 1. Plotting these Good 1 quantities against the Income levels and inferring the shape of the curve from these three points, we obtain the Engel Curve shown in Figure 6.13.

6.5 Income Effects - Mathematical Derivation

As with the demand function, we can solve for an individual's Engel Curve using a mathematical approach instead of a graphical approach. The steps we take are:

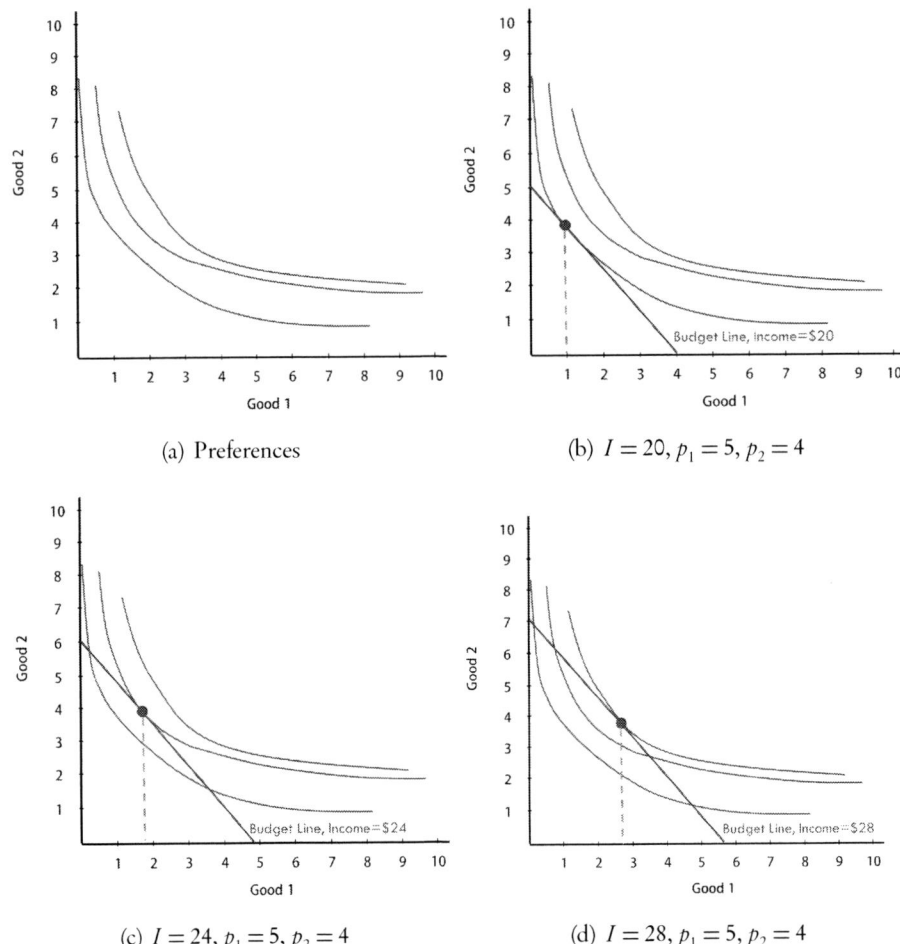

(a) Preferences

(b) $I = 20, p_1 = 5, p_2 = 4$

(c) $I = 24, p_1 = 5, p_2 = 4$

(d) $I = 28, p_1 = 5, p_2 = 4$

Figure 6.12: Example 6.5

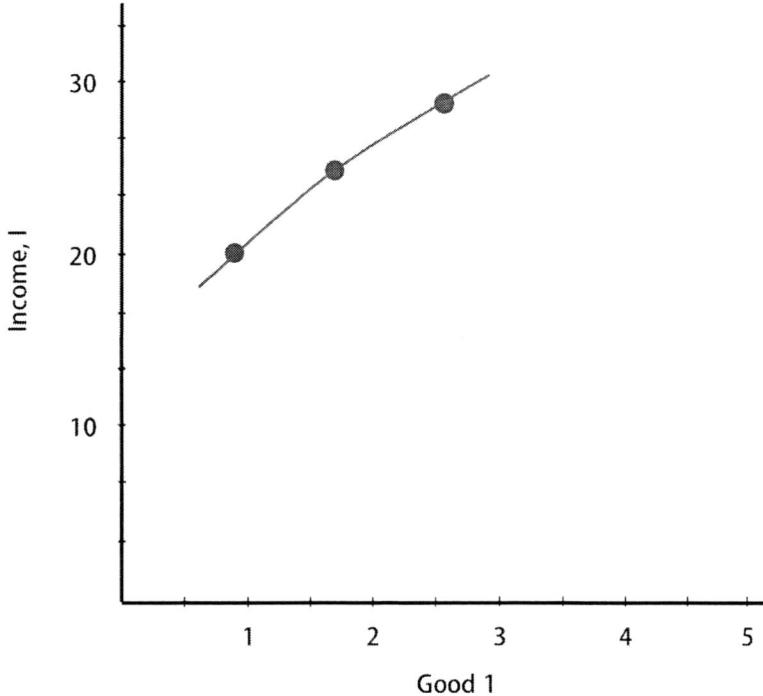

Figure 6.13: Example 6.5 Engel Curve

1. Set up a constrained optimization problem using the specified utility function and a general budget line of the form $I - p_1 x_1 - p_2 x_2$. Note I, p_1, and p_2 are left as constants.

2. Solve the constrained optimization problem for the optimal x_1^* and x_2^* using one of the mathematical techniques we have established. Your results will be in terms of I, p_1, and p_2 and are called your *Demand Functions*.

3. (Optional) To more easily plot your Good 1 *Engel Curve*, solve your optimal x_1 solution for I. Plug in points for x_1 and plot the corresponding values of I. To more easily plot your Good 2 *Engel Curve*, solve your optimal x_2 solution for I. Plug in points for x_2 and plot the corresponding values of I.

Example 6.6 (Engel Curve Derivation):

Question: Assume an individual's preferences can be represented by the Cobb-Douglas utility function, $U(x_1, x_2) = x_1^{1/2} x_2^{1/2}$. Graph her Engel curve for Good 1.

Answer:

1. Set up a constrained optimization problem using the specified utility function and a general budget line of the form $I - p_1 x_1 - p_2 x_2$. Note I, p_1, and p_2 are left as constants.

$$\mathcal{L} \equiv x_1^{1/2} x_2^{1/2} + \lambda(I - p_1 x_1 - p_2 x_2)$$

2. Solve the constrained optimization problem using one of the mathematical techniques we have established.

Replicating the steps in Example 6.1,

$$x_1^* = \frac{I}{2p_1} \tag{6.11}$$

$$x_2^* = \frac{I}{2p_2} \tag{6.12}$$

3. (Optional) To more easily plot your Good 1 *Engel Curve*, solve your optimal x_1 solution for I. Plug in points for x_1 and plot the corresponding values of I.

For a given price level, p_1, we could directly plug in I values into Eqn. (6.11), solve for the corresponding x_1^*, then plot our (x_1^*, I) values to graph our Engel Curve. We will take our optional approach and solve for I then plug in our x_1^* values.

Solving Eqn. (6.11) for I,

$$I = 2p_1 x_1^* \tag{6.13}$$

For a given price level, p_1, we can now graph our demand curves by plugging in values of x_1^* and plotting our corresponding values of I. For instance, if $p_1 = \$1$, when $x_1^* = 1/2$, $I = 2(1)(1/2) = 1$. When $x_1^* = 1$, $I = 2(1)(1) = 2$. When $x_1^* = 2$, $I = 2(1)(2) = 4$. If we plot these and other points, we generate the Engel curve shown in Figure 6.14 that is specific to $p_1 = 1$.

Note if we wanted to plot the Engel curve for Good 2, we would solve Eqn. (6.12) for I and plot (x_2^*, I) points.

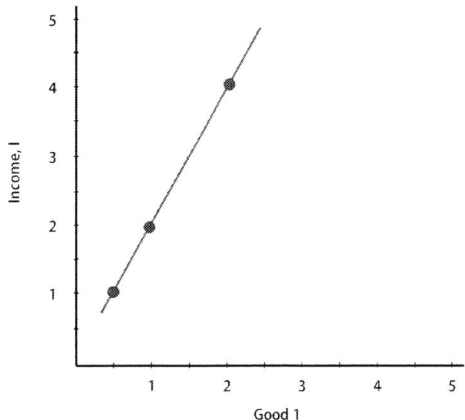

Figure 6.14: Example 6.6 Engel Curve

Note when we change income, the relative prices stay the same and we only experience an income effect. It is important to note that the income effect measured using a direct Income change is not the same as the income effect measured using the techniques established in Section 6.3. However, the sign of the change will be the same. In particular, $\frac{\partial x_1^*}{\partial I}$ tells us how the consumption of Good 1 will change with a change in income. If $\frac{\partial x_1^*}{\partial I} > 0$, the good is normal. In other words, an increase in income will lead to an increase in consumption. If $\frac{\partial x_1^*}{\partial I} < 0$, the good is inferior.

We can also graphically determine the sign of the Income Effect by looking at the Engel Curve. If an Engel Curve is upward sloping ($\frac{\partial I}{\partial x_1^*} > 0$), the good is normal. If the Engel Curve is downward sloping ($\frac{\partial I}{\partial x_1^*} < 0$), the good is inferior.

6.6 Elasticity

6.6.1 General Definition

Of particular importance when answering the question "with a defined set of preferences, how will an individual's choice change as their budget set changes?" is the concept of elasticity.

Definition 6.8 (Elasticity):
Elasticity$_{A,B}$, or *the elasticity of A with respect to B*, is the percent change in A that results from a percent change in B. Formally,

$$
\begin{aligned}
\epsilon_{A,B} &= \frac{\%\Delta A}{\%\Delta B} \\[2mm]
&= \frac{\frac{\Delta A}{A}}{\frac{\Delta B}{B}} \\[2mm]
&= \frac{\Delta A}{\Delta B}\frac{B}{A}
\end{aligned}
\qquad (6.14)
$$

Example 6.7 (Elasticity):
Question: Assume if an individual works out (W) for 1 hour a day, he can bench-press (B) 200 pounds. Under a different training regimen, he finds out that if he works out (W) for 1.5 hours a day, he can bench-press (B) 225 pounds. What is his elasticity of bench-press weight with respect to workout length?

Answer:

$$
\begin{aligned}
\epsilon_{B,W} &= \frac{\Delta B}{\Delta W}\frac{W}{B} \\[2mm]
&= \frac{(225-200)}{(1.5-1)}\frac{1}{200} \\[2mm]
&= 0.25
\end{aligned}
$$

In other words, a 1% change in workout hours will result in a 0.25% change in bench-press weight given that the individual is currently working out 1 hour a day and bench-pressing 200 pounds.

With extremely small changes in A and B, we can write Eqn. (6.14) in its differential form. Specifically,

$$
\epsilon_{A,B} = \frac{\partial A}{\partial B}\frac{B}{A}
\qquad (6.15)
$$

where $\frac{\partial A}{\partial B}$ is the derivative of A with respect to B.

Example 6.8 (Elasticity):

Question: Assume an econometrician determined an individual's bench-press weight follows the equation:

$$B = 100 + 50W - 15T + 30P \tag{6.16}$$

where B is the amount the individual can bench press (in pounds), W is the length of time spent working out per day (in hours), T is the amount of time spent watching TV per day (in hours) and P is the amount of performance-enhancing drugs the individual takes (in mL). What is his elasticity of bench-press weight with respect to workout length when W=2, T=1, and P=1?

Answer: Using the differential form of elasticity,

$$\epsilon_{B,W} = \frac{\partial B}{\partial W}\frac{W}{B} \tag{6.17}$$

Using Eqn. (6.16) and plugging in W=2, T=1, and P=1, we find the current bench-press weight is

$$B = 100 + 50(2) - 15(1) + 30(1) = 215$$

To determine the derivative of B with respect to W, we take the partial derivative of Eqn. (6.16) with respect to W,

$$\frac{\partial B}{\partial W} = 50$$

Plugging these values and W=2 into Eqn. (6.17),

$$\begin{aligned}
\epsilon_{B,W} &= \frac{\partial B}{\partial W}\frac{W}{B} \\
&= (50)\frac{2}{215} \\
&= 0.47
\end{aligned}$$

In other words, a 1% change in workout hours will result in a 0.47% change in bench-press weight given the fact that the individual is currently working out for 2 hours a day, watching 1 hour of TV a day, and taking 1 mL of performance-enhancing drugs.

Example 6.9 (Elasticity):
  Question: Assume an econometrician determined an individual's bench-press weight follows the equation:

$$B = 100 + 50W - 15T + 30P \tag{6.18}$$

where B is the amount the individual can bench press (in pounds), W is the length of time spent working out per day (in hours), T is the amount of time spent watching TV per day (in hours) and P is the amount of performance-enhancing drugs the individual takes (in mL). What is his elasticity of bench-press weight with respect to workout length in terms of W, T, and/or P?

Answer: Using the differential form of elasticity,

$$\epsilon_{B,W} = \frac{\partial B}{\partial W}\frac{W}{B} \tag{6.19}$$

To determine the derivative of B with respect to W, we take the partial derivative of Eqn. (6.18) with respect to W,

$$\frac{\partial B}{\partial W} = 50$$

Plugging this value and Eqn. (6.19) into Eqn. (6.19),

$$\epsilon_{B,W} = \frac{\partial B}{\partial W}\frac{W}{B}$$
$$= (50)\frac{W}{100 + 50W - 15T + 30P}$$

Note we plugged in Eqn. (6.18) for B in our elasticity equation to ensure the elasticity was in terms of W, T, and P.

6.6.2 Demand Elasticity

Of particular importance to economists is the concept of Demand Elasticity. Demand Elasticity tells us the percent change of quantity demanded that will occur due to a percent change of a specific variable. For instance, Demand Elasticity allows us to determine how sensitive one product is to the price of another product, how much market power a particular firm has, the potential effectiveness of advertising expenditures, and more.

Definition 6.9 (Demand Elasticity):

$\epsilon_{Demand,B}$, or *the demand elasticity with respect to B*, is the percent change in quantity demanded that results from a percent change in B. Formally,

$$\epsilon_{Demand,B} = \frac{\%Demand}{\%\Delta B}$$

$$\epsilon_{Demand,B} = \frac{\partial Demand}{\partial B} \frac{B}{Demand} \qquad (6.20)$$

The Demand Elasticities with respect to specific values of B have been given names due to their prevalence in the Economics literature.

Definition 6.10 (Own-Price Elasticity):

$\epsilon_{Demand,Price}$, or *Own-Price Elasticity*, is the percent change in quantity demanded that results from a percent change in the good's price. Formally,

$$\epsilon_{Demand, Price} = \frac{\%Demand}{\%\Delta Price}$$

$$\epsilon_{Demand, Price} = \frac{\partial Demand}{\partial Price} \frac{Price}{Demand}$$

or, as is most commonly seen,

$$\epsilon_{x_i,p_i} = \frac{\partial x_i}{\partial p_i} \frac{p_i}{x_i} \qquad (6.21)$$

Own-Price Elasticity tells us the % change in the demand for Good i (where i is name of the good) per a percent change in its own price, p_i.

Definition 6.11 (Cross-Price Elasticity):

$\epsilon_{Demand, Price\ of\ Other\ Good}$, or *Cross-Price Elasticity*, is the percent change in quantity demanded that results from a percent change in another good's price. Formally,

$$\epsilon_{Demand,\ Price\ of\ Other\ Good} = \frac{\%Demand}{\%\Delta Price\ of\ Other\ Good}$$

$$\epsilon_{Demand,\ Price\ of\ Other\ Good} = \frac{\partial Demand}{\partial Price\ of\ Other\ Good}\frac{Price\ of\ Other\ Good}{Demand}$$

or, as is most commonly seen,

$$\epsilon_{x_i, p_j} = \frac{\partial x_i}{\partial p_j}\frac{p_j}{x_i} \qquad (6.22)$$

Cross-Price Elasticity tells us the % change in the demand for Good i (where i is name of the good) per a percent change in another good's price, p_j.

Definition 6.12 (Income Elasticity):

$\epsilon_{Demand, Income}$, or *Income Elasticity*, is the percent change in quantity demanded that results from a percent change in an individual's income. Formally,

$$\epsilon_{Demand,\ Income} = \frac{\%Demand}{\%\Delta Income}$$

$$\epsilon_{Demand,\ Income} = \frac{\partial Demand}{\partial Income}\frac{Income}{Demand}$$

or, as is most commonly seen,

$$\epsilon_{x_i, I} = \frac{\partial x_i}{\partial I}\frac{I}{x_i} \qquad (6.23)$$

Income Elasticity tells us the % change in the demand for Good i (where i is name of the good) per a percent change in an individual's income, I.

Definition 6.13 (Own-Advertising Elasticity):

$\epsilon_{Demand, Advertising}$, or *Own-Advertising Elasticity*, is the percent change in quantity demanded that results from a percent change in the good's advertising expenditure. Formally,

$$\epsilon_{\text{Demand, Advertising}} = \frac{\%\text{Demand}}{\%\Delta\text{Advertising}}$$

$$\epsilon_{\text{Demand, Advertising}} = \frac{\partial\,\text{Demand}}{\partial\,\text{Advertising}}\frac{\text{Advertising}}{\text{Demand}}$$

or, as is most commonly seen,

$$\epsilon_{x_i, A_i} = \frac{\partial x_i}{\partial A_i}\frac{A_i}{x_i} \tag{6.24}$$

Advertising Elasticity tells us the % change in the demand for Good i (where i is name of the good) per a percent change in the expenditures spent on advertising for that good, A_i.

Example 6.10 (Demand Elasticity):

Question: Find the Own-Price, Cross-Price, and Income-Elasticity of the x_1 demand function generated by the Cobb-Douglas preferences $U(x_1, x_2) = x_1^{1/2}x_2^{1/2}$ in terms of p_1, p_2, and I.

Answer: In Example (6.1) we found

$$x_1^* = \frac{I}{2p_1} \tag{6.25}$$

• Own-Price Elasticity

Taking the derivative of x_1 with respect to p_1,

$$\frac{\partial x_1}{\partial p_1} = -\frac{I}{2p_1^2}$$

Plugging this value and Eqn. (6.25) into Eqn. (6.21),

$$\epsilon_{x_1, p_1} = -\frac{I}{2p_1^2} \frac{p_1}{\frac{I}{2p_1}}$$

$$= -1$$

Thus, an individual's consumption of x_1 will always change by the same percentage as p_1 (but in the opposite direction). In other words, the individual will spend a constant share of her income on the good.

- Cross-Price Elasticity

Taking the derivative of x_1 with respect to p_2,

$$\frac{\partial x_1}{\partial p_2} = 0$$

Plugging this value and Eqn. (6.25) into Eqn. (6.22),

$$\epsilon_{x_1, p_2} = 0\left(\frac{p_2}{\frac{I}{2p_1}}\right)$$

$$= 0$$

Thus, an individual's consumption of x_1 is independent of the price of Good 2, p_2.

- Income Elasticity

Taking the derivative of x_1 with respect to I,

$$\frac{\partial x_1}{\partial I} = \frac{1}{2p_1}$$

Plugging this value and Eqn. (6.25) into Eqn. (6.23),

$$\epsilon_{x_1, I} = \frac{1}{2p_1}\left(\frac{I}{\frac{I}{2p_1}}\right)$$

$$= 1$$

Thus, an individual's consumption of x_1 will always change by the same percentage as I. As shown with Own-Price Elasticity, the individual will spend a constant share of her income on the good.

Chapter 7

Uncertainty

Using the tools we have developed, you should now feel comfortable examining a variety of scenarios concerning consumer behavior. Using specific utility functions and more advanced budget lines, more exotic questions can be answered within this framework, such as how an individual will allocate her consumption over time or how an increase in wage will effect the number of hours a worker will choose to work. For all of these questions, the techniques we have developed would prove sufficient.

Unfortunately, questions such as these have only limited applications. Consider, for instance, the question as to which job to take after college. Should you take a consulting job that pays extremely well, but guarantees you will have to work long hours and travel constantly? Should you take a job that pays less but avoids travel? Should you take a job that is near your parents? In order to answer these questions using the tools we have developed, we would have to assume that you have all the information necessary to correctly rank your preferences. However, who really knows how happy a certain option will make them one year from now? What if you find someone with whom you want to spend a lot of time? What if you get married? What if you have a child? What if you have triplets? What if your selection of job affects your likelihood of getting married? Depending on each of these possibilities, you might select one job over another.

In cases where we are uncertain of the outcome of a given choice, our existing theoretical framework proves lacking. Assume, for instance, that the bundles over which preferences exist are not actual things, but lotteries over things. For instance, you could ask yourself "do I prefer a high-paying job that requires me to travel and gives me a 10% chance of getting married in 5 years or a low-paying

PREFERENCES OVER LOTTERIES

job that gives me a 20% chance of getting married?". As lotteries are technically things themselves (if it helps, imagine you are selecting between a lottery ticket that gives you a 10% of getting married and another lottery ticket that is giving you a 20% chance of getting married), it is possible to use our existing framework. Assuming preferences over these imaginary lottery tickets are complete and transitive (which is a reasonable assumption), we can state "a utility representation exists". We might even be able to claim the monotonicity property holds, so that "an increasing utility representation exists". However, consider how many types of lotteries exist in a world with just 2 goods. One lottery would be "10% chance of good 1, 90% chance of good 2". Another would be "10.1% chance of good 1, 89.9% chance of good 2". Another would be "10.01% chance of good 1, 89.99% chance of good 2". It should quickly become clear that with only 2 goods in the world, there are an infinite number of possible lotteries over which preferences must exist. As such, any utility representation we attempt to use must have an infinite number of variables, making mathematical manipulation highly untractable.

As the point of economics is to study individual choice-making in a simplified framework, using a utility function with an infinite number of variables seems counterproductive. There are certainly mathematical tools to address this scenario, but they are hardly simple and their implications tend to be overly general. Instead, we will make use of a fundamental finding in economics, known as the *expected utility theorem*. In particular, this theorem states that when preferences over lotteries display specific properties, a "simple" utility representation exists.

7.1 Preferences Over Lotteries

Before defining specific preferences over lotteries, we must first formally define what a lottery is

Definition 7.1 (Lottery):
Consider the bundles of goods, $x_1, x_2, \ldots, x_n$. A *lottery* over the bundles is a set of probabilities, $(p_1, p_2, \ldots, p_n)$, such that

1. $p_1 + p_2 \cdots + p_n = 1$

2. $p_i \geq 0$

3. p_i is the probability the consumer receives bundle x_i.

Note probabilities are written in their decimal representation where 30% = 0.3, for instance. Thus $(.1, .9)$, is the lottery that assigns probability 10% to bundle 1 and 90% to bundle 2.

As previously mentioned, because lotteries are themselves "things", we can assume preferences over lotteries are complete and transitive in the same manner as Section 3. We can also define properties specific to lotteries.

◇ † Continuity (of Lotteries)

> **Definition 7.2 (Continuity):**
> Loosely, preferences over lotteries are *continuous* if, whenever $(p_1, p_2, \ldots, p_n) \succeq (q_1, q_2, \ldots, q_n)$ and $(p_1, p_2, \ldots, p_n) \approx (t_1, t_2, \ldots, t_n)$, then $(t_1, t_2, \ldots, t_n) \succeq (q_1, q_2, \ldots, q_n)$

Note this is essentially identical to the non-lottery definition of continuity. It basically states if one lottery is preferred to another lottery, and we take a third lottery whose probabilities are sufficiently close to the first, it will also be preferred to the second lottery. As an example, consider the following bundles:

x_1: attending class

x_2: not attending class

x_3: getting attacked by a bear on the way to class

Assume you prefer the lottery $(1, 0, 0)$ to $(0, 1, 0)$. In other words, you prefer the "sure-thing" lottery that ensures you go to class to the lottery that ensures you do not go to class. Continuity implies that you would also then prefer $(.99, 0, .1)$ to $(0, 1, 0)$. In other words, even if there was a possibility of a bear attack, as long as the possibility was small enough you would still go to class.

◇ † Independence

To describe independence, we must first introduce the concept of "mixing" lotteries.

1 2 345
.2 .2 .2 .2 .2

1 2 3 4 5
.5 .5 0.

$\left(\frac{1}{3}\right)(.2)+\left(\frac{2}{3}\right)(.5)$

Definition 7.3 (Mixing):
Given two lotteries, $(p_1, p_2, \ldots, p_n)$ and $(t_1, t_2, \ldots, t_n)$, a *mixture* of these two lotteries is the new lottery $(\alpha p_1 + (1-\alpha)t_1, \alpha p_2 + (1-\alpha)t_2, \ldots, \alpha p_n + (1-\alpha)t_n)$ where $0 \le \alpha \le 1$.

Intuitively, mixing two lotteries can best be explained by considering two lottery tickets. Each lottery ticket is itself a lottery. An example of mixing the two lotteries is saying "I will roll a die. If I roll a 1, 2, 3, or 4, you will get the first lottery ticket. If I roll a 5 or 6, you will get the second lottery ticket."

Definition 7.4 (Independence):
Preferences over lotteries display *independence* if, whenever $(p_1, p_2, \ldots, p_n) \succeq (q_1, q_2, \ldots, q_n)$, then $(p_1, p_2, \ldots, p_n)$ mixed with $(t_1, t_2, \ldots, t_n)$ is still weakly preferred to $(q_1, q_2, \ldots, q_n)$ mixed with $(t_1, t_2, \ldots, t_n)$ in the same manner.

In other words, assume one lottery, $(p_1, p_2, \ldots, p_n)$, is preferred to another lottery, $(q_1, q_2, \ldots, q_n)$. I then state "Now let us consider a third lottery. $(t_1, t_2, \ldots, t_n)$. You have two options:

- With probability α you receive lottery $(p_1, p_2, \ldots, p_n)$. With probability $(1-\alpha)$ you receive lottery $(t_1, t_2, \ldots, t_n)$.

- With probability α you receive lottery $(q_1, q_2, \ldots, q_n)$. With probability $(1-\alpha)$ you receive lottery $(t_1, t_2, \ldots, t_n)$.".

Independence requires you prefer the first option no matter the value of α and no matter the value of $(t_1, t_2, \ldots, t_n)$.

While seemingly intuitive, independence is a surprisingly strong assumption. In particular, is neglects many aspects of human emotion such as regret, disappointment, and the desire to have uncertainty resolved as early as possible. Consider, for example, Machina's Paradox, in which an individual is first given a choice between "a trip to Venice", "watching an amazing movie about Venice", or "staying home (and not watching the movie)". The individual's preferences are such that "a trip to Venice" ≻ "watching an amazing movie about Venice" ≻ "staying home". Next, the individual is given a choice between lotteries of the form (probability of a trip to Venice, probability of watching an amazing movie about

Venice, probability of staying home). In particular, she is given a choice between $(.99, 0.01, 0)$ and $(.99, 0, 0.01)$. In other words, she is offered one lottery with a high probability of going to Venice and a very low probability of instead watching an amazing moving about Venice. She is offered another lottery with an equally high probability of going to Venice and an equally low probability of instead staying home (and not watching the movie). Consider what lottery you would prefer. If you were almost assured a trip to Venice, but instead had horrible luck and ended up not going, would you want to watch an amazing movie about Venice? How disappointed would you be sitting through the movie, thinking about all the sights you are not experiencing? Unfortunately, the Independence Axiom requires you to prefer the lottery where you would have to sit through the movie.

Example 7.1 († Machina's Paradox):
Question: Prove Machina's Paradox violates the Independence Axiom.

Answer: Note preferences over the goods can be represented by $(1, 0, 0) \succ (0, 1, 0) \succ (0, 0, 1)$. In other words, receiving the trip as a sure-thing lottery is preferred to watching the movie as a sure-thing lottery is preferred to staying home and not watching the movie as a sure thing lottery. Independence then requires mixing maintains these preferences. Assume we mix $(0, 1, 0)$ with $(1, 0, 0)$ where $\alpha = 0.01$, resulting in the lottery $(.99, 0.01, 0)$. Likewise, mix $(0, 0, 1)$ with $(1, 0, 0)$ in the exact same way, resulting in the lottery $(.99, 0, 0.01)$. Because $(0, 1, 0) \succ (0, 0, 1)$, independence states that these mixtures must result in the same preferences. i.e. $(.99, 0.01, 0) \succ (.99, 0, 0.01)$. However, this means an individual would want to sit at home and watch a movie about the city in which she "should" be visiting. This seems highly unlikely.

Because of these obvious shortcomings of the Independence Axiom, it is one of the more controversial assumptions in Economics. However, it is also one of the most commonly used. The reasons are twofold. First, it is considered a normative assumption. In other words, this is how people "should" act. Secondly, and considerably more importantly, assuming independence allows us to use one of the most important theorems in Economics, the Expected Utility Theorem.

7.2 Expected Utility Theorem

Why does the independence axiom invalidate this?

Theorem 7.1 (Expected Utility Theorem):
If preferences over lotteries are complete, transitive, continuous, and satisfy the independence axiom, then $(p_1, p_2, \ldots, p_n) \succeq (q_1, q_2, \ldots, q_n)$ *if and only if*

$$\sum_{i=1}^{n} p_i u_i \geq \sum_{i=1}^{n} q_i u_i$$

where the u_i's are known as von Neumann-Morgenstern (vNM) utilities and can be interpreted as the cardinal utility received from good i.

Definition 7.5 (Expected Utility):
For a given lottery, $(p_1, p_2, \ldots, p_n)$, the form $\sum_{i=1}^{n} p_i u_i$ is known as its *expected utility*.

Assume, for instance, that we are offered a lottery over the two events, "a trip to Paris, France" and "a Trip to Shelby, NC". The Expected Utility Theorem states that we can assign utilities to each event that have a cardinal interpretation. For instance, if $u(\text{Paris}) = 10$ and $u(\text{Shelby}) = 1$, then we can state "going to Paris is 10 times better than going to Shelby". Equally importantly, if we were offered two lottery tickets, one of which has a prize of "going to France" and one of which has a prize of "going to Shelby", the tickets would only be equivalent if the Shelby ticket was 10 times more likely to win.

Example 7.2 (Expected Utility):
Question: Assume the requirements for the Expected Utility Theorem hold (from this point forward, always assume these requirements hold). An individual has vNM utilities of the form:

$$u(\text{going to class and getting a good grade on a pop quiz}) \;=\; 5$$
$$u(\text{going to class and learning, but not having a pop quiz}) \;=\; 1$$
$$u(\text{sleeping in}) \;=\; 2$$

The individual believes there is a 10% chance of a pop quiz. Should he go to class?

Answer: With lotteries of the form, (probability of going to class and getting a good grade on a pop quiz, probability of going to class and learning but not having a pop quiz, probability of sleeping in), the individual is facing the two lotteries $(0.1, 0.9, 0)$ and $(0, 0, 1)$. The individual should go to class if $(0.1, 0.9, 0) \succeq (0, 0, 1)$. We can use the Expected Utility Theorem to determine if this is the case. In particular, $(0.1, 0.9, 0) \succeq (0, 0, 1)$ if and only if

$$\sum_{i=1}^{n} p_i u_i \geq \sum_{i=1}^{n} q_i u_i$$
$$\Rightarrow (0.1)(5) + (0.9)(1) + (0)(2) \geq (0)(5) + (0)(1) + (1)(2)$$

Note this condition does not hold. In particular, $(0.1)(5) + (0.9)(1) + (0)(2) = 1.4$. $(0)(5) + (0)(1) + (1)(2) = 2$. Thus, according to the Expected Utility Theorem, the individual should NOT go to class.

Example 7.3 (Expected Utility):
Question: Now assume the professor starts noticing that no one is attending his class. He therefore decides to make the class more interesting. How much more interesting would he need to make the class in order to get the student in Example 7.2 to start attending class? In particular, what value of β, below, would make the student indifferent to staying at home and coming to class?

$$u(\text{going to class and getting a good grade on a pop quiz}) = 5$$
$$u(\text{going to class and learning, but not having a pop quiz}) = \beta$$
$$u(\text{sleeping in}) = 2$$

The individual believes there is a 10% chance of a pop quiz.

Answer: With lotteries of the form, (probability of going to class and getting a good grade on a pop quiz, probability of going to class and learning but not having a pop quiz, probability of sleeping in), the individual is facing the two lotteries $(0.1, 0.9, 0)$ and $(0, 0, 1)$. The individual should go to class if $(0.1, 0.9, 0) \succeq (0, 0, 1)$. We can use the Expected Utility Theorem to determine if this is the case. In particular, $(0.1, 0.9, 0) \succeq (0, 0, 1)$ if and only if

$$\sum_{i=1}^{n} p_i u_i \geq \sum_{i=1}^{n} q_i u_i$$
$$\Rightarrow (0.1)(5) + (0.9)(\beta) + (0)(2) \geq (0)(5) + (0)(\beta) + (1)(2)$$

Per the problem statement, we need this condition to hold with equality. Setting up the equality and solving for β,

$$
\begin{aligned}
(0.1)(5) + (0.9)(\beta) + (0)(2) &= (0)(5) + (0)(\beta) + (1)(2) \\
\Rightarrow .5 + .9\beta &= 2 \\
\Rightarrow \beta &= \frac{1.5}{.9} = \frac{5}{3}
\end{aligned}
$$

Thus, the professor needs to make the student's utility from attending class rise from 1 to $\frac{5}{3}$. Or, in words, he needs to make the class 66.7% more interesting.

Example 7.4 (Expected Utility):

Question: Unfortunately, this professor has no idea how to make his class more interesting. Thus, he decides to take a different approach. In particular, he decides to have more pop quizzes. On what percentage of days must he have a pop quiz in order to get the student in Example 7.2 to start attending class? In particular, what value of γ, below, would make the student indifferent to staying at home and coming to class?

$$
\begin{aligned}
u(\text{going to class and getting a good grade on a pop quiz}) &= 5 \\
u(\text{going to class and learning, but not having a pop quiz}) &= 1 \\
u(\text{sleeping in}) &= 2
\end{aligned}
$$

The individual believes there is a $\gamma\%$ chance of a pop quiz.

Answer: With lotteries of the form, (probability of going to class and getting a good grade on a pop quiz, probability of going to class and learning but not having a pop quiz, probability of sleeping in), the individual is facing the two lotteries $(\gamma, 1-\gamma, 0)$ and $(0, 0, 1)$. The individual should go to class if $(\gamma, 1-\gamma, 0) \succeq (0, 0, 1)$. We can use the Expected Utility Theorem to determine if this is the case. In particular, $(\gamma, 1-\gamma, 0) \succeq (0, 0, 1)$ if and only if

$$
\sum_{i=1}^{n} p_i u_i \geq \sum_{i=1}^{n} q_i u_i
$$
$$
\Rightarrow (\gamma)(5) + (1-\gamma)(1) + (0)(2) \geq (0)(5) + (0)(1) + (1)(2)
$$

Per the problem statement, we need this condition to hold with equality. Setting up the equality and solving for γ,

$$(\gamma)(5)+(1-\gamma)(1)+(0)(2) = (0)(5)+(0)(1)+(1)(2)$$
$$\Rightarrow 5\gamma+1-\gamma = 2$$
$$\Rightarrow \gamma = \frac{1}{4}$$

Thus, the professor needs to hold a pop quiz once every 4 class periods.

It should be noted that while a monotonic transformation of an expected utility function will maintain an individual's preferences, only a linear transformation will maintain its expected utility structure. Thus, if given a set of vNM utility functions $u_1, u_2, \ldots, u_n$, the only transformations that will allow the use of Theorem 7.1 are those of the form $au_1 + b, au_2 + b, \ldots, au_n + b$ where a and b are constants.

7.3 Attitudes Toward Risk

Most individuals spend thousands of dollars a year on car insurance, but rarely find it necessary to file a claim. Individuals in "safe" neighborhoods spend thousands of dollars to install security systems that are only triggered by the occasional cat wandering around at night. Individual investors are frequently advised to diversify their portfolios, avoiding specializing in companies that can potentially have magnificent gains. Why do individuals behave this way? Why do some individuals avoid risk at all costs? How do insurance agencies make billions of dollars?

To answer these questions, we will use the expected utility framework developed in the previous section. In particular, we will examine lotteries over amounts of money, so individual valuations of particular goods are all identical, allowing us to isolate the risk-specific behavior of individuals.

7.3.1 Expected Value

analogous to expected utility

Definition 7.6 (Expected Value):
The *expected value* of a lottery, $(p_1, p_2, \ldots, p_n)$, over the monetary prizes $(v_1, v_2, \ldots, v_n)$ is

1. The average amount of money you expect to win.

2. $\sum_{i=1}^{n} p_i v_i$

Obviously, in a lottery you will only win one of the prizes. However, the expected value tells you the average amount you will win if you played the lottery repeatedly.

> **Example 7.5 (Expected Value):**
> **Question:** An individual buys a raffle ticket that pays \$10 with 10% probability, \$20 with 50% probability, and \$30 with 40% probability. What is the expected value of the raffle ticket?
>
> **Answer:** Using Defn. 7.6,
>
> $$EV = \sum_{i=1}^{n} p_i v_i$$
> $$= (0.1)(\$10) + (0.5)(\$20) + (0.4)(\$30)$$
> $$= \$23$$

Note the *expected value* tells us how much *money*, in expectation, the lottery will give us. This is in contrast to the *expected utility* which tells us, in expectation, how much *utility* the lottery will give us. The difference between these two values tells us how much an individual dislikes risk.

Consider a multinational firm facing an acquisition that offers the following lottery: with 50% chance the aquisition will be successful and the firm will make \$1,000,000 in profits; with 50% chance the aquisition will fail and the firm will lose \$500,000 in profits. Many business experts would argue this is a good business strategy for the firm. In particular, in expectation they will make \$250,000 on a \$500,000 investment, a 50% rate of return! Even if this aquisition fails, a multinational firm will likely have so many assets that they will not be noticeably affected.

Now consider personally facing the same lottery. Would you take it? Most individuals who are not excessively wealthy would emphatically pass. The reason stems from the loss the individual would incur upon losing compared to the gain incurred upon winning. If, for instance, you lost the gamble, you would immediately be $500,000 in debt. It could potentially take you years to pay off this debt, possibly causing you to live your entire life barely scraping by. If, however, you won the lottery, you would have a fantastic nest egg of $1,000,000. However, you would likely still need to work and your style of living, while better, would not be life-changing. Putting this concept in the terms we have developed, the utility lost from losing the lottery significantly outweighs the utility gained from winning the lottery. This concept is at the heart of risk aversion.

Consider Figure 7.1 which shows an individual's vNM utility for money who originally has $40,000. The utility the individual receives from this wealth is shown by point b. Now consider a lottery that gives the individual $30,000 with probability 50% and takes away $30,000 with probability 50%. For instance, assume the individual is considering investing in a risky stock with a potentially high rate of return. Note this lottery has an expected value of $0. If the individual receives the $30,000, he ends up with the utility shown by point c. However, if he loses the $30,000, he ends up with the utility shown by point a. It is obvious that the utility lost by losing the gamble is signficantly more than the utility gained by winning the gamble. Since he has an equal possibility of each outcome, this outcome has an expected utility less than 0. If given the opportunity, the individual would prefer to not accept the lottery and avoid its risk. This individual is *risk averse*.

Now consider Figure 7.2 which shows a large firm's individual vNM utility for money that originally has $40 million and a utility shown by point b. Like the individual above, the firm is facing a $30,000 lottery with an expected value of $0. If the firm receives the $30,000, it ends up with the utility shown by point c. If it loses the $30,000, it ends up with the utility shown by point a. Note in this case the utility gained by winning the lottery is equal to the utility lost by losing the lottery. A large firm with millions of dollars in assets does not "feel" a $30,000 loss the same way an individual does. Since the firm has an equal possibility of each outcome and each outcome offsets the other, this outcome has an expected utility equal to 0. If given the opportunity, the firm is indifferent to accepting the lottery and rejecting the lottery. This firm is *risk neutral*.

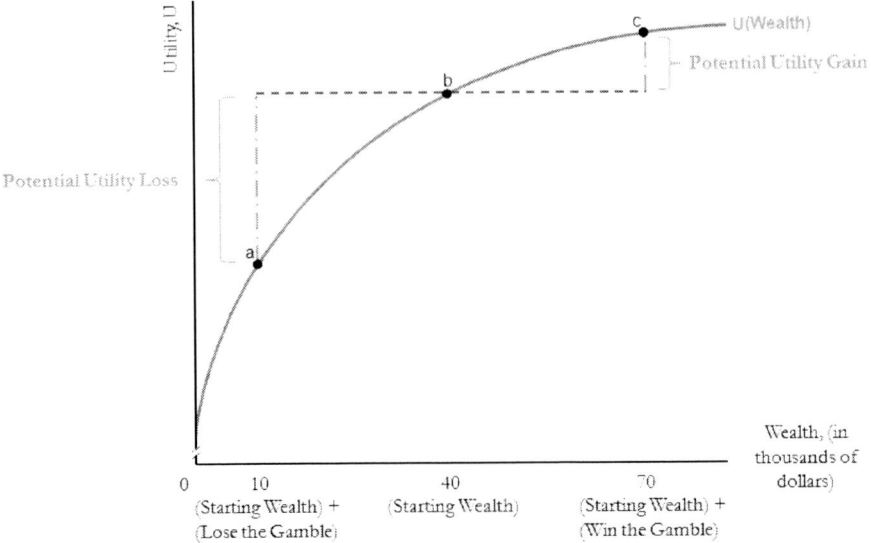

Figure 7.1: Risk Averse Preferences

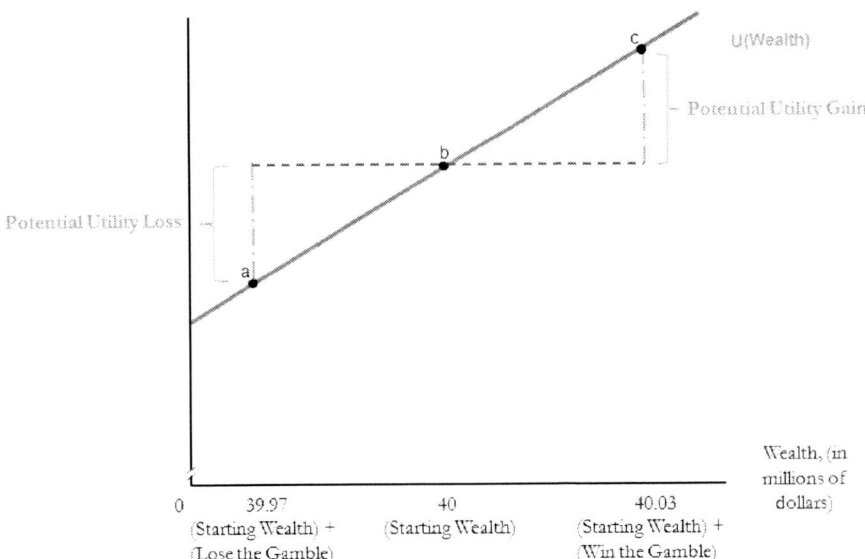

Figure 7.2: Risk Neutral Preferences

Finally, consider Figure 7.3 which shows a gambler's individual vNM utility for money that originally has $40,000 and a utility shown by point b. Again, the individual is facing a $30,000 lottery with an expected value of $0. If the individual receives the $30,000, he ends up with the utility shown by point c. If he loses the $30,000, he ends up with the utility shown by point a. Note in this case the utility gained by winning the lottery is greater to the utility lost by losing the lottery. The gambler gets a huge "high" by winning the gamble. Since the individual has an equal possibility of each outcome, this outcome has an expected utility greater than 0. If given the opportunity, the individual would accept the lottery and embrace its risk. This individual is *risk loving*.

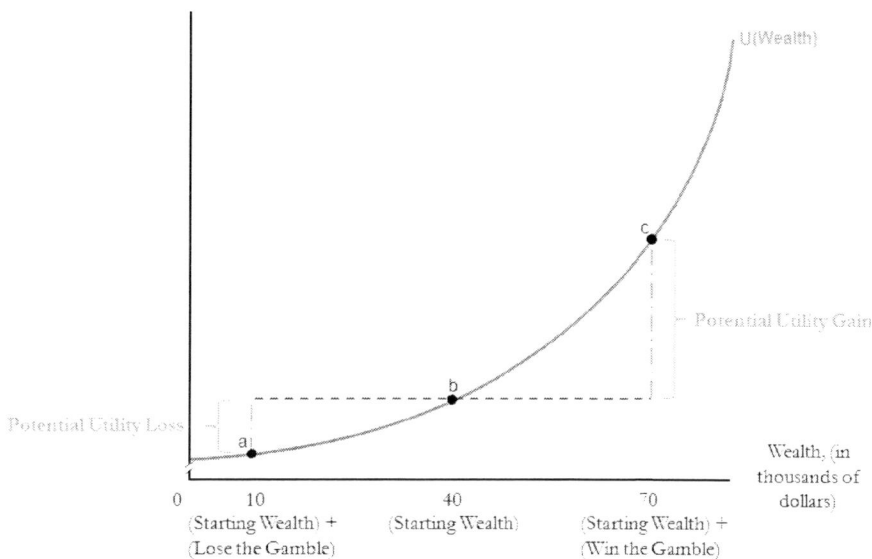

Figure 7.3: Risk Loving Preferences

Note the crucial role the curvature of the vNM utility functions play in each of the above three figures. In particular, the risk averse individual has a strictly concave utility function. The risk neutral individual has a linear (neither strictly concave nor strictly convex) utility function. The risk loving individual has a strictly convex utility function. By examining the curvature of an individual's utility function, we can therefore determine his attitude towards risk.

To determine the curvature of an individual's utility function, we use the following definitions of concavity and convexity.

Definition 7.7 (Strict Concavity):
A function, $f(x)$, is *strictly concave* if

1. $f''(x) < 0$

2. The curve is above the secant line drawn between any two points.

3. The tangent line to the curve "falls" as x increases.

4. **(Informal)** The function curves inward.

Definition 7.8 (Strict Convexity):
A function, $f(x)$ is *strictly convex* if

1. $f''(x) > 0$

2. The curve is below the secant line drawn between any two points.

3. The tangent line to the curve "rises" as x increases.

4. **(Informal)** The function curves outward.

Combining these results, we can now fully characterize the concept of risk aversion, risk neutrality, and risk loving.

Definition 7.9 (Risk Aversion):
An individual is *risk averse* if

1. $u(x)$ is strictly concave

2. $u''(x) < 0$

Definition 7.10 (Risk Neutral):
An individual is *risk neutral* if

1. $u(x)$ is neither strictly concave nor strictly convex.

2. $u''(x) = 0$

Definition 7.11 (Risk Loving):
An individual is *risk loving* if

1. $u(x)$ is strictly convex.

2. $u''(x) > 0$

Example 7.6 (Attitudes Toward Risk):
Question: An individual has a vNM utility function over money, $u(x) = x^{1/2}$, where x is money. Is the individual risk averse, risk neutral, or risk loving?

Answer: To determine the individual's risk preferences, we need only take the second derivative of his vNM utility function for money.

$$
\begin{aligned}
u'(x) &= \frac{1}{2}x^{-1/2} \\
\Rightarrow u''(x) &= -\frac{1}{4}x^{-3/2}
\end{aligned}
$$

For all positive values of x, $u''(x) < 0$. Thus, the individual's utility function is concave and they are risk averse.

7.4 Risk Premium

A risk adverse individual prefers to avoid risk where possible. A natural question that arises is "how much would he be willing to pay to avoid this risk". This is the question at the heart of the insurance industry. It turns out answering this question is surprisingly easy.

Using the expected utility theorem, we are able to determine the expected utility of a particular lottery. An individual would be willing to pay any fee such that their expected utility of paying the fee and avoiding the lottery is greater than or equal to the expected utility of the lottery. Formally,

Definition 7.12 (Risk Premium):
Consider a risk averse individual with vNM utility for money, $u(x)$. The *risk premium* of a particular lottery with expected value, EV, is

1. The value, r, such that $u(EV - r) = EU$ where EU is the expected utility of the lottery.

2. The amount *less* than the expected value she would accept in exchange for the lottery.

3. **(Informal)** The "fee" paid to avoid the risk inherent to the lottery.

Example 7.7 (Risk Premium):
Question: An individual has a vNM utility function over money, $u(x) = x^{1/2}$, where x is money. She faces a lottery that pays \$10 with probability 0.2 and \$100 with probability 0.8. What is her risk premium?

Answer: We know the risk premium, r, satisfies $u(EV - r) = EU$ To use this equation, we must first solve for the lottery's expected utility, EU. Using Definition 7.5,

$$EU = \sum_{i=1}^{n} p_i u_i$$
$$\Rightarrow EU = (0.2)(10)^{1/2} + (0.8)(100)^{1/2} = 8.632$$

We must also solve for the lottery's expected value, EV. Using Defn. 7.6,

$$EV = \sum_{i=1}^{n} p_i v_i$$
$$\Rightarrow EV = (0.2)(\$10) + (0.8)(\$100) = \$82$$

Thus,

$$
\begin{aligned}
u(\text{EV} - r) &= \text{EU} \\
\Rightarrow (82 - r)^{1/2} &= 8.632 \\
\Rightarrow (82 - r) &= 74.5 \\
\Rightarrow r &= \$7.48
\end{aligned}
$$

The individual would be willing to accept $7.48 less than the lottery's expected value to avoid its risk. In other words, she would be willing to sell the lottery ticket for $74.5.

Chapter 8

Production

Having formalized the decision-making process of an individual, we now turn our attention to firms. In one way, firms are just a specific type of "individual". In particular, they are "individuals" whose preferences follow very specific patterns. In general, economists assume this pattern is "higher profits are preferred". Obviously, in some cases profits are not a firm's sole concern, and theorists have examined many scenarios where this is the case. For our analysis, however, this assumption is appropriately widespread and realistic.

The manner in which the theory of the firm diverges from the theory of the consumer is the nature of "consumption". An individual actually consumes the bundles in question. Utility is gained when a consumer eats an orange, drives a car, wears jewelry, etc. With gambles over money, utility is gained from consuming the goods the money can actually purchase. Unfortunately, a firm cannot physically "consume" a good. General Electric, for instance, cannot eat an orange.

What a firm can do, however, is "consume" goods in the process of producing another good which can be sold for a profit. Since we have assumed profit is the sole determinant of the firm's preferences, this "consumption" once again determines the firm's "utility". As an example of firm consumption, consider the goods Ford must "consume" in order to make a car. It consumes steel, labor, electrical circuitry, electricity, warehouse space, lawyers, engineers, etc. By purchasing each of these goods, Ford receives utility in the form of profits through the sale of automobiles. This is essentially equivalent to an individual purchasing a good and receiving utility in the form of consumption pleasure. However, whereas the link between "purchasing goods" and "consumption pleasure" is considered an innate primitive in consumer theory, the link between "purchasing goods" and "profits" is a much more complex process.

In particular, this link will depend crucially on the type of technology being used to convert the input goods ("purchased goods") into output goods ("goods sold for profit"). Given a specific level of physical inputs, Ford can produce different amounts of automobiles depending on how many hours a day it operates, how much automated equipment it uses, whether it follows best practices, etc. The cost of these decisions will depend crucially on whether the staff is unionized, the transport costs of its steel inputs, whether it is receiving bulk discounts, etc. Producer theory is concerned with how a firm will maximize profits given this technological link between inputs and outputs.

8.1 Production Set

To model a firm's "technological link" between inputs and outputs, economists use the concept of production set.

> **Definition 8.1 (Production Set):**
> A firm's *production set* is every combination of inputs $(x_1, x_2, \ldots, x_n)$ and output (y) that is technologically possible. Notationally, an element of the production set is written $(x_1, x_2, \ldots, x_n, y)$.

For instance, assume a computer manufacturer has only two inputs, labor (L) and capital (K). Assume that using 5 workers and 3 automated machines (a type of capital) allows the firm to produce 4 computers. Then (5, 3, 4) would be an element of the production set. Note that (5, 3, 3) would also be an element of the production set, since if it is technologically possible to have 5 workers with 3 automated machines produce 4 computers, it is possible to have 5 workers with 3 automated machines produce less than 4 computers.

In order to get a better understanding of production sets, we will consider a firm that uses only one input and produces one output. In such a case, the production set can be illustrated via. a two dimensional picture, as in Figure 8.1.

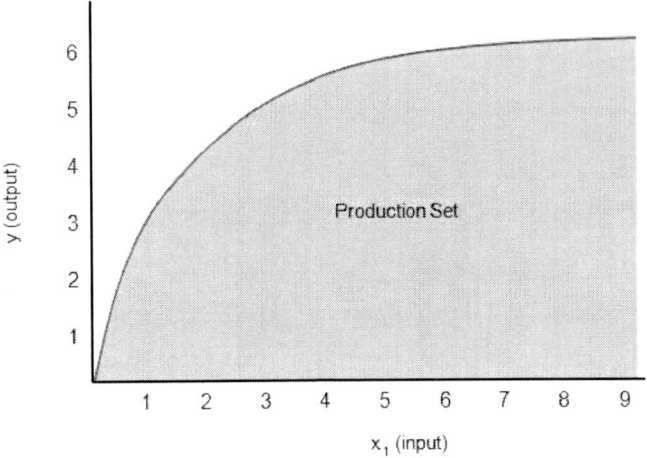

Figure 8.1: 1 Input, 1 Output Graphical Production Set

Note that all economically pertinent information related to the firm's technological abilities are contained within the production set. It tells us exactly how many inputs are required to produce each level of output. As we did with consumers' preferences, we can attribute specific properties to a firm's technological abilities.

8.2 Properties of Production Sets

We will define properties of production sets using terminology specific to one input, x_1, and one output, y. These terms easily generalize to technologies of multiple inputs and outputs.

◊ **No Free Lunch**

Definition 8.2 (No Free Lunch):
A production set displays the *No Free Lunch* property if, whenever $y > 0$, $x > 0$.

If a firm's production set displays the No Free Lunch property, it does not have a technology that allows them to produce "something from nothing". Figure 8.2

demonstrates this property.

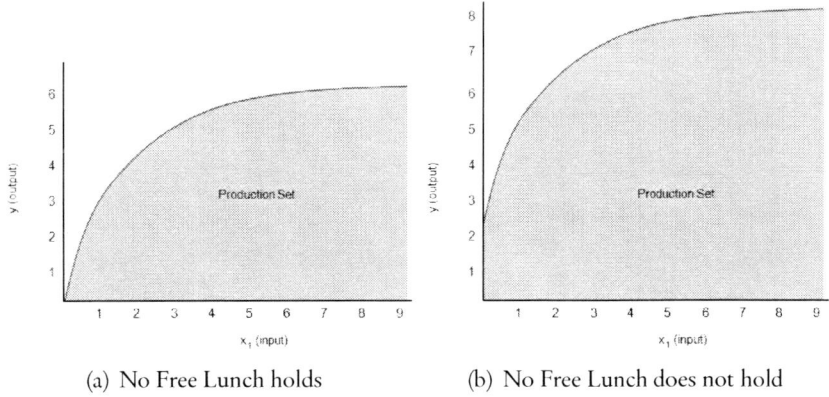

(a) No Free Lunch holds   (b) No Free Lunch does not hold

Figure 8.2: No Free Lunch Property

◇ **Possibility of Inaction**

Definition 8.3 (Possibility of Inaction):
A production set has the *possibility of inaction* if $(0,0)$ is an element of the set.

The possibility of inaction implies no costs have been sunk into production. In other words, the firm can decide to produce nothing at zero cost. Figure 8.3 demonstrates this property.

◇ **Free Disposal**

Definition 8.4 (Free Disposal):
A production set exhibits *free disposal* if, whenever (x_1, y) is an element of the set, then $(x_1 + \epsilon, y)$ is also part of the set.

In other words, the free disposal property states that a firm can dispose of "extra" inputs without having to sacrifice any output.

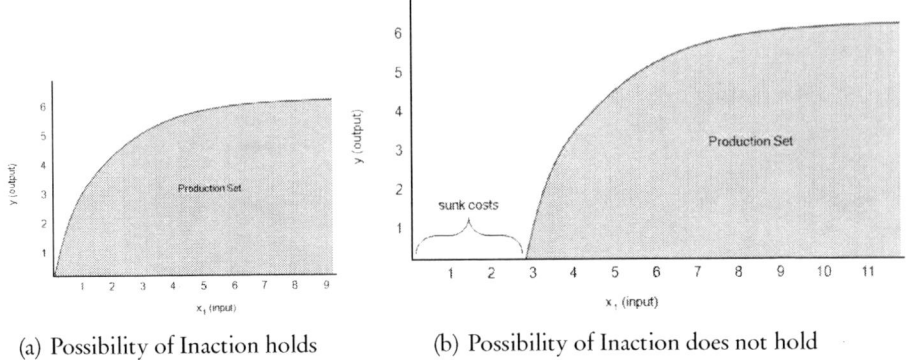

(a) Possibility of Inaction holds   (b) Possibility of Inaction does not hold

Figure 8.3: Possibility of Inaction Property

◇ **Returns to Scale**

Definition 8.5 (Increasing Returns to Scale - Global):
A production set has *increasing returns to scale* (or *increasing returns*) if, whenever (x_1, y) is an element of the production set, $(\alpha x_1, \alpha y + \epsilon)$ is also an element of the production set for all $\alpha > 1$, where ϵ is some value greater than 0.

Definition 8.6 (Decreasing Returns to Scale - Global):
A production set has *decreasing returns to scale* (or *decreasing returns*) if, whenever (x_1, y) is an element of the production set, $(\alpha x_1, \alpha y)$ is not an element of the production set for all $\alpha > 1$.

Definition 8.7 (Constant Returns to Scale - Global):
A production set has *constant returns to scale* (or *constant returns*) if, whenever (x_1, y) is an element of the production set, $(\alpha x_1, \alpha y)$ is also an element of the production set for all $\alpha > 1$, but $(\alpha x_1, \alpha y + \epsilon)$ is not, for all $\epsilon > 0$.

Returns to scale indicate whether a firm can scale up its production technology.[1] Increasing returns to scale implies that scaling up a firm's inputs will result in a proportionately larger increase in its outputs. Decreasing returns to scale implies that scaling up a firm's inputs will result in a proportionately smaller increase its outputs. Constant returns to scale implies scaling up a firm's inputs will result in a proportionate increase in its outputs.

As demonstrated by the general growth of firms and the number of corporate mergers, most firm technologies do not display decreasing returns. Instead, they display increasing returns, which indicates a firm can scale up its production technology. Consider, for instance, Samuel Adams in 1985. Originally, it was a small microbrew with few employees and a small brewery. If the firm "duplicated itself" and built an identical brewery with the same number of employees, it would likely be able to double its output, indicating increasing returns to scale. More importantly, it could likely more than double its output by building one large brewery instead of two smaller breweries and allowing employees to specialize in specific aspects of the production process.

The ability to produce more efficiently by scaling up production is one of the reasons we see mergers and firm growth. As a company gets larger, it is able to invest in more productive technology such as automated machinery. Knowledge of best practices within the firm can be distributed, making all employees more productive. Individuals can specialize in specific tasks, improving their abilities.

Generally, we see firms have increasing returns to scale up to a point. Eventually the firm can get so large that inefficiencies and redundancies lower productivity. This effect can be seen clearly in Table 8.1 and Figure 8.4, which shows per employee sales data for three large automobile manufacturers as reported in The Economist (1992). It seems apparent that Ford's size was roughly "efficient" at the time of the report. Chrysler, a smaller company, was likely undersized, and could have seen efficiency gains by scaling up to Ford's size. GM, on the other hand, was likely oversized, and could have seen efficiency gains by scaling down.

As in the automotive industry, when firms show a particular type of returns to scale up to a point, we define them as follows.

---

[1] An alternative definition of returns to scale involves determining if a production technology can be scaled down. When a production set displays the Possibility of Inaction and No Free Lunch the definitions coincide.

	Sales (in billions of dollars)	Employees (in thousands)	Sales per Employee (in thousand dollars)
Chrysler	29.4	123	238.8
Ford	88.3	333	265.4
General Motors	123.1	756	162.7

Table 8.1: Automotive Efficiencies in 1992

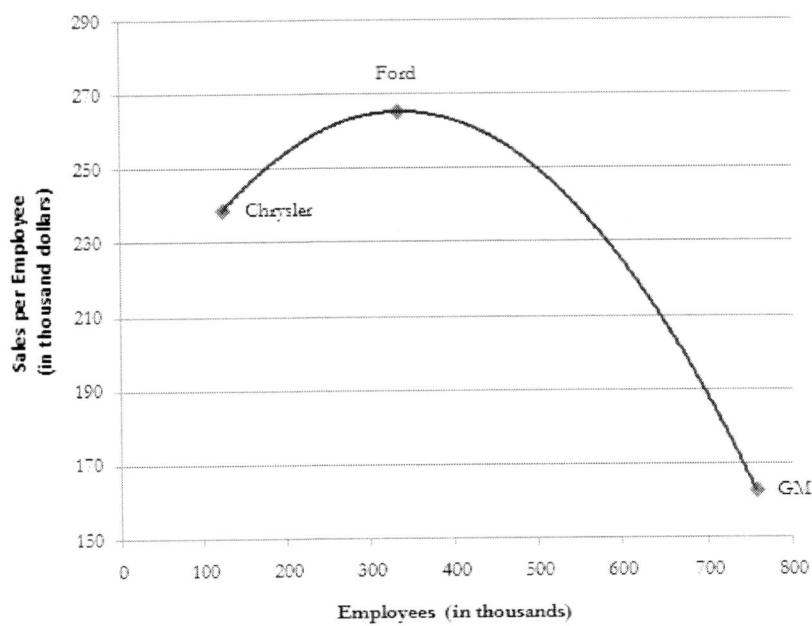

Figure 8.4: Automobile Sales per Employee (1992)

Definition 8.8 (Increasing Returns to Scale - Local):
A production set has *local increasing returns to scale* (or *local increasing returns*) at (x_1, y) if $(\alpha x_1, \alpha y + \epsilon)$ is also an element of the production set for $\alpha \in [1, \beta]$ where $\beta > 1$ and ϵ is some value greater than 0.

Definition 8.9 (Decreasing Returns to Scale - Local):
A production set has *local decreasing returns to scale* (or *local decreasing returns*) at (x_1, y) if $(\alpha x_1, \alpha y)$ is not an element of the production set for $\alpha \in [1, \beta]$ where $\beta > 1$.

Definition 8.10 (Constant Returns to Scale - Local):
A production set has *local constant returns to scale* (or *local constant returns*) at (x_1, y) if $(\alpha x_1, \alpha y)$ is also an element of the production set but $(\alpha x_1, \alpha y + \epsilon)$ is not for all $\epsilon > 0$ and $\alpha \in [1, \beta]$ where $\beta > 1$.

Figure 8.5 shows production sets with various economies of scales.

⋄ **Convexity**

Definition 8.11 (Convexity):
A production set exhibits *convexity* if, whenever (x_1, y_1) and (x_2, y_2) are elements of the set, then $(\alpha x_1 + (1 - \alpha)x_2, \alpha y_1 + (1 - \alpha)y_2)$ is also part of the set where $0 \leq \alpha \leq 1$.

Convexity implies that using a balanced production plan is weakly more efficient than using an unbalanced production plan. Consider an automotive production plant using human workers and automated machines. Assume 10 human workers could produce 10 automobile frames a day. Likewise, assume 10 automated machines can produce 50 automobile frames a day. It is reasonable to assume that 9 automated machines could produce 45 automobiles a day and 1 worker could produce 1 automobile frame per day. This fulfills the definition of convexity. More importantly, it is not unreasonable to believe that 9 automated machines and 1 worker could produce more than 46 automobile frames in a day. Specifically, if the human worker kept the automated machines running efficiently and quickly fixed any necessary repairs, the combination of inputs might result in an increase in productivity. Strict convexity captures this concept.

It should be noted that convexity of the production set and the possibility of inaction imply decreasing returns to scale.

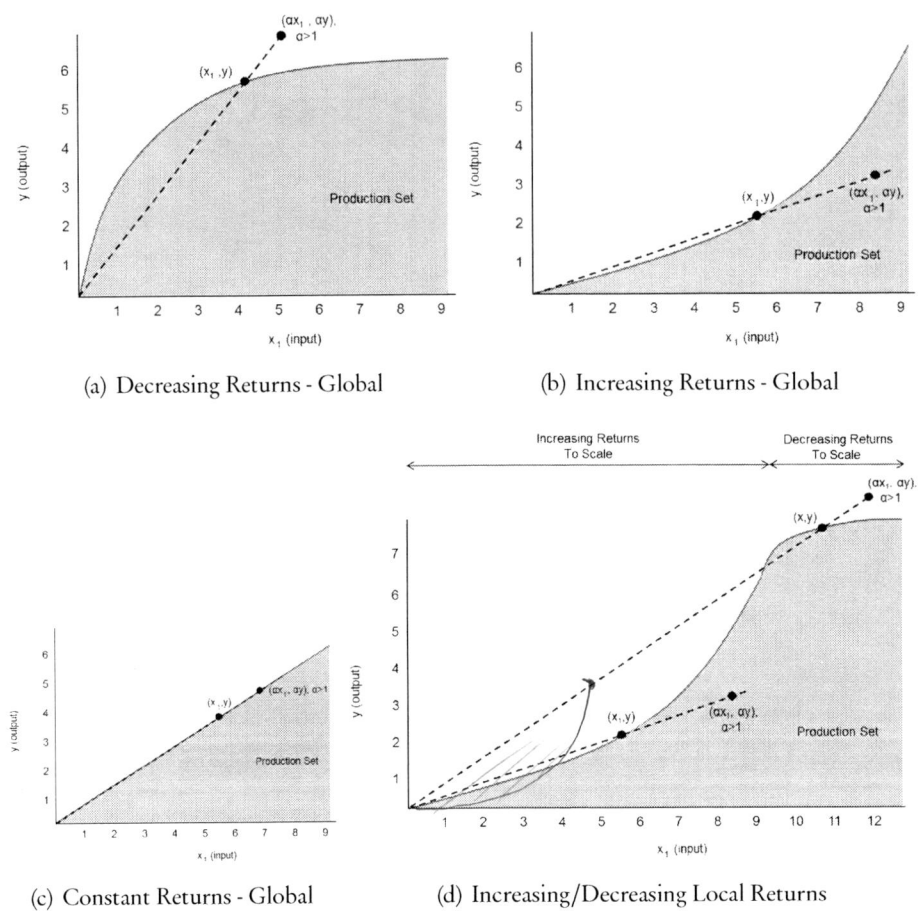

Figure 8.5: Economies of Scale

8.3 Efficiency and the Production Function

Having defined specific properties of production sets (note other properties exist, but are beyond the scope of this class), we can now incorporate additional mathematical concepts to simplify our analysis. We will first consider a manner in which we can "summarize" the production set. Specifically, we will determine if a function exists which can be used to fully describe the production technology. Note the similarities between this exercise and our earlier results of summarizing individual preferences in the form of a utility function.

Note that for a given level of input(s), the production set defines every possible level of outputs that can be produced. It is sensible to assume that, as economists, we are only concerned with the efficient level of output.

> **Definition 8.12 (Efficient Production):**
> A firm displays *efficient production* if, given a level of inputs, x_1, they are producing the largest amount of output, y, possible.

While it is possible a firm hires 10 workers and tells 5 of them to "kick back and relax", it does not seem likely. Thus, assuming firms are producing at their efficient levels is a reasonable assumption. It is important to note the difference between "efficient production" and the "efficient (optimal) level of inputs". Efficient production implies that, given the level of inputs, the firm is doing as well as it can. Having the optimal level of inputs implies that the firm has selected the level of inputs to maximize its profits *and* is is using those inputs efficiently. In Table 8.1, for instance, General Motors was not using an optimal number of inputs (employees). However, it was using its overly large workforce efficiently in that it was likely not instructing its workforce to not work. Note also that inputs include items such as best practices, information technologies, strategy consultants, etc. Thus, even if General Motors could have organized its workforce in a more productive manner, this would have required the additional inputs of human resource consultants, organizational experts, etc.

Note that if we focus on efficient production, we no longer are concerned with the full production set. Instead, we are only concerned with the boundary of the production set. In our one-input case, this boundary can be represented by a single-variable function.

Definition 8.13 (Production Function):
Given a fixed level of inputs, x_1, a firm's *production function*, $f(x_1)$, gives the maximum amount of output, y, the firm can produce. In other words, $y = f(x_1)$ is the amount of output, y, than can efficiently be produced given x_1.

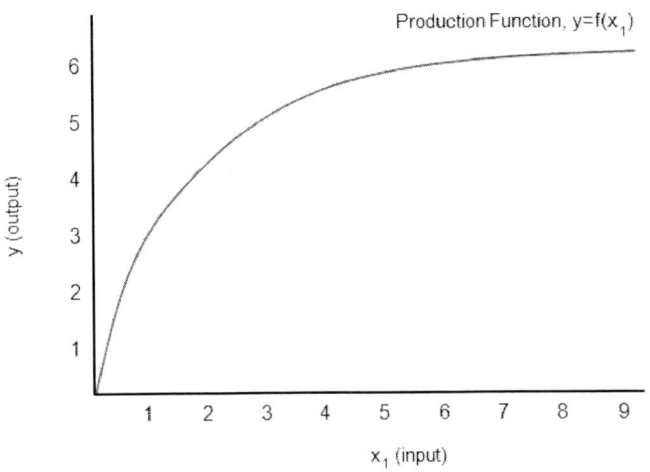

Figure 8.6: Production Function

Note the similarities between the production function and the budget line. The budget line tells us the maximum amount of goods that can be purchased given a budget set. The production function tells us the maximum amount of goods that can be produced given a production set.

8.4 Properties of Production Functions

Theorem 4.1 tells us for any rational preferences, we can construct a representative utility function. Existence of a production function is much easier. In particular, it only requires the assumption that "for any level of inputs, some maximal output can be produced". This assumption is innocuous, allowing us to focus our attention on production functions instead of their underlying production sets.

That being said, in much the same way that the properties of underlying preferences affect the properties of the utility function, the properties of the underlying production set affect the properties of the production function.

Theorem 8.1 (f(x) and Free Disposal):
A production set has the Free Disposal property if and only if the production function is weakly increasing in its inputs.

The logic behind Theorem 8.1 is straightforward. In particular, if a given level of inputs allows the production of some maximal level of outputs, then any higher level of inputs will allow at least that level of production, since (in the worst case scenario), the extra inputs can simply be disposed of.

Theorem 8.2 (f(x) and No Free Lunch):
A production set has the No Free Lunch property if and only if $f(\vec{0}) = 0$, where $f(x)$ is the production function.

In other words, if there are no inputs used, no output can be produced.

Theorem 8.3 (f(x) and the Possibility of Inaction):
A production set has the Possibility of Inaction property if and only if $f(\vec{0}) \geq 0$ and $\vec{0}$ is in the domain of $f(x)$.

In other words, it is possible to use no inputs and produce no outputs.

Theorem 8.4 (f(x) and Convexity of the Production Set):
A production set is convex if and only if its production function is concave.

Consider the fact that we said a production set displaying convexity and the possibility of inaction implies decreasing returns to scale. Note the curvature of the production function in Figure 8.5(a), which shows a production set exhibiting decreasing returns to scale. In particular, the production function is concave.

Theorem 8.5 (f(x) and Decreasing Returns to Scale - Global):
A production set displays global decreasing returns to scale if and only if
$f(tx) < tf(x)$ *for all* $t > 1$.

Consider, for instance, if we doubled the amount of each input in a decreasing returns to scale production technology. Using Theorem 8.5, this implies $f(2x) \leq 2f(x)$. In other words, doubling all inputs results in less than double the output. We are unable to scale up the technology.

Theorem 8.6 (f(x) and Increasing Returns to Scale - Global):
A production set displays global increasing returns to scale if and only if
$f(tx) > tf(x)$ *for all* $t > 1$.

In the case of increasing returns to scale, it must be the case that doubling all inputs results in more than double the output. Scaling up is possible and results in a higher per-input productivity.

Theorem 8.7 (f(x) and Constant Returns to Scale - Global):
A production set displays global constant returns to scale if and only if
$f(tx) = tf(x)$ *for all* $t > 1$.

In the case of constant returns to scale, doubling the inputs results in doubling the outputs.

Example 8.1 (Returns to Scale):
Question: Consider the 2-input Constant Elasticity of Substitution (CES) production function, $y = f(x_1, x_2) = (x_1^\rho + x_2^\rho)^{\frac{1}{\rho}}$. Does it represent an increasing, decreasing, or constant production technology?

Answer: Using Theorems 8.5 - 8.7, we must determine the relationship between $f(tx_1, tx_2)$ and $tf(x_1, x_2)$.

$$
\begin{aligned}
f(tx_1, tx_2) &= \left((tx_1)^\rho + (tx_2)^\rho\right)^{\frac{1}{\rho}} \\
\Rightarrow &= \left(t^\rho x_1^\rho + t^\rho x_2^\rho\right)^{\frac{1}{\rho}} \\
\Rightarrow &= \left(t^\rho (x_1^\rho + x_2^\rho)\right)^{\frac{1}{\rho}} \\
\Rightarrow &= t^{\frac{\rho}{\rho}} \left(x_1^\rho + x_2^\rho\right)^{\frac{1}{\rho}} \\
\Rightarrow &= t \left(x_1^\rho + x_2^\rho\right)^{\frac{1}{\rho}} \\
\Rightarrow &= tf(x_1, x_2)
\end{aligned}
$$

Since $f(tx_1, tx_2) = tf(x_1, x_2)$, the CES production function represents a constant returns to scale production technology.

Note that analogous theorems exist for local returns to scale.

Theorem 8.8 (Production Function Decreasing Returns to Scale - Local):
A production set displays local decreasing returns to scale at x if and only if $f(tx) < tf(x)$ *for all* $t \in [1, \beta]$ *where* $\beta > 1$.

Theorem 8.9 (Production Function Increasing Returns to Scale - Local):
A production set displays local increasing returns to scale at x if and only if $f(tx) > tf(x)$ *for all* $t \in [1, \beta]$ *where* $\beta > 1$.

Theorem 8.10 (Production Function Constant Returns to Scale - Local):
A production set displays local constant returns to scale at x if and only if $f(tx) = tf(x)$ *for all* $t \in [1, \beta]$ *where* $\beta > 1$.

8.5   Ordinal vs. Cardinal

In the last example, we used a CES production function. Note the form of this function is identical to the form of a CES utility function. There is, however, a crucial difference that must be noted. A utility function is an ordinal representation of preferences. Its construction ensures that more preferred bundles will result in higher utilities, but it does not offer a cardinal interpretation of "utility". "5 utils" does not have an inherent meaning outside our analysis. The production function, on the other hand, tells us the maximum of output that can be produced given a fixed number of inputs. This function does have a cardinal meaning. To say "5 employees working 10 hours can produce 6 automobile frames" means something very specific. A production function is specific to the underlying technology. As such, a monotonic transformation of a production function does not represent the underlying technology in the same manner a monotonic transformation of a utility function represents the underlying preferences.

Theorem 8.11:

A production function that is a monotonic transformation of another production function does NOT represent the same underlying production technology.

8.6   Multidimensional Production Functions

To this point, we have concentrated on single-input production technologies. Obviously, this has been an extreme simplification. In general, multiple inputs are required to produce a good. Building a house, for instance, requires wood, nails, cement, workers, architects, plumbers, electricians, etc.

Luckily, working with multidimensional production functions is no more difficult than dealing with multidimensional utility functions. In fact, most properties of production functions have natural analogs to properties of utility functions.

8.6.1 Marginal Productivity

Definition 8.14 (Marginal Productivity - Verbal):
The *marginal productivity* of an input good is the extra amount of output that can be produced with an extra unit of the input good.

Note the similarities between this concept and marginal utility. In particular, marginal utility answers the question "how much extra utility can be gained from one extra consumption good". Marginal productivity answers the question "how much extra output can be gained from one extra input good". In an identical way that marginal utility can be computed using a partial derivative, so can marginal productivity.

Definition 8.15 (Marginal Productivity - Calculus):
The *marginal productivity* of input good, x_1, is $MP_{x_1} = \frac{\partial f}{\partial x_1}$.

8.6.2 Marginal Rate of Technical Substitution (MRTS)

When multiple goods can be used in the production of an output, consider the tradeoff that can be made between the input goods. For instance, if we once again focus on the construction of automobile bodies, if one human laborer is laid off, for how many more hours will an automated machine have to work to offset the loss? Alternatively, if one extra human laborer is hired, for how many more hours can an automated machine be turned off and still have the total output remain the same? This tradeoff is called the marginal rate of technical substitution (MRTS).

Definition 8.16 (MRTS - Verbal):
- The *marginal rate of technical substitution* (MRTS) is the maximum amount of one input good that a firm will sacrifice to obtain one more unit of another input good.

- Assume one unit of an input good is taken away. The *marginal rate of technical substitution* is the number of units of the other input good the firm must be given to keep its output level the same.

Recall that we were able to visualize the MRS by plotting indifference curves. In particular, an indifference curve represents all bundles that make a consumer equally happy. The slope of a specific indifference curve tells us the manner in which the individual is able to trade the goods and maintain the same utility. As such, the slope of the indifference curve tells us the MRS.

In the same way, consider a curve that shows us all combinations of bundles that allow a firm to produce the same level of output. Figure 8.7, for instance, shows all combinations of human hours and automated machine hours that can produce 4 automobile frames. We call such a graph an isoquant.

Definition 8.17 (Isoquant):
An *isoquant* is the graphical set of all bundles of input goods that a firm views as equally desirable.

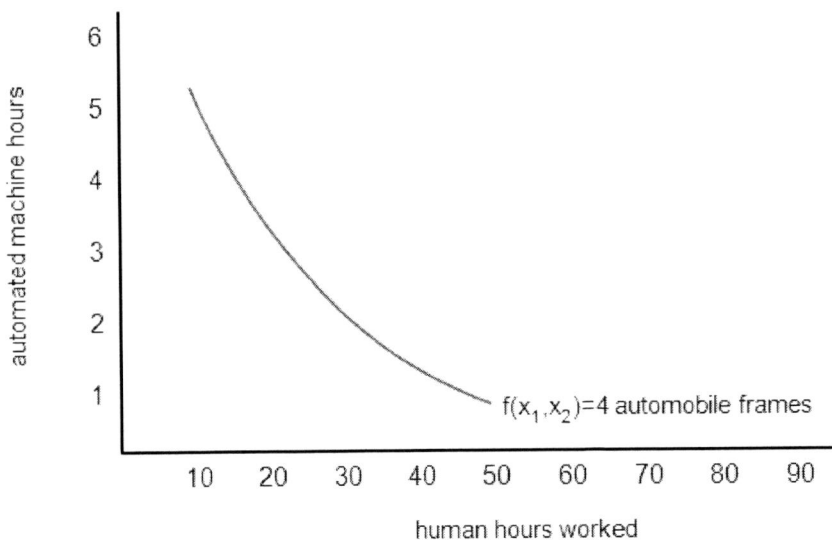

Figure 8.7: 2 Input Good Isoquant

Given the similarities between isoquants and indifference curves, it should be clear that the slope of an isoquant will tell us the manner in which a firm is be able to trade the input goods and maintain the same output. Because isoquants and indifference curves are mathematically identical with the only difference being the "name" of the underlying function (utility vs. production), we can use identical techniques to solve for the mathematical representation of the MRTS. In particular,

---

Theorem 8.12 (MRTS):
The following are all characterizations of the marginal rate of technical substitution between input goods x_1 and x_2

1. *$MRTS_{x_1,x_2}$ is the maximum amount of input good x_2 that a firm will sacrifice to obtain one more unit of input good x_1.*

2. *$MRTS_{x_1,x_2}$ is the slope of the isoquant, $x_2(x_1)$.*

3. *$MRTS_{x_1,x_2} = -\dfrac{MP_{x_1}}{MP_{x_2}} = -\dfrac{f_1}{f_2}$*

8.6.3 Properties of Isoquants

Isoquants have essentially the same properties as indifference curves. In particular, isoquants cannot cross, isoquants slope downward, isoquants must be thin, and an isoquant farther from the origin represents greater output. Whereas the properties of indifference curves generally result from the monotonicity property and transitivity, the properties of isoquants result from efficiency. As an example, consider Figure 8.8. If isoquants could cross, a point such as e could exist that is common to two isoquants. However, an isoquant represents the single efficient level of output given the level of inputs. In our Figure, $q = 6$ cannot be on an isoquant passing through the input levels represented by e, since $q = 10$ is obviously more efficient given the same input levels.

8.6.4 Substitutability of Inputs

Having established the similarities between indifference curves and isoquants, it is not surprising that the curvature of an isoquant has roughly the same interpretation as the curvature of an indifference curve. Consider, for instance, a utility function of the form $U(x_1,x_2) = x_1 + x_2$ that represents perfect substitutes, where an individual is indifferent between bundle x_1 and bundle x_2. A production function of the same form, $f(x_1,x_2) = x_1 + x_2$, also represents perfect substitutes. In

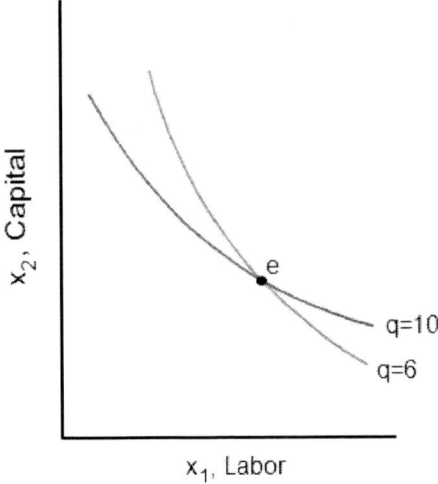

Figure 8.8: Crossing Isoquants

this case, however, it is the firm that is indifferent between using a unit of x_1 and a unit of x_2 in their production process. The isoquants and indifference curves look identical.

As expected, the more alike two goods are in the production process, the more their isoquants "look like" lines (i.e. they "look more like" perfect substitutes). The more two goods require each other to be useful to the production process, the more L-shaped their isoquants (i.e. they "look more like" perfect complements).

Examples of perfect substitutes in a cereal-making production process are corn purchased from Iowa and corn purchased from Nebraska. The firm is indifferent between one ear of Iowa corn and one ear of Nebraska corn. Examples of perfect complements are a human and a bulldozer. The human cannot lift thousands of pounds without the bulldozer, and the bulldozer cannot operate without a driver. Examples of imperfect substitutes/complements are general human labor and general capital equipment. A factory worker cannot be replaced with automated machines, since the worker's ability to repair equipment, organize operations, etc. cannot be duplicated with machines. Likewise, automated machines cannot be replaced with factory workers, since the level of precision in machinery is difficult to reproduce. However, neither input relies entirely on the other. A human would still be partially productive without automated machines. An automated machine would still be partially productive without humans optimizing its performance. Figure 8.9 demonstrates these examples.

Figure 8.9: Substitutability of Inputs

8.7 Using Isoquants to Determine Economies of Scale

By strictly using an isoquant representation of a production technology, we can determine the economies of scale. Consider Figure 8.10. Starting at point a, we find that one unit of each of the input goods results in 1 unit of the output good. If we double both input goods, we arrive at point b. The isoquant passing through point b corresponds to 3 units of the output good. Thus, in this region, $f(2x_1, 2x_2) = 3f(x_1, x_2)$. In other words, we are in an area of increasing returns to scale. Doubling the inputs results in more than a doubling of the output.

> **Example 8.2 (Isoquants and Economies of Scale):**
> **Question:** In figure 8.10, determine the economies of scale when passing from point b to c and from c to d.
>
> **Answer:** From point b, if we once again double both input goods, we arrive at point c. The isoquant passing through point c corresponds to 6 units of the output good. Thus, in this region, $f(2x_1, 2x_2) = 2f(x_1, x_2)$. In other words, we are in an area of constant returns to scale. Doubling the inputs results in a doubling of the output. Finally, if we double both input goods again, we arrive at point d. The isoquant passing through point d corresponds to 8 units of the output good. Thus, in this region, $f(2x_1, 2x_2) = 1.33f(x_1, c_2)$. In other words,

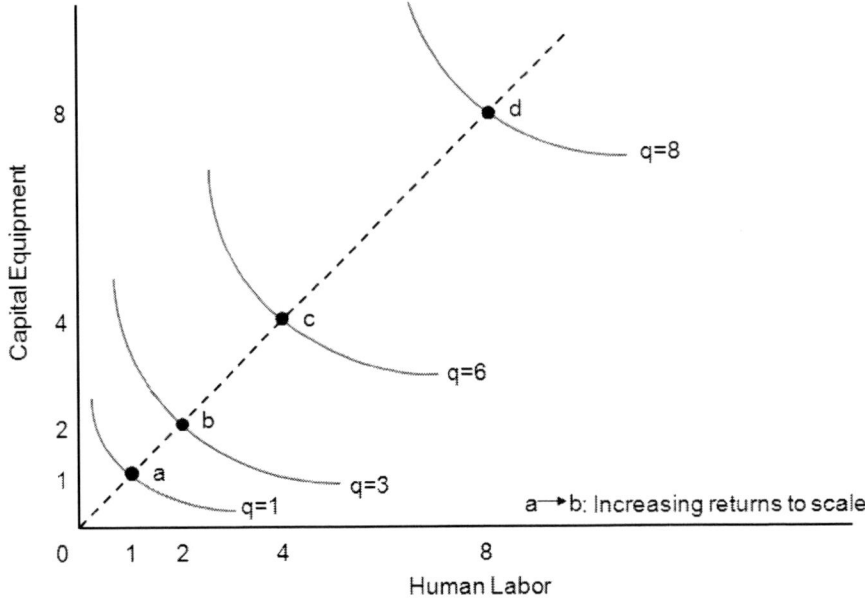

Figure 8.10: Isoquants and Economies of Scale

we are in an area of decreasing returns to scale. Doubling the inputs results in less than a doubling of the output.

Chapter 9

Cost Minimization

Having formalized a firm's production technology through the concept of a production set and its corresponding production function, we can now begin to answer specific questions firms face on a daily basis. The first, and most direct question we will address is "with a given set of input prices and a production technology, what is the cheapest way for a firm to produce q units of output?".

9.1 Isocost Lines

In order to answer this question, we need to formalize the concept of Cost. Consider a production process that uses x_1 units of Input Good 1 and x_2 units of Input Good 2. The price per unit of Input Good 1 is w_1 and the price per unit of Input Good 2 is w_2.[1] Assuming Input Goods 1 and 2 are the only inputs necessary for production, the total cost, C, will satisfy the equation

$$C = w_1 x_1 + w_2 x_2 \tag{9.1}$$

If we want to determine all the bundles of Input Goods that will cost exactly $\overline{C}$, where $\overline{C}$ is a fixed cost level, we can rearrange Eqn. 9.1 to find

$$x_2 = -\frac{w_1}{w_2} x_1 + \frac{\overline{C}}{w_2} \tag{9.2}$$

---

[1] We use the letter, w, to represent the prices of input goods necessary to produce a specific output good. We use p to represent the price for which the output good is sold to consumers (which naturally coincides with the price consumers have to pay for the good).

Thus, for every x_1 level, Eqn. 9.2 tells us exactly how much x_2 a firm can purchase to achieve a total cost equaling $\overline{C}$. We define the line defined by Eqn. 9.2 as an *isocost line*.

> **Definition 9.1 (Isocost Line):**
> An *Isocost Line* is the set of all bundles that cause a firm to achieve a fixed cost level, $\overline{C}$.

It is worth noting the similarities between Eqn. 9.2 and the consumer's Budget Line, Eqn. 5.2. In particular, the consumer's Budget Line tells us all the combinations of x_1 and x_2 that cause an individual to spend exactly I. Equation 9.2 tells us all the combinations of x_1 and x_2 that cause the firm to spend exactly $\overline{C}$. As the formulations of these lines are mathematically identical with the only difference being a change in the variable names, it is not surprising that the properties of a budget line discussed in Chapter 5 have direct analogues to the properties of an isocost line.

With x_1 on the x-axis and x_2 on the y-axis:

- Eqn. 9.2 is in a "slope-intercept" form of a line, $x_2 = mx_1 + b$ with $m = -\frac{w_1}{w_2}$ and $b = \frac{\overline{C}}{w_2}$.

- The y-axis intercept is equal to $\frac{\overline{C}}{w_2}$. This should make intuitive sense, since the y-axis intercept of the isocost line tells us how many units of x_2 we can purchase if our total cost is $\overline{C}$ and we spend all our money on Input Good 2. Naturally, this will be the total cost divided by the price per unit of Input Good 2.

- The x-axis intercept is equal to $\frac{\overline{C}}{w_1}$. This can be solved from Eqn. 9.2 or can be intuitively found using the same logic as the y-axis intercept.

- The slope of the isocost line is $-\frac{w_1}{w_2}$.

Example 9.1 (Isocost Line):
Question: Assume the price of labor is $3.00 and the price of capital is $4.00. Graphically, with labor on the x-axis and capital on the y-axis, what does the

isocost line relating to a total cost of $\overline{C} = 12$ look like?

Answer: As shown in Figure (9.1), the isocost line is just all combinations of labor and capital that cost exactly $12.

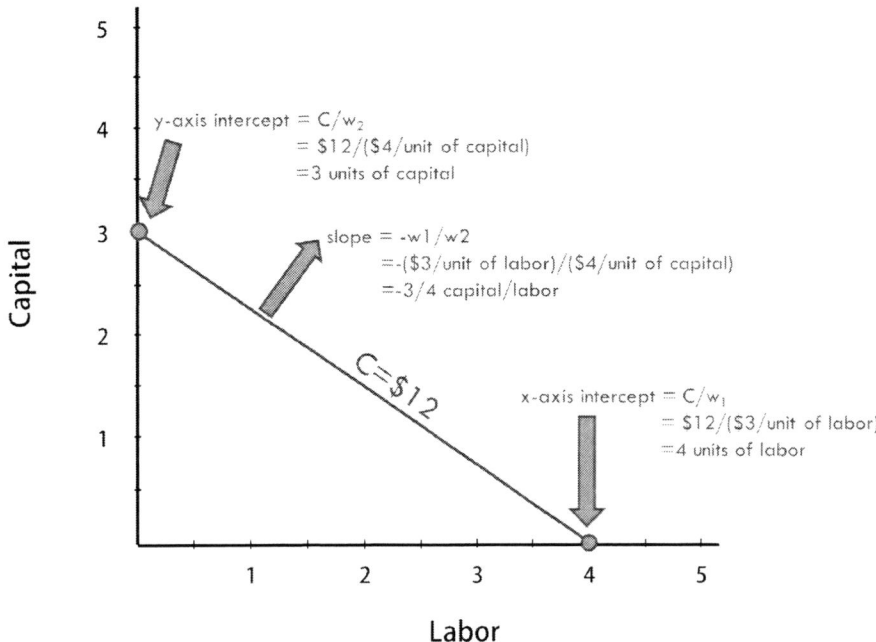

Figure 9.1: Example (9.1) - Graphical Representation of the Isocost Line

Example 9.2 (Isocost Line Adjustments):
Question: Assume the price of labor is $3.00 and the price of capital is $4.00. Graphically, with labor on the x-axis and capital on the y-axis, what does the isocost line relating to a total cost of $\overline{C} = 24$ look like?

Answer: As shown in Figure (9.2), the isocost line is just all combinations of labor and capital that cost exactly $24.

The last two examples illustrate the point that each isocost line is specific to one total cost level. As this cost increases, isocosts move away from the origin in

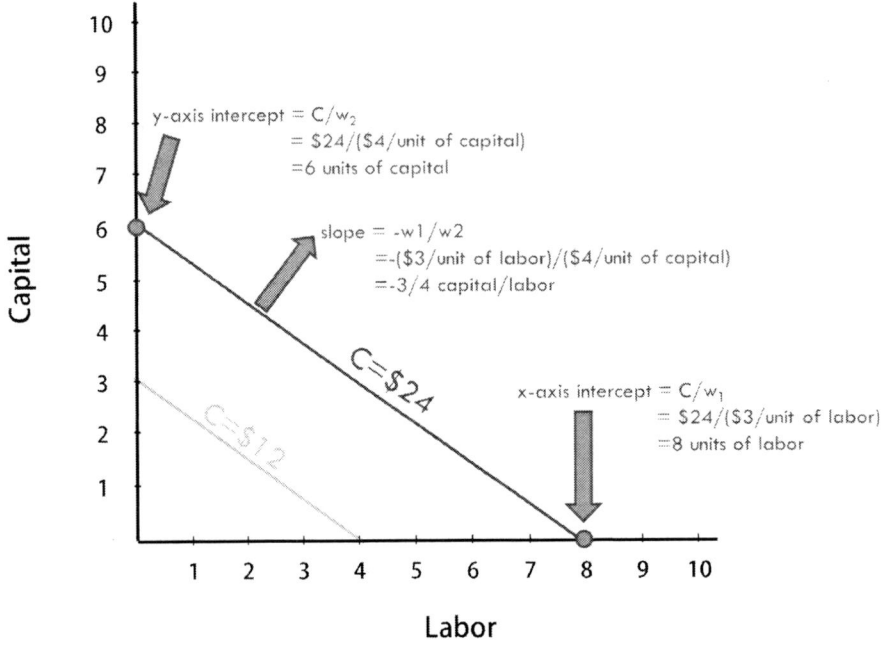

Figure 9.2: Example (9.2) - Isocost Line Adjustments

parallel shifts. Specifically, if we look at Eqn. 9.2 and again recognize this is in the "slope-intercept" form of a line, the slope, $-\frac{w_1}{w_2}$ is unaffected by the total cost level. Instead, only the intercepts change, with higher costs resulting in higher intercepts.

9.1.1 Factor Price Ratio

Analogous to the Marginal Rate of Transformation, the slope of the isocost line tells us by how much x_2 can increase if 1 unit of x_1 is taken away, while keeping total costs constant.

Example 9.3 (Isocost Slope):
Question: Assume the price of labor is $3.00 and the price of capital is $4.00. If 1 unit of labor is given up, how much additional capital can be purchased?

Answer: If 1 unit of labor is given up, the firm can gain $3.00 (since that is the price of labor). It can then purchase $3.00/($4/capital) = 3/4 units of capital.

Note this is identical to the statement "the slope of the isocost line is $-\frac{w_1}{w_2} = -\frac{3}{4}$".

It should be clear that this tradeoff is very similar to the tradeoff made when studying the marginal rate of technical substitution (MRTS). The MRTS tells us how much additional x_2 is required to offset a 1 unit reduction of x_1 for the firm *so that it produces the same level of output*. The slope of an isocost line tells us how much additional x_2 must be purchased given a 1 unit reduction of x_1 *to maintain the same total costs*. For the budget line, we call this tradeoff the Marginal Rate of Transformation. For an isocost line, we call this tradeoff the *Factor Price Ratio*.

> **Definition 9.2 (Factor Price Ratio):**
> The slope of an isocost line is also called the *Factor Price Ratio*.

9.2 Cost Minimization - Graphical

Having formalized the concept of production through production sets/production functions/isoquants and the concept of costs through isocost lines, we now have the tools to address our original question, "with a given set of input prices and a production technology, what is the cheapest way for a firm to produce q units of output?" The approach we will take is very similar to the approach we took to find the optimal consumption bundle for a consumer.

> **Example 9.4 (Cost Minimization):**
> **Question:** Consider a firm trying to produce 100 cars in a given day, and it takes labor and capital to produce a car. The isoquant specific to producing 100 cars is shown in Figure 9.3. The input price of labor is $20 per employee. The input price of capital is $40 per unit of capital. What is the cheapest manner in which the firm can produce 100 cars?
>
> **Answer: ?**

To answer this question, we first recall that by definition of an isoquant, we must be using a labor/capital mix on the isoquant shown in Figure 9.3. Any other labor/capital mix will lie on a different isoquant, resulting in a different output

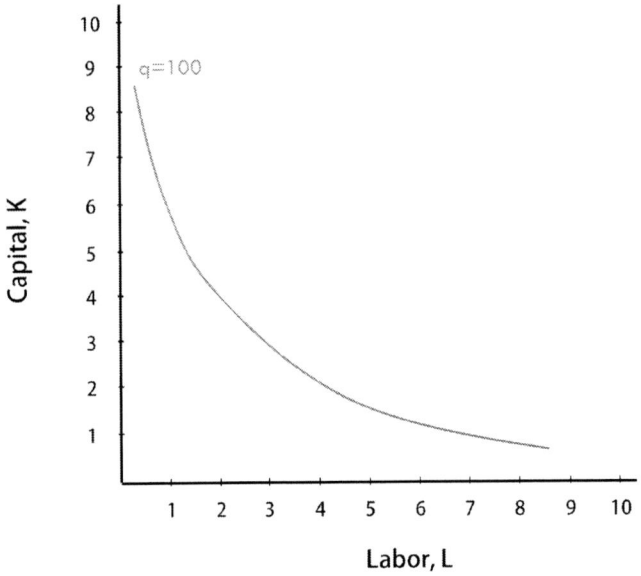

Figure 9.3: Example (9.4) - Production Technology

level. We will now examine specific points on the isoquant to determine which causes total cost to be minimized.

Example 9.5 (Cost Minimization - Low Labor/High Capital Blend):
Question: Will the firm in Example 9.4 minimize costs by selecting the labor/capital mix represented by point A, as shown in Figure 9.4(a)?

Answer: One way to approach this problem is to calculate the costs, $C = w_1 L_A + w_2 K_A$, at point A, $(L_A, K_A) = (2,4)$ and attempt to find another point on the isoquant with lower total points. However, as we need to find the point that results in the *lowest* possible cost, we will take a more systematic approach. In particular, we will identify the isocost line passing through point A and make a graphical argument as to whether a lower isocost line passes through another point on the isoquant. Recall that lower isocost lines represent lower total costs, so if a point with a lower isocost line is on the same isoquant, we will still be producing 100 cars but at a lower total cost.

To find the isocost line passing through point A, we could solve for the total cost by calculating $C = w_1 L_A + w_2 K_A = (\$20)(2) + (\$40)(4) = \$120$ and use Eqn. (9.2). However, an easier approach is to use the Factor Price Ratio. Specifically, for a given set of input prices, recall that all isocost lines have the same slope, specifically the Factor Price Ratio which equals $-\frac{w_1}{w_2}$. As the price of labor is \$20 and the price of capital is \$40, this implies that the isocost line passing through point A will have a slope of $-\frac{20}{40} = -1/2$. If we draw a line having a slope of -1/2 passing through point A, we generate the isocost line as shown in Figure 9.4(b).

Compare this isocost line to the isocost line passing through point B, as shown in Figure 9.5. In particular, we know the isocost line passing through point B must have the same slope as the isocost passing through point A. It is then immediately clear that the isocost line passing through B is lower than the isocost line passing through A, implying a lower cost. Thus, point A could not have been the cost-minimizing labor/capital blend.

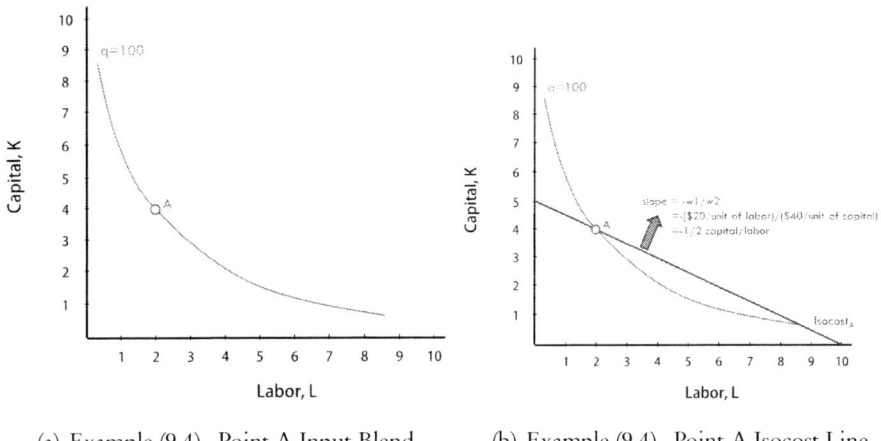

(a) Example (9.4) - Point A Input Blend   (b) Example (9.4) - Point A Isocost Line

Figure 9.4: Cost Minimization Problem

Example 9.6 (Cost Minimization - Intermediate Blend):
Question: Having established that the labor/capital blend represented by point B in Figure 9.5 is a lower-cost alternative to the labor/capital blend represented by point A, we can then ask if the firm in Example 9.4 will minimize costs by selecting the labor/capital mix represented by point *B*.

Answer: Using an identical approach as used in Example 9.5, we can move down the isoquant to point C, as shown in Figure 9.6. This is once again on a lower isocost line, implying the labor/capital mix represented by point B could not be cost-minimizing.

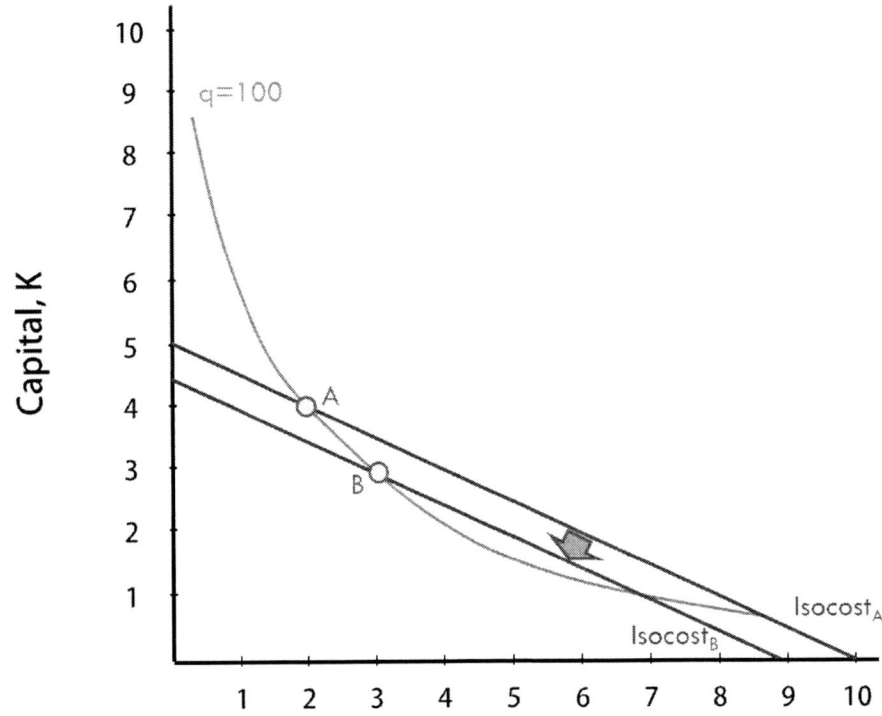

Figure 9.5: Example (9.4) - Point B Isocost Line

Continuing with this logic, we can continue to "move down" the isoquant until we are at the lowest possible isocost line. Specifically, the labor/capital mix that ensures we produce 100 cars (as indicated by the fact we are on the $q = 100$ isoquant) at the lowest possible cost is point D, (4.8, 1.6), as shown in Figure 9.7. To determine the lowest cost to produce 100 cars, we can directly compute the cost as $C = w_1 L_D + w_2 K_D = (\$20)(4.8) + (\$40)(1.6) = \$160$. Alternatively, we can compute the cost of any point on the isocost line, as all points by definition incur the same cost. For instance, if we note that the isocost line passing through point D also passes through (0,4), we can compute the cost as $C = (\$20)(0) + (\$40)(4) = \$160$.

From Figure 9.7, we see a very important property concerning the cost-minimizing input mix. In particular, when the cost-minimizing input mix contains positive amounts of each good, the isoquant corresponding to the desired output level is tangent to an isocost line containing the cost-minimizing point. In other words,

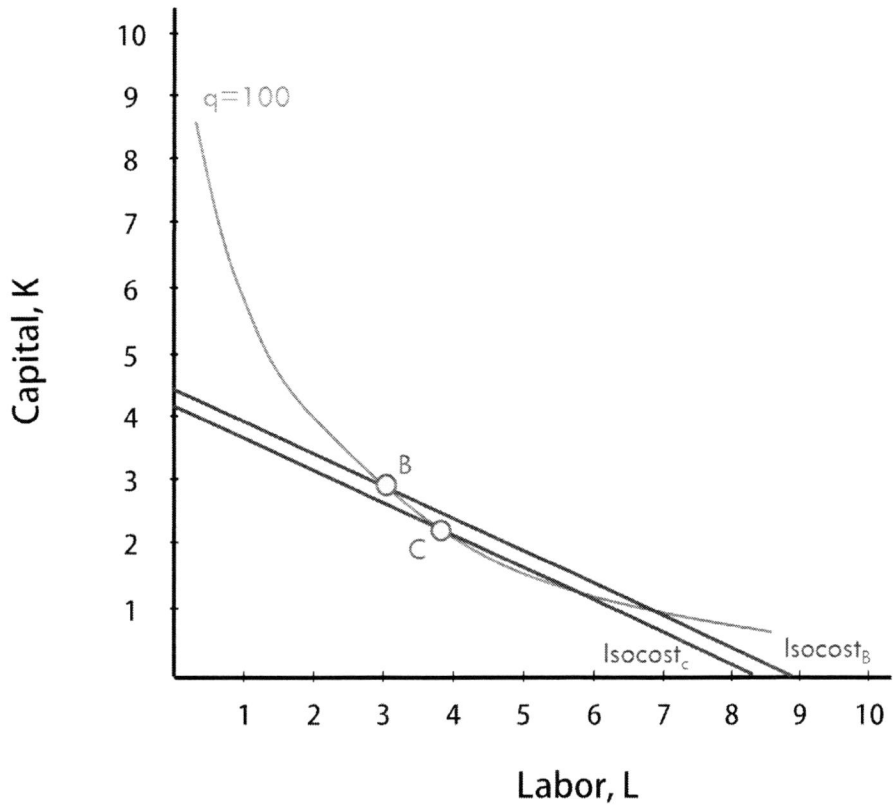

Figure 9.6: Example (9.6) - Point C Isocost Line

the slope of the isocost line is identical to the isoquant at the cost-minimizing point. Using Theorem 8.12 and Definition 9.2, this is identical to recognizing that at the cost-minimizing bundle the marginal rate of technical substitution equals the factor price ratio. Or, intuitively, the rate at which the firm is willing to exchange the goods is equal to the rate at which the factor input market is willing to exchange the goods.

Combining our findings,

Theorem 9.1 (Interior Solution to the Cost-Minimization Problem):
An interior solution to the cost-minimization problem of a firm wanting to

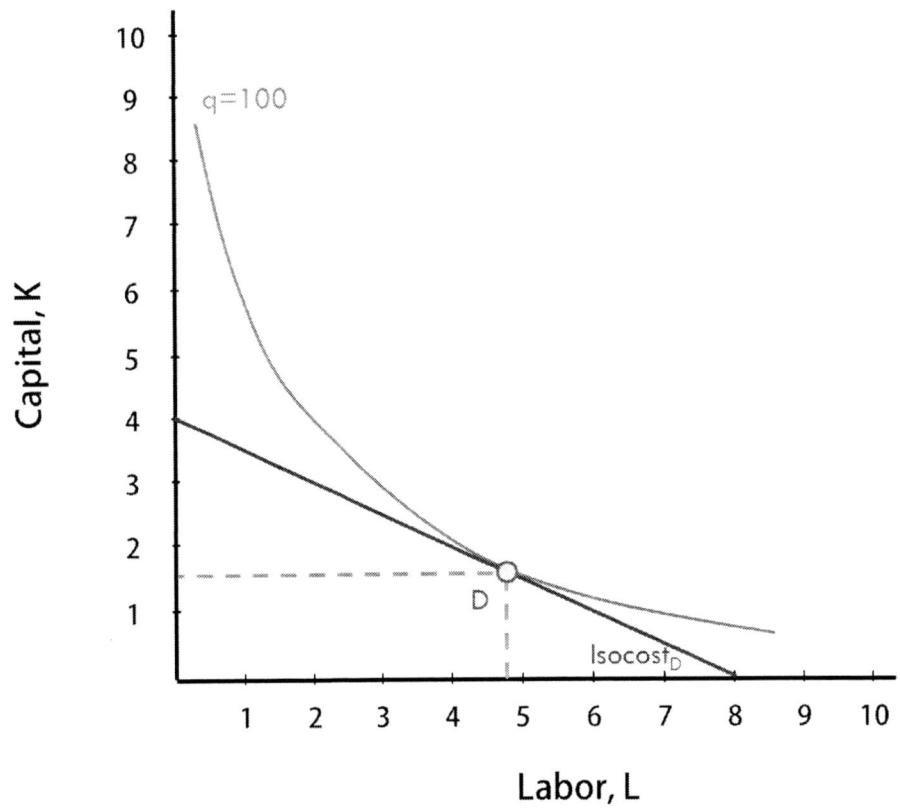

Figure 9.7: Example (9.4) - Cost Minimizing Labor/Capital Mix

produce q units of output has the following properties.

1. *The interior optimum must lie on the isoquant representing the input blends that can be used to efficiently produce q units of output.*

2. *The isocost line is tangent to the isoquant at the interior optimum.*

3. *The slope of the isoquant is identical to the slope of the isocost line at the interior optimum.*

4. $MRTS_{x_1,x_2}(x_1^*, x_2^*) = -\frac{w_1}{w_2}$ *where* (x_1^*, x_2^*) *is the interior optimum.*

5. $-\dfrac{f_1(x_1^*,x_2^*)}{f_2(x_1^*,x_2^*)} = -\dfrac{w_1}{w_2}$ *where* (x_1^*, x_2^*) *is the interior optimum and* $f(x_1, x_2)$ *is the production function generating the specified isoquant.*

As with the consumer problem, it is possible the cost-minimizing input bundle will not be an interior solution, and we must check the corner solutions to determine whether this is the case.

9.2.1 Relationship to the Consumer Problem

In working through the graphical approach to cost minimization, you likely noticed many similarities to the consumer's constrained optimization problem. The two approaches are extremely similar, with one fundamental difference. As shown in Figure 9.8, the consumer problem involves finding the indifference curve that is tangent to a fixed budget line. The producer problem involves finding an isocost curve that is tangent to a fixed isoquant. The consumer equivalent would be to find, for a given set of prices, the lowest income level that would ensure a fixed level of happiness as represented by a single indifference curve. This alternate approach to the consumer problem is known as the "Expenditure Minimization Problem" and generates demand functions known as "Hicksian Demand Functions". This is in contrast to our approach, which is known as the "Utility Maximization Problem" and generates demand functions known as "Marshallian Demands". Clearly, these approaches are related, but there are subtle differences beyond the scope of this book. However, it is important to note that our cost-minimization approach is mathematically different than if we had simply relabeled "consumers" as "firms", "indifference curves" as "isoquants", and "budget lines" as "isocost lines".

9.3 Cost Minimization - Calculus

As with the utility maximization problem, we can take a calculus-based approach to solve for the interior optimum of the producer's cost-minimization problem. We will make minimal assumptions on the production function, $f(x_1, x_2)$. Specifically, we will assume that it is continuous (which roughly implies small changes in inputs will result in small changes in outputs), concave (which implies the production set is convex), and increasing (which implies the production set has the

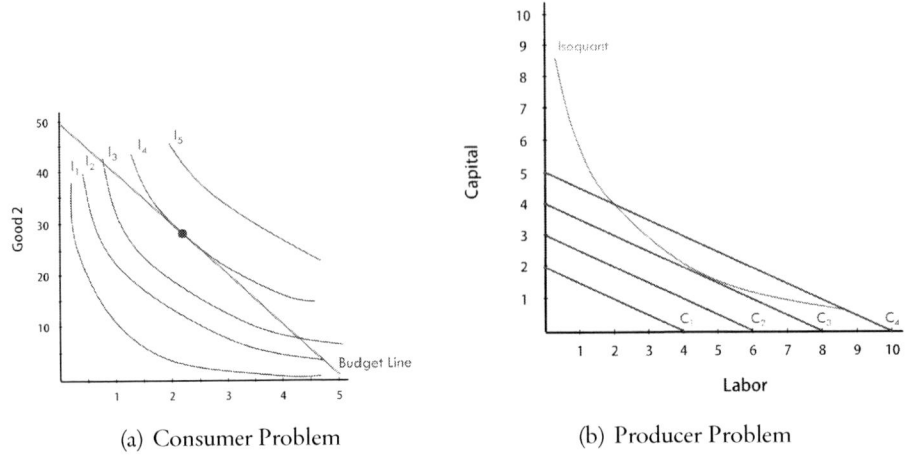

Figure 9.8: Consumer v. Producer Problem

Free Disposal property). The problem of minimizing the firm's costs subject to producing exactly q units of output is called the *cost-minimization problem* or *producer's problem*.

Definition 9.3 (Cost-Minimization Problem):
The *Cost-Minimization Problem* (or *producer's problem*) is the constrained optimization problem:

$$\min_{x_1,x_2} w_1 x_1 + w_2 x_2 \text{ such that (s.t.) } q = f(x_1,x_2)$$

In words, the producer's problem states "find the bundle of input goods, (x_1^*, x_2^*), that makes the firm's total costs as low as possible such that the desired output level is achieved." To find the interior cost-minimizing bundle, we can once again use the Lagrangian Approach.[2] To use this technique on the producer's problem for input prices, (w_1, w_2), and a quantity level, q:

---

[2]While the consumer problem is a maximization problem and the producer problem is a minimization problem, the Lagrangian technique will work in either scenario. To gain intuition on why this might be the case, assume producers maximize $-w_1 x_1 - w_2 x_2$ instead of minimizing $w_1 x_1 + w_2 x_2$. The problem is then transformed into a maximization problem with no inherent change to the underlying analysis.

1. Create the Lagrangian equation:

$$\mathcal{L} \equiv w_1 x_1 + w_2 x_2 + \lambda\big(q - f(x_1, x_2)\big)$$

2. Take the first order conditions of $\mathcal{L}$ with respect to the original choice variables (x_1 and x_2 in this case) *and* the Lagrangian multiplier, λ:

$$\frac{\partial \mathcal{L}}{\partial x_1} = 0 : w_1 - \lambda^* f_1(x_1^*, x_2^*) = 0$$

$$\frac{\partial \mathcal{L}}{\partial x_2} = 0 : w_2 - \lambda^* f_2(x_1^*, x_2^*) = 0$$

$$\frac{\partial \mathcal{L}}{\partial \lambda} = 0 : q - f(x_1^*, x_2^*) = 0$$

3. **Solve for the optimal** x_1^*, x_2^*, λ^*:

As with the consumer problem, we cannot solve for explicit values of x_1^*, x_2^*, and λ^* without an explicit production function. However, we can simplify the first order conditions:

$$w_1 - \lambda^* f_1(x_1^*, x_2^*) = 0 \;\Rightarrow\; \lambda^* = \frac{w_1}{f_1(x_1^*, x_2^*)}$$

$$w_2 - \lambda^* f_2(x_1^*, x_2^*) = 0 \;\Rightarrow\; \lambda^* = \frac{w_2}{f_2(x_1^*, x_2^*)}$$

Note that since $\frac{w_1}{f_1(x_1^*, x_2^*)}$ and $\frac{w_2}{f_2(x_1^*, x_2^*)}$ both equal λ, they must equal each other as well. Therefore, these equations further reduce to

$$\frac{w_1}{f_1(x_1^*, x_2^*)} = \frac{w_2}{f_2(x_1^*, x_2^*)}$$

$$\Rightarrow \frac{f_1(x_1^*, x_2^*)}{f_2(x_1^*, x_2^*)} = \frac{w_1}{w_2}$$

4. **Check the corner solutions.**

Once again, we have derived the same condition we derived using graphical methods in Theorem 9.1!

Example 9.7 (Cobb-Douglas Cost-Minimization):

Question: Assume a firm has a Cobb-Douglas production function of the form $f(x_1, x_2) = x_1^{1/4} x_2^{3/4}$. If the price of input good 1 is \$1 and the price of input good 2 is \$2, what is the cost-minimizing mix of inputs necessary to produce 10 units of output?

Answer: We are attempting to solve the minimization problem,

$$\min_{x_1, x_2} x_1 + 2x_2 \text{ s.t. } q = x_1^{1/4} x_2^{3/4}$$

We must first set up the Lagrangian function:

$$\mathcal{L} = x_1 + 2x_2 + \lambda(10 - x_1^{1/4} x_2^{3/4}) \tag{9.3}$$

Next, we must set up the first order conditions.

$$\frac{\partial \mathcal{L}}{\partial x_1} = 0 : 1 - \lambda^* \frac{1}{4} x_1^{*-3/4} x_2^{*3/4} = 0$$

$$\frac{\partial \mathcal{L}}{\partial x_2} = 0 : 2 - \lambda^* \frac{3}{4} x_1^{*1/4} x_2^{*-1/4} = 0$$

$$\frac{\partial \mathcal{L}}{\partial \lambda} = 0 : 10 - x_1^{*1/4} x_2^{*3/4} = 0 \tag{9.4}$$

Solving these first order conditions will give us the optimal (x_1^*, x_2^*).

$$1 - \lambda^* \frac{1}{4} x_1^{*-3/4} x_2^{*3/4} = 0 \quad \Rightarrow \quad \lambda^* = \frac{1}{\frac{1}{4} x_1^{*-3/4} x_2^{*3/4}} \tag{9.5}$$

$$2 - \lambda^* \frac{3}{4} x_1^{*1/4} x_2^{*-1/4} = 0 \quad \Rightarrow \quad \lambda^* = \frac{2}{\frac{3}{4} x_1^{*1/4} x_2^{*-1/4}} \tag{9.6}$$

Noting that since Eqns. 9.5 and 9.6 both equal λ^*, they must also equal each other:

$$\frac{1}{\frac{1}{4}x_1^{*-3/4}x_2^{*3/4}} = \frac{2}{\frac{3}{4}x_1^{*1/4}x_2^{*-1/4}}$$

$$\Rightarrow x_1^* \frac{1}{\frac{1}{4}x_2^{*3/4}} = \frac{2}{\frac{3}{4}x_2^{*-1/4}}$$

$$\Rightarrow x_1^* \frac{1}{\frac{1}{4}} = x_2^* \frac{2}{\frac{3}{4}}$$

$$\Rightarrow 4x_1^* = x_2^* \frac{8}{3}$$

$$\Rightarrow x_1^* = \frac{2x_2^*}{3} \tag{9.7}$$

We can now plug this result into Eqn. 9.4 (our third first order condition) to solve for x_2^*:

$$10 - x_1^{*1/4}x_2^{*3/4} = 0 \Rightarrow 10 - \left(\frac{2x_2^*}{3}\right)^{1/4}x_2^{*3/4} = 0$$

$$\Rightarrow 10 - \left(\frac{2}{3}\right)^{1/4}x_2^* = 0$$

$$\Rightarrow \left(\frac{2}{3}\right)^{1/4}x_2^* = 10$$

$$\Rightarrow x_2^* = 10\left(\frac{3}{2}\right)^{1/4} = 11.07$$

To solve for x_1^*, we plug x_2^* back into Eqn. 9.7.

$$x_1^* = \frac{2x_2^*}{3}$$

$$\Rightarrow x_1^* = \frac{2(11.07)}{3}$$

$$\Rightarrow x_1^* = 7.38$$

Thus, our cost-minimizing interior bundle is (7.38, 11.07). To ensure we have an interior solution, we must now compare the cost of our interior bundle to the cost of producing 10 units of output using only one input. Note, however, that it is impossible to produce any units of output unless both input goods are strictly greater than zero. Thus, we do not have a corner solution.

9.4 Factor Demand Functions

With the tools we have developed up to this point, we now have the ability to answer the very general question, "with a defined production technology, how can a firm produce a given level of output most cheaply given fixed input prices". This is a very powerful question to be able to answer, but expanding the question to ask "how will a firm's cost-minimizing input blend change as industry conditions change" can allow us to predict how firms will respond to future changes, which gives us the ability to examine the potential effects of industry, policy, and input price changes.

The technique we will use to determine how firms will respond to industry changes is virtually identical to the procedure we used to derive the consumer's demand functions. Specifically, we will solve the firm's cost-minimization problem for an arbitrary set of input good prices and output level and derive the firm's *Factor Demand Functions*.[3]

> **Definition 9.4 (Factor Demand Function):**
> A *Factor Demand Function* specifies the relationship between the prices of input goods, the quantity of output produced, and the amount of an input good a firm will utilize when minimizing their costs.

9.4.1 Factor Demand Function - Mathematical Derivation

The steps we take to derive a firm's factor demand functions are:

1. Set up the firm's cost-minimization problem using unspecified input good prices and an unspecified output quantity level. The Lagrangian function will be in the form $\mathscr{L} \equiv w_1 x_1 + w_2 x_2 + \lambda\big(q - f(x_1, x_2)\big)$ where q, w_1, and w_2 are left as constants.

2. Solve the cost-minimization problem for the optimal x_1^* and x_2^* using one of the techniques we have established. Your results will be in terms of q, w_1, and w_2 and are called your *Factor Demand Functions*.

---

[3]As with the consumer demand curves, we could also take a strictly graphical approach whereby we graphically solve for the firm's cost-minimizing input blend at different price levels and plot the (x_1^*, w_1) combinations. As this approach is more tedious and less precise, we only focus on the mathematical derivation.

Example 9.8 (Factor Demand Function Derivation):

Question: Assume a firm's production technology follows the CES production function, $f(x_1, x_2) = (x_1^{1/2} + x_2^{1/2})^2$. What are the firm's x_1 and x_2 factor demand functions?

Answer: Following the steps above,

1. **Set up the firm's cost-minimization problem using unspecified input good prices and an unspecified output quantity level. The Lagrangian function will be in the form $\mathcal{L} \equiv w_1 x_1 + w_2 x_2 + \lambda(q - f(x_1, x_2))$ where $q, w_1,$ and w_2 are left as constants:**

$$\mathcal{L} \equiv w_1 x_1 + w_2 x_2 + \lambda(q - (x_1^{1/2} + x_2^{1/2})^2)$$

2. **Solve the cost-minimization problem for the optimal x_1^* and x_2^* using one of the techniques we have established. Your results will be in terms of $q, w_1,$ and w_2 and are called your *Factor Demand Functions*.**

Taking the first order conditions,

$$w_1 - \lambda 2(x_1^{*1/2} + x_2^{*1/2})\left(\frac{1}{2}x_1^{*-1/2}\right) = 0 \qquad (9.8)$$

$$w_2 - \lambda 2(x_1^{*1/2} + x_2^{*1/2})\left(\frac{1}{2}x_2^{*-1/2}\right) = 0 \qquad (9.9)$$

$$q - (x_1^{*1/2} + x_2^{*1/2})^2 = 0 \qquad (9.10)$$

Solving for λ in Eqn. (9.8),

$$\lambda = \frac{w_1}{2(x_1^{*1/2} + x_2^{*1/2})(\frac{1}{2}x_1^{*-1/2})} \qquad (9.11)$$

Solving for λ in Eqn. (9.9),

$$\lambda = \frac{w_2}{2(x_1^{*1/2} + x_2^{*1/2})(\frac{1}{2}x_2^{*-1/2})} \qquad (9.12)$$

Setting λ from Eqn. (9.11) equal to λ from Eqn. (9.12),

$$\frac{w_1}{2(x_1^{*1/2} + x_2^{*1/2})(\frac{1}{2}x_1^{*-1/2})} = \frac{w_2}{2(x_1^{*1/2} + x_2^{*1/2})(\frac{1}{2}x_2^{*-1/2})} \qquad (9.13)$$

Cancelling terms and simplifying Eqn. (9.13), we find

$$\Rightarrow \frac{w_1}{2\left(\frac{1}{2}x_1^{*-1/2}\right)} = \frac{w_2}{2\left(\frac{1}{2}x_2^{*-1/2}\right)}$$

$$\Rightarrow \frac{w_1}{x_1^{*-1/2}} = \frac{w_2}{x_2^{*-1/2}}$$

$$\Rightarrow x_1^{*1/2} = \frac{w_2}{w_1}x_2^{*1/2}$$

$$\Rightarrow x_1^* = \left(\frac{w_2}{w_1}\right)^2 x_2^* \qquad (9.14)$$

Plugging Eqn. (9.14) into Eqn. (9.10),

$$q - \left(\left(\left(\frac{w_2}{w_1}\right)^2 x_2^*\right)^{1/2} + x_2^{*1/2}\right)^2 = 0$$

$$q - \left(\frac{w_2}{w_1}x_2^{*1/2} + x_2^{*1/2}\right)^2 = 0$$

$$\Rightarrow q = \left(\frac{w_1 + w_2}{w_1}x_2^{*1/2}\right)^2$$

$$\Rightarrow q = \left(\frac{w_1 + w_2}{w_1}\right)^2 x_2^*$$

$$\Rightarrow x_2^* = \left(\frac{w_1}{w_1 + w_2}\right)^2 q \qquad (9.15)$$

which is the firm's factor demand function for Good 2. Plugging Eqn. (9.15) into Eqn. (9.14),

$$x_1^* = \left(\frac{w_2}{w_1}\right)^2 \left(\frac{w_1}{w_1 + w_2}\right)^2 q$$

$$\Rightarrow x_1^* = \left(\frac{w_2}{w_1 + w_2}\right)^2 q \qquad (9.16)$$

which is the firm's factor demand function for Good 1.

As with demand functions, we can use a firm's factor demand functions to answer questions such as "if the price of an input good increases, by how much will a firm decrease its usage in its production process?". Perhaps more importantly, a firm's factor demand functions allow us to quantitatively analyze a firm's cost function.

9.5 Cost Function

Definition 9.5 (Cost Function):
A *Cost Function* specifies the relationship between the prices of input goods, the quantity of output produced, and the total minimum cost a firm will incur with its production process.

Recall a firm's Factor Demand Functions specify the cost-minimizing input blend for each possible set of input prices and output quantity. As such, to determine the minimum cost of producing a specific quantity of output, we need only determine the price of purchasing the number of input goods specified by the Factor Demand Functions.

9.5.1 Cost Function - Mathematical Derivation

The steps we take to derive a firm's cost function are:

1. Using mathematical techniques, solve for the firm's Factor Demand Functions, $x_1(w_1, w_2, q)$ and $x_2(w_1, w_2, q)$.

2. The cost function will equal the total cost of the $x_1(w_1, w_2, q)$ and $x_2(w_1, w_2, q)$ input goods. Specifically, $C(w_1, w_2, q) = w_1 x_1(w_1, w_2, q) + w_2 x_2(w_1, w_2, q)$.

Example 9.9 (Cost Function Derivation):
Question: Assume a firm's production technology follows the CES production function, $f(x_1, x_2) = \left(x_1^{1/2} + x_2^{1/2} \right)^2$. What is the firm's cost function?
Answer: Following the steps above,

1. **Using mathematical techniques, solve for the firm's Factor Demand Functions, $x_1(w_1, w_2, q)$ and $x_2(w_1, w_2, q)$.**

In Example 9.8, we found

$$x_1(w_1, w_2, q) = \left(\frac{w_2}{w_1 + w_2} \right)^2 q$$

$$x_2(w_1, w_2, q) = \left(\frac{w_1}{w_1 + w_2} \right)^2 q.$$

2. The cost function will equal the total cost of the $x_1(w_1, w_2, q)$ and $x_2(w_1, w_2, q)$ input goods. Specifically, $C(w_1, w_2, q) = w_1 x_1(w_1, w_2, q) + w_2 x_2(w_1, w_2, q)$.

Plugging in our Factor Demand Functions,

$$C(w_1, w_2, q) = w_1 \left(\frac{w_2}{w_1 + w_2} \right)^2 q + w_2 \left(\frac{w_1}{w_1 + w_2} \right)^2 q$$

Example 9.10 (Cost Function Derivation):

Question: Assume a firm's production technology follows the CES production function, $f(x_1, x_2) = \left(x_1^{1/2} + x_2^{1/2} \right)^2$. If the price of input good 1 is \$1 and the price of input good 2 is \$2, what is the minimum cost at which the firm can produce a given output level, q?

Answer: From Example 9.9, we found

$$C(w_1, w_2, q) = w_1 \left(\frac{w_2}{w_1 + w_2} \right)^2 q + w_2 \left(\frac{w_1}{w_1 + w_2} \right)^2 q$$

Plugging in $w_1 = \$1$ and $w_2 = \$2$,

$$
\begin{aligned}
C(q) &= 1 \left(\frac{2}{1+2} \right)^2 q + 2 \left(\frac{1}{1+2} \right)^2 q \\
\Rightarrow &= \frac{4q}{9} + \frac{2q}{9} \\
\Rightarrow &= \frac{2q}{3}
\end{aligned}
$$

9.6 Cost Specifications

Example 9.10 demonstrates the fact that if input prices are fixed, the Cost Function of a firm only relies on the quantity of output goods it produces. In many scenarios, it is reasonable to assume that input prices are fixed (especially for a short period of time). As such, we often see a firm's Cost Function written as $C(q)$ instead of $C(w_1, w_2, q)$.

When analyzing how a firm's costs will change with its quantity, we oftentimes focus on different cost measures.

9.6.1 Marginal/Average Costs

Definition 9.6 (Marginal Cost - MC):
A firm's *Marginal Cost* is

1. $\frac{\partial C(q)}{\partial q}$

2. **Informal** The amount the firm's costs will increase by producing one extra unit of the good.

3. **Informal** The cost of producing one specific unit of output.

Definition 9.7 (Average Cost - AC):
A firm's *Average Cost* is

1. $\frac{C(q)}{q}$

2. **Informal** The average cost of producing one unit of output.

There is clearly a relationship between a firm's marginal costs and average costs. To intuitively understand this, assume the average height of an individual in a particular class is 6' tall. Assume one more individual walks in the classroom and the average height of the class increases. How tall must the individual be? Clearly, in order to increase the average height of the class, the marginal height of the individual (the height of one extra individual) must be above the average. Mathematically, we can find the same relationship between MC and AC.

Theorem 9.2 (Relationship Between MC And AC):

1. A firm's Average Costs are increasing if and only if the firm's Marginal Costs are greater than the firm's Average Costs. Mathematically, $\frac{\partial AC}{\partial q} > 0$ if and only $MC > AC$.

2. A firm's Average Costs are decreasing if and only if the firm's

> *Marginal Costs are less than the firm's Average Costs. Mathematically,* $\frac{\partial AC}{\partial q} < 0$ *if and only* $MC < AC$.
>
> 3. *A firm's Average Costs are constant if and only if the firm's Marginal Costs are equal to the firm's Average Costs. Mathematically,* $\frac{\partial AC}{\partial q} = 0$ *if and only* $MC = AC$.

We will prove the first statement of the theorem, as the other statements follow identical logic. By definition,

$$AC(q) = \frac{C(q)}{q}$$

In order for AC to be increasing, it must be the case that its derivative must be positive. Mathematically,

$$\frac{\partial AC(q)}{\partial q} = \frac{C'(q)}{q} - \frac{C(q)}{q^2} > 0$$

Multiplying both sides by q and slightly rearranging, we find that in order for AC to be increasing, it must be the case that

$$C'(q) > \frac{C(q)}{q}$$

By definition, this is identical to the condition

$$MC > AC$$

as claimed. Graphically, Theorem 9.2 implies that cost curves must have a shape similar to those in Figure 9.9

9.6.2 Average Costs and Returns to Scale

As we will see in the next Chapter, marginal costs play a key role in profit-maximizing behavior. However, average costs are also extremely valuable. First, they are easily measured, unlike marginal costs. A firm's average cost can be calculated by dividing its yearly expenditures by the quantity of output it produced. Isolating the cost of a single marginal unit is much more difficult. Second, in many cases a firm's average cost is a good approximate for its marginal costs. If,

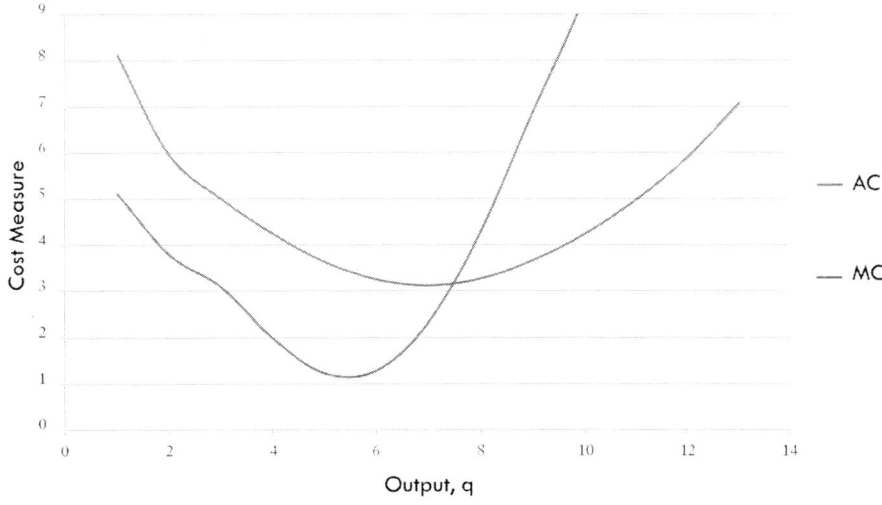

Figure 9.9: Average Cost and Marginal Cost

for instance, a firm produces a large number of units and its marginal costs increase at a slow rate in a relevant range (for instance, if it costs Ford the same amount to produce its 1000th car or its 5000th car), then the firm's average costs will approximate its marginal costs, as shown in Figure 9.10. Lastly, whether a firm's average costs are increasing, decreasing, or constant tells us if the production technology is displaying increasing, decreasing, or constant returns to scale. In particular,

---

Theorem 9.3 (Average Costs and Returns to Scale):

1. *If a firm's average costs are decreasing, it is in a range of increasing returns to scale.*

2. *If a firm's average costs are increasing, it is in a range of decreasing returns to scale.*

3. *If a firm's average costs are constant, it is in a range of constant returns to scale.*

To intuitively determine why this is the case, consider the case of decreasing average costs. As we have established, decreasing average costs imply that marginal

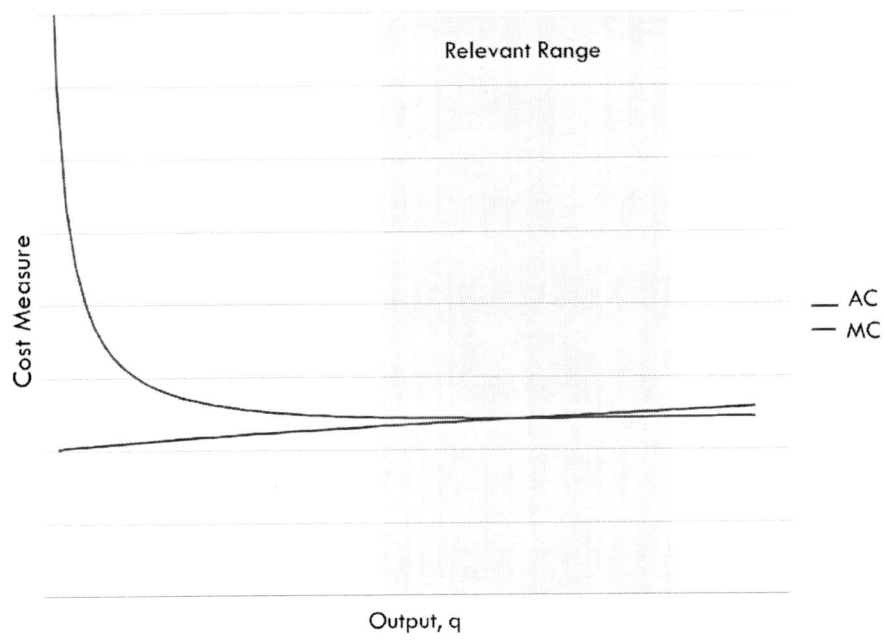

Figure 9.10: Relevant Range - AC ~ MC

costs are below average costs. In other words, the cost of producing new units of the output good is lower than the cost of producing the previous units of the output good. In other words, it requires fewer inputs to produce the same number of outputs. Or, put another way, with an identical number of inputs, we can produce more units of output. This is exactly the definition of increasing returns to scale.

Figure 9.11 shows the relationship between AC and returns to scale. In general, we assume cost curves roughly approximate this shape. Specifically, we assume that small firms have increasing returns to scale as labor/capital is progressively more productive, oftentimes through specialization. As firms become mature, they tend to reach a range of constant returns to scale, in which they can scale up/down fairly easily. If firms continue to grow, they tend to reach a period of decreasing returns to scale, in which the administrative overhead required to run a large firm makes it progressively more costly.

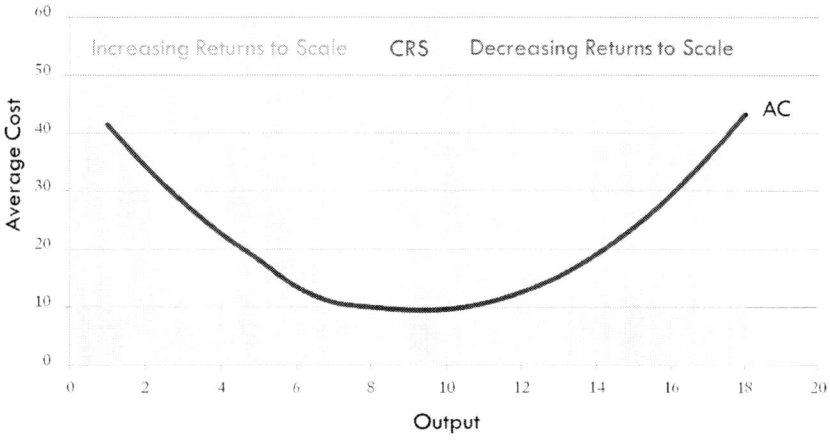

Figure 9.11: Average Cost and Returns to Scale

9.6.3   Fixed/Variable Costs

Two other important cost specifications are *fixed* and *variable* costs.

> **Definition 9.8 (Fixed Costs - FC):**
> A firm's *Fixed Costs (FC)* are
>
> 1. The incurred costs that are unrelated to the level of output. For instance, rental space, administrative overhead, etc.
>
> 2. The part of the Cost function that is unaffected by q.

> **Definition 9.9 (Variable Costs - VC):**
> A firm's *Variable Costs* are
>
> 1. The incurred costs that are directly related to the level of output. For instance, the cost of electricity, input goods, etc.
>
> 2. The part of the Cost function that is directly affected by q.

Example 9.11 (Fixed vs. Variable Costs):
Question: Assume a firm's cost function is $C(q) = 100 + 2q + q^2$. What are the firm's fixed and variable costs?

Answer: The part of the cost function that is unrelated to q is 100. This is therefore our fixed costs. The part of the cost function that is directly related to q is $2q + q^2$. This is our variable costs.

Note a firm's total costs can always be decomposed into its fixed and variable costs. In addition, we can take average measures of each component cost.

Definition 9.10 (Average Fixed Cost - AFC):
A firm's *Average Fixed Cost* is

1. $\frac{FC}{q}$

2. **Informal** The average fixed cost of producing one unit of output.

Definition 9.11 (Average Variable Cost - AVC):
A firm's *Average Variable Cost* is

1. $\frac{VC(q)}{q}$

2. **Informal** The average variable cost of producing one unit of output.

As can be seen from the definition of AFC, as output increases AFC will decrease since the fixed costs are spread over a larger number of units. AVC, however, will not necessarily have this property as a firm's variable costs will likely increase as the production level increases.

9.7 Short-Run v. Long-Run

Oftentimes in economics we are concerned with *short-run* versus *long-run* analysis.

Definition 9.12 (Short-Run):
A firm's *Short-Run* is the time period in which some inputs are fixed, such as factory space.

Definition 9.13 (Long-Run):
A firm's *Long-Run* is the time period in which all inputs are variable.

In comparing the Short-Run and Long-Run, note that no specific time frame is mentioned. Instead, the time it takes to make all inputs variable can be thought of as the time it would take to completely exit a market, which can differ greatly between industries. Consider a hot-dog vendor who decides to rent his hot-dog cart at the start of every month. Once he has agreed to rent his cart for a month, he has to incur the cost whether or not he sells any hot-dogs. Thus, it is a fixed cost and he is "in the industry" whether he wants to be or not. However, in the next month he could decide whether to renew his cart rental, making it a variable input. As such, at the start of the next month he could decide to fully exit the industry. Compare this to a chemical company who has purchased a large chemical factory. The short-run for the company can be very long indeed if it takes years for the company to be able to sell its factory. In the meantime, the input good of factory space is fixed and cannot be adjusted.

Mathematically, differentiating between the short-run and long-run is surprisingly easy. In particular, in the short-run certain input goods are fixed. In the long-run, all input goods are variable. As such, in the short-run a firm can only maximize over a subset of input goods. To solve for the short-run cost curve,

1. **Create the Lagrangian equation, with all non-variable input goods treated as constants.**

2. Take the first order conditions of $\mathcal{L}$ with respect to *only* the variable input goods and the Lagrangian multiplier, λ.

3. Solve for the factor demand functions of the variable input goods.

4. **The short-run cost function will equal the total cost of the variable *and fixed* input goods.**

Example 9.12 (Short-Run Cost-Minimization):

Question: Assume a firm has a Cobb-Douglas production function of the form $f(x_1, x_2) = x_1^{1/4} x_2^{3/4}$. If the level of input good 2 is fixed, what is the firm's short-run cost function?

Answer: We are attempting to solve the minimization problem,

$$\min_{x_1} w_1 x_1 + w_2 x_2 \text{ s.t. } q = x_1^{1/4} x_2^{3/4}$$

Note that we are only minimizing over x_1, as the level of input good 2 is fixed. Mathematically, we treat it as a constant. We must first set up the Lagrangian function:

$$\mathcal{L} = w_1 x_1 + w_2 x_2 + \lambda(q - x_1^{1/4} x_2^{3/4}) \tag{9.17}$$

Next, we must set up the first order conditions. As there is only once choice variable, we will only take the first order condition with respect to x_1 and λ.

$$\frac{\partial \mathcal{L}}{\partial x_1} = 0 : w_1 - \lambda^* \frac{1}{4} x_1^{*-3/4} x_2^{3/4} = 0 \tag{9.18}$$

$$\frac{\partial \mathcal{L}}{\partial \lambda} = 0 : q - x_1^{*1/4} x_2^{3/4} = 0 \tag{9.19}$$

Solving these first order conditions will give us the cost-minimizing (x_1^*). Note in this case Eqn. (9.19) can be used to directly solve for x_1^*. Intuitively, with only one choice variable and an increasing production technology, there is only one way to produce exactly q units of output. With additional variable inputs, we would need to solve the full system of equations.

$$
\begin{aligned}
q - x_1^{*1/4} x_2^{3/4} &= 0 \\
\Rightarrow x_1^{*1/4} &= \frac{q}{x_2^{3/4}} \\
\Rightarrow x_1^* &= \frac{q^4}{x_2^3} \tag{9.20}
\end{aligned}
$$

The total short-run cost of our production process is therefore

$$C_{SR}(q, w_1, w_2) = w_1 \frac{q^4}{x_2^3} + w_2 x_2$$

Recall x_2 is a constant, which is why it appears in our short-run cost function. In our long-run cost function, we would solve for our optimal x_2, and it would therefore not explicitly appear.

Chapter 10

Profit Maximization

Let us take a step back and examine what questions we have answered. From the consumer's demand function, we are able to determine how much a consumer (or the market as a whole) will demand of a particular good given a specific price. From the firm's cost-minimization problem, we have determined how a firm will produce a specific amount of output good at the lowest cost.

We have yet to answer the fundamental question, "how much output will a firm produce?" or, equivalently, "what price will the firm set, recognizing it can only sell a quantity level as dictated by the market demand function?". To answer this question, we address a fundamentally important decision facing any firm. Specifically, "what output level should the firm produce in order to maximize profits?".[1] In order to analyze the incentives firms face in their decision-making, we will examine a simple baseline scenario. Extending the baseline model to incorporate more advanced concepts such as the benefit to research & development can be done within this analytical framework using modified models.

---

[1]While we generally consider profits in monetary terms, this analysis does not require this restriction. For instance, if the "profits" of a particular non-profit firm is the number of vaccinations administered in Sub-Saharan Africa, we could modify our "revenue" as defined, below, and identical analysis can be performed.

10.1 Baseline Monopolistically Competitive Model

Definition 10.1 (Monopolistically Competitive Model):
The *Baseline Monopolistically Competitive Model* (BMC Model) is
a model of profit-maximization in which

1. Consumers purchase goods according to their demand functions.

2. A firms cost-minimizes by selecting inputs according to its factor demand functions.

3. Firms select quantity (or price) to maximize their profits, where profit, Π, is measured as total revenues - total cost.

4. Firms set the same price for each customer.

5. A firm has some degree of market power, by which it can increase the price of its output good without losing all of its customers.

In general, these assumptions are viewed as fairly innocuous. The first assumption assumes that consumers are rational. The second assumption assumes that firms operate "on their cost functions", and do not systematically operate inefficiently. The third assumption assumes firms care only about monetary profit, but this assumption can easily be relaxed with no changes to the underlying analysis. The fourth assumption assumes firms cannot, for instance, charge higher prices to higher-valued customers. Again, this assumption can be easily relaxed and is done in models of price discrimination. The final assumption is specific to this model, and assumes that a firm has some degree of monopoly power. This power can be a result of many factors:

• **Natural Monopolies:** In certain scenarios, only a single firm can realistically operate in a given industry. Consider, for instance, the power industry. For a particular city, two power companies could not find it profitable to install the necessary transformers, power lines, and meters if each company only sold to half of the market. Instead, only 1 firm can feasibly be profitable and we would expect to see only a single firm operating. Clearly, if only one firm is operating in a given market, it has the ability to adjust prices without losing its entire customer base to competitors.

- **Patents:** In an effort to incentivize welfare-enhancing innovations, governments offer patent protection by which firms who create new products obtain government-granted monopoly power for a fixed number of years.

- **Strategic Barriers to Entry:** If a firm has extremely low costs, then any potential rival risks being undercut on price and losing its customer base. If the cost disparity is large enough, this might disincentivize new firms from entering a specific market, giving the low-cost firm market power.

- **Network Effects:** Some products, such as Facebook, only have value if many consumers use it. As such, industries with network effects tend to see very few entrants, as new rivals do not have the necessary customer base to offer significant value to its users.

- **Customer Loyalty:** Customers oftentimes are willing to pay increased prices in order to use a known product. Whether it be due to loyalty, happiness with the product, or specific product characteristics, a loyal customer base gives the producing firm a degree of market power over its customers.

10.1.1 Profit Function

To mathematically analyze a firm's profit-maximizing price, we must first derive the firm's *Profit Function*

> **Definition 10.2 (Profit Function):**
> 1. A *Profit Function* specifies the relationship between the quantity of output a firm produces and the total profit the firm will receive.
>
> 2. Alternatively, a *Profit Function* specifies the relationship between the output price a firm sets and the total profit the firm will receive.

Both definitions of the profit function are mathematically equivalent, as once a price is set, consumers' demand functions dictate the level of output a firm can feasibly sell. In our baseline model, a firm's profit function can be calculated according to the general profit definition:

> **Definition 10.3 (Profit):**
> A firm's *Profit* is Revenue - Cost

Profit as a Function of Price

To produce a specified level of output, q, we have analyzed how to determine a firm's cost. Specifically, it will cost the firm $C(q)$. To determine the revenue, note if a firm sells q units at a price of $\$p$ per unit it will receive $\$pq$ in total revenue. However, the price, $\$p$, the firm sets will directly influence how many units it can sell. As the BMC model assumes, consumers will consume the good according to their demand functions which (according to the Law of Demand) decrease as prices increase. If we recognize that firms can only sell q units of output if its consumers want to purchase q units of output and consumers will want to purchase exactly $x(p)$ units of the good, where $x(p)$ is the market demand function, then it must be the case that $q = x(p)$. As $q = x(p)$ is clearly a function of p, we can write the firm's total revenue as $\$pq(p)$ where $q(p) = x(p)$ and its total cost as $C\Big(q(p)\Big)$. Plugging these functions into Definition 10.3, we obtain a *firm's profit function as a function of price.*

Definition 10.4 (Profit Function as a Function of Price):
A firm's *Profit Function as a Function of Price* equals

$$\Pi(p) = pq(p) - C\Big(q(p)\Big)$$

where $q(p) = x(p)$ is the market demand function (how much of the good the consumers in the market will consume at a given price).[a]

---

[a]To derive the market demand functions from individual demand functions, simply add the individual demand functions at each price. For instance, if the first consumer has an individual demand for Good 1 of $x_1^1 = \frac{10}{p_1}$ and the second consumer has an individual demand for Good 1 of $x_1^2 = \frac{5}{p_1}$ then the market demand at price p_1 is $\frac{10}{p_1} + \frac{5}{p_1} = \frac{15}{p_1}$.

Oftentimes, we will see $q(p)$ written as $D(p)$ to represent the market demand, but the meaning is the same.

Definition 10.5 (Profit as a Function of Price - Alternate):
A firm's *Profit Function as a Function of Price* equals

$$\Pi(p) = pD(p) - C\Big(D(p)\Big) \qquad (10.1)$$

where $D(p) = x(p)$ is the market demand function.

Profit as a Function of Quantity

As noted above, we can also view the profit function as a function of quantity since once a price is set, consumers' demand functions dictate the level of output a firm can feasibly sell. Specifically, we use the *inverse demand function* to determine the price a firm must set to sell exactly q units of output.

Definition 10.6 (Inverse Demand Function):
1. An *Inverse Demand Function*, $p(q)$ specifies the relationship between the quantity of output a firm wants to sell and the price that ensures they will sell that quantity.

2. Mathematically, if the demand function is $x(p)$, the *Inverse Demand Function* is $p^{-1}(x)$, the inverse of the demand function.

Recall from Chapter 6 that to more easily plot demand curves, we optionally solved our optimal value of x_1 (for instance) for p_1 and plugged in points for x_1 to find the price that would ensure exactly x_1 units of Good 1 would be consumed. While not explicitly stated, we were solving for the inverse demand functions.

> **Example 10.1 (Inverse Demand Function):**
> **Question:** Assume the market demand equals $x(p) = 10 - p^2$. Find the inverse demand function.
>
> **Answer:** To find the inverse demand function, define $q \equiv x(p)$. Plugging into the market demand and solving for p,
>
> $$\begin{aligned} q &= 10 - p^2 \\ p^2 &= 10 - q \\ p &= (10 - q)^{1/2} \end{aligned}$$

The inverse demand function is then $p(q) = (10 - q)^{1/2}$.

Using our inverse demand function, we can also write our profit function as a function of quantity.

> **Definition 10.7 (Profit Function as a Function of Quantity):**
> A firm's *Profit Function as a Function of Quantity* equals
>
> $$\Pi(q) = p(q)q - C(q) \qquad (10.2)$$
>
> where $p(q)$ is the market inverse demand function.

10.1.2   BMC Model Profit Maximization

We now have the framework under which we can answer the question "How will a firm with market power behave in an effort to maximize profits?". We will examine this question using the Profit Function as a Function of Quantity for tractability reasons, but an equivalent analysis can be performed using the Profit Function as a Function of Price. As the BMC Model assumes, the monopolistically competitive firm will charge the same price for each unit of output it produces, and the price will be dictated by the market inverse demand curve.

One thing to note in this model is that the firm is not constrained in the amount of output it selects. In other words, there is no budget set or production requirement imposed upon the firm as in our Consumer and Cost-Minimization problems. In particular, the firm can select any output level it desires. Mathematically, this means we will not require a Lagrangian approach, but will instead use standard First-Order-Condition analysis.

The steps we take to find a firm's profit-maximizing behavior when profit is a function of quantity are:

1. Set up the firm's Profit Function as a function of quantity.

2. Take the first order condition(s) of the firm's profit function as a respect to the variable of choice. When the profit function is a function of quantity, the variable of choice is quantity.

3. Solve the first order condition(s) to solve for the firm's profit-maximizing quantity.

4. If necessary, plug the profit-maximizing quantity level into the inverse market demand to determine the profit-maximizing price level.

5. If necessary, plug the profit-maximizing quantity and/or price levels into the profit function to determine the profit-maximizing profit level.

The steps we take to find a firm's profit-maximizing behavior when profit is a function of price are:

1. Set up the firm's Profit Function as a function of price.

2. Take the first order condition(s) of the firm's profit function as a respect to the variable of choice. When the profit function is a function of price, the variable of choice is price.

3. Solve the first order condition(s) to solve for the firm's profit-maximizing price.

4. If necessary, plug the profit-maximizing price level into the market demand to determine the profit-maximizing quantity level.

5. If necessary, plug the profit-maximizing quantity and/or price levels into the profit function to determine the profit-maximizing profit level.

Example 10.2 (Profit-Maximization):

Question: A firm faces a market demand of $D(p) = 10 - p$ and has a cost function of $C(q) = 1 + q^2$. What quantity/price level will maximize the firm's profit if we view the profit function as a function of quantity? What are the total profits the firm will achieve?

Answer: Following the steps above,

1. **Set up the firm's Profit Function as a function of quantity.**

   Per Eqn. (10.2), the profit function as a function of quantity is $\Pi(q) = p(q)q - C(q)$. To find the price as a function of quantity, we need to solve for the market inverse demand function from the market demand. To find the inverse demand function, define $q \equiv D(p)$. Plugging into the market demand and solving for p,

$$q = 10 - p$$
$$\Rightarrow p = 10 - q$$

The inverse demand function is then $p(q) = 1 - q$. Plugging this and the cost function into Eqn. (10.2),

$$\Pi = (10 - q)q - (1 + q^2) \tag{10.3}$$

2. **Take the first order condition(s) of the firm's profit function as a respect to the variable of choice. When the profit function is a function of quantity, the variable of choice is quantity.**

To more easily take the first order condition of Eqn. (10.3), we will first expand the terms.

$$\begin{aligned} \Pi &= (10 - q)q - (1 + q^2) \\ &= 10q - q^2 - 1 - q^2 \\ &= 10q - 2q^2 - 1 \tag{10.4} \end{aligned}$$

Taking the first order condition of Eqn. (10.4) with respect to quantity,

$$\frac{\partial \Pi}{\partial q} = 10 - 4q^* = 0 \tag{10.5}$$

3. **Solve the first order condition(s) to solve for the firm's profit-maximizing quantity.**

Solving Eqn. (10.5) for q^*,

$$10 - 4q^* = 0$$
$$\Rightarrow q^* = \frac{5}{2} \tag{10.6}$$

Thus, the firm's profit-maximizing quantity level is $q^* = \frac{5}{2}$ units of output.

4. **If necessary, plug the profit-maximizing quantity level into the inverse market demand to determine the profit-maximizing price level.**
To solve for the profit-maximizing price level, we plug $q^* = \frac{5}{2}$ into the inverse market demand function, $p(q) = 10 - q$.

$$p^* \equiv p(q^*) = 10 - \frac{5}{2}$$
$$= \frac{15}{2}$$

Thus, the firm's profit-maximizing price level is $p^* = \frac{15}{2}$.

5. **If necessary, plug the profit-maximizing quantity and/or price levels into the profit function to determine the profit-maximizing profit level.**

To solve for the profit-maximizing profit level, we plug $q^* = \frac{5}{2}$ into the profit function, $\Pi(q) = (10 - q)q - (1 + q^2)$.

$$\Pi^*(q) \equiv \Pi(q^*) = \frac{15}{2}\frac{5}{2} - \left(1 + \left(\frac{5}{2}\right)^2\right)$$
$$= \frac{75}{4} - \frac{29}{4}$$
$$= \frac{46}{4}$$
$$= \frac{23}{2}$$

Thus, the firm's profit-maximizing profit level is $\Pi^* = \frac{23}{2}$.

Let us now verify that we get the same profit-maximizing price/quantity combination if we view the firm's profit as a function of price.

Example 10.3 (Profit-Maximization):
Question: A firm faces a market demand of $D(p) = 10 - p$ and has a cost function of $C(q) = 1 + q^2$. What quantity/price level will maximize the firm's profit if we view the profit function as a function of price? What are the total profits the firm will achieve?

Answer: Following the steps above,

1. **Set up the firm's Profit Function as a function of price.**

Per Eqn. (10.1), the profit function as a function of price is $\Pi(p) = pD(p) - C(D(p))$. Thus, we need only plug in the market demand function to find our profit function.

$$\Pi \;=\; p(10-p) - \left(1 + (10-p)^2\right) \tag{10.7}$$

2. **Take the first order condition(s) of the firm's profit function as a respect to the variable of choice. When the profit function is a function of price, the variable of choice is price.**

To more easily take the first order condition of Eqn. (10.7), we will first expand the terms.

$$\begin{aligned} \Pi \;&=\; p(10-p) - \left(1 + (10-p)^2\right) \\ &=\; 10p - p^2 - 1 - (10-p)^2 \end{aligned} \tag{10.8}$$

Taking the first order condition of Eqn. (10.8) with respect to price,

$$\frac{\partial \Pi}{\partial p} \;=\; 10 - 2p^* - 2(10 - p^*)(-1) = 0 \tag{10.9}$$

3. **Solve the first order condition(s) to solve for the firm's profit-maximizing quantity.**

Solving Eqn. (10.9) for p^*,

$$\begin{aligned} 10 - 2p^* - 2(10 - p^*)(-1) \;&=\; 0 \\ \Rightarrow 10 - 2p^* + 20 - 2p^* \;&=\; 0 \\ \Rightarrow 30 - 4p^* \;&=\; 0 \\ \Rightarrow p^* \;&=\; \frac{30}{4} \\ \Rightarrow p^* \;&=\; \frac{15}{2} \end{aligned}$$

Thus, the firm's profit-maximizing price level is $p^* = \frac{15}{2}$.

4. **If necessary, plug the profit-maximizing price level into the market demand to determine the profit-maximizing quantity level.**
To solve for the profit-maximizing quantity level, we plug $p^* = \frac{15}{2}$ into the market demand function, $D(p) = 10 - p^*$.

$$\begin{aligned} q^* \equiv D(p^*) \;&=\; 10 - \frac{15}{2} \\ &=\; \frac{5}{2} \end{aligned}$$

Thus, the firm's profit-maximizing quantity level is $q^* = \frac{5}{2}$.

5. **If necessary, plug the profit-maximizing quantity and/or price levels into the profit function to determine the profit-maximizing profit level.**

To solve for the profit-maximizing profit level, we plug $p^* = \frac{15}{2}$ into the profit function, $\Pi(p) = p(10 - p) - (1 + (10 - p)^2)$

$$
\begin{aligned}
\Pi^*(p) \equiv \Pi(p^*) &= \frac{15}{2}\frac{5}{2} - \left(1 + \left(\frac{5}{2}\right)^2\right) \\
&= \frac{75}{4} - \frac{29}{4} \\
&= \frac{46}{4} \\
&= \frac{23}{2}
\end{aligned}
$$

Thus, the firm's profit-maximizing profit level is $\Pi^* = \frac{23}{2}$.

10.1.3 First Order Condition Analysis

As we noted above, the firm is not constrained in the amount of output it selects. This introduces the question "why doesn't the firm raise its price if it has some degree of market power"? One of the major benefits of using mathematical techniques to work through our analogy is the ability to analyze, in detail, the marginal incentives affecting the firm's behavior. To see how we can use the first order conditions to relate our analogy back to the marginal incentives faced by the firm, let us first work through a general profit-maximization model.

Example 10.4 (Profit-Maximization - General):
Question: A firm faces a market demand of $D(p)$ and has a cost function of $C(q)$. What quantity/price level will maximize the firm's profit if we view the profit function as a function of quantity?

Answer: Following the steps above,

1. **Set up the firm's Profit Function as a function of quantity.**

Per Eqn. (10.2), the profit function as a function of quantity is $\Pi(q) = p(q)q - C(q)$. To find the price as a function of quantity, we need to solve for the market inverse demand function from the market demand. As we are not given an explicit market demand function, we will use the general form $p(q)$, recognizing it is defined as the inverse demand function of $D(p)$. Thus, our profit function is

$$\Pi(q) = p(q)q - C(q) \tag{10.10}$$

2. **Take the first order condition(s) of the firm's profit function as a respect to the variable of choice. When the profit function is a function of quantity, the variable of choice is quantity.**

Taking the first order condition of Eqn. (10.10) with respect to quantity,

$$\frac{\partial \Pi}{\partial q} = p'(q)q + p(q) - C'(q) = 0 \tag{10.11}$$

3. **Solve the first order condition(s) to solve for the firm's profit-maximizing quantity.**

As we are not given explicit functions, we cannot solve for a closed-form solution. However, we know the profit-maximizing quantity will satisfy Eqn. (10.11).

4. **If necessary, plug the profit-maximizing quantity level into the inverse market demand to determine the profit-maximizing price level.**

Again, we are not given explicit functions, but we can rearrange Eqn. (10.11) to isolate our price. In particular,

$$p'(q)q + p(q) - C'(q) = 0$$
$$\Rightarrow p(q) = C'(q) - p'(q)q$$

We now know the conditions which need to hold for the firm to be profit-maximizing, but the true benefit of taking a mathematical approach is gaining insight into what tensions the firm is facing. Let look at Eqn. (10.11) more deeply. In particular, the derivative of the firm's profit with respect to quantity intuitively tells us "how much additional profit will the firm receive if it increases output by one unit". The first order condition requires that this value must be 0. In other words, the firm cannot get additional profit by increasing (or decreasing) its output. Let us look at the marginal incentives of increasing quantity as shown in the first order condition.

First, recall that a firm's profit is simply total revenue - total cost. Thus, when we look at a firm's marginal profit with respect to quantity, $p'(q)q + p(q) - C'(q)$, we can decompose it into two separate effects, the marginal revenue and the marginal cost. Recall the revenue in the general profit formulation is $p(q)q$. Thus, the term $p'(q)q + p(q)$ (which is the marginal revenue) can be interpreted as the marginal change in profit due to a change in revenue. The cost in the general profit formulation is $-C(q)$. Thus, the term $-C'(q)$ (which is the marginal cost) can be interpreted as the marginal change in profit due to a change in the costs.

When we examine Eqn. (10.11), we can now see the tradeoff the firm is facing. As it increases output, for instance, three marginal effects are occurring. From the cost side, we see that an increase in quantity will result in profits changing by $-C'(q)$. Recall $-C'(q)$ is the marginal cost the firm faces, which is exactly the extra cost the firm incurs when it produces one extra unit of the good. Thus, by producing an extra unit, profits go down by exactly the amount it costs to produce the unit.

On the revenue side, however, we see a more subtle story. Specifically, two effects are occurring. First, when the firm increases quantity by one, marginal profits increase by $p(q)$. In other words, the firm's profits will increase by the increased revenue the firm will receive by selling its one additional unit of output for the price, $p(q)$. However, a second effect is occurring that is the key to why a firm with market power does not continually increase quantity. Specifically, the final effect the firm is facing when it increases its output by one unit is $p'(q)q$. This tells us the firm's profits will change by the number of units the firm is selling times the change in price it must incur. Why must a firm change its price to sell an additional unit of the good? The reason is that in order to incentive a new customer to purchase its good who currently does not want to purchase its good, the firm must lower its price. As we are assuming the firm is setting a single price for all units of the good, this means that it must drop its price on all units sold. Thus, its profits change by $p'(q)q$, the amount the price must change times the amount of units it is selling. Recall the law of demand implies that in order for quantity demanded to go up, price must go down. Thus, $p'(q) < 0$, and this effect is negative.

Putting the three marginal effects of the FOC together, we see that when a firm decides whether to lower its price to increase its quantity sold, it must balance the cost of producing extra units, the benefit of having additional customers, and the cost of giving up revenues from existing customers.

10.1.4 Profit-Maximizing Markup

In balancing these marginal effects, it should not be surprising that the customers' sensitivity to price will play an important role. In particular, if customers are extremely price sensitive, then the price drop necessary to incentivize new customers might be extremely small, making the lost-revenue, $p'(q)q$, effect very small. In such a case, we would not be surprised to see large output levels (and subsequently low prices). If, however, customers are not price sensitive, then a large price drop would be necessary to incentivize new customers to purchase the good, since price is not a main driver in customers' purchasing decisions. Therefore, the lost-revenue effect would be large, incentivizing firms to keep prices high.

A useful measure of customer price sensitivity is the own-price elasticity of demand, which we recall from Chapter 6 is the percent change in quantity per percent change in price. If a change in price results in a large change in quantity demanded (i.e. price-sensitive or "elastic" customers), this elasticity is very large in magnitude. If a change in price results in a small change in quantity (i.e. price-insensitive or "inelastic" customers), this elasticity is very small in magnitude. As it turns out, this measure is not only useful in determining profit-maximizing firm behavior, it can be used to directly calculate a firm's optimal markups. To see this, we first rewrite Eqn. (10.11), which is a firm's general first order conditions when profit is a function of quantity:

$$p'(q)q + p(q) - C'(q) = 0$$

Rewriting $p'(q)$ as $\frac{\partial p}{\partial q}$, $p(q)$ as p and rearranging,

$$p - C'(q) = -\frac{\partial p}{\partial q}q$$

If we divide both sides by p, we find

$$\frac{p - C'(q)}{p} = -\frac{\partial p}{\partial q}\frac{q}{p}$$

Recall the definition of own-price elasticity is $\epsilon = \frac{\partial q}{\partial p}\frac{p}{q}$. This is exactly the negative of the reciprocal of the right side of the equation. In addition, as own-price elasticity is always negative per the Law of Demand, $-\frac{1}{\epsilon} = \frac{1}{|\epsilon|}$ Thus,

$$\frac{p - C'(q)}{p} = \frac{1}{|\epsilon|} \qquad (10.12)$$

Note intuitively what the left side of the equality means. In particular, it is the percent of the sales price that is markup over marginal costs. Due to the analytic tractability of solving for this value from the own-price elasticity and the intuitive appeal, this term is commonly used in economics and is called the *Lerner Index*.

Definition 10.8 (Lerner Index):
A firm's *Lerner Index* for a product is

1. The percent of the sales price that is markup over marginal costs.

2. $L = \frac{P - MC}{P}$ where P is the sales price of the good and MC is the marginal cost.

3. A measure used by economists and regulators to measure market power.

4. For a profit maximizing firm, $\frac{1}{|\epsilon|}$, where ϵ is the own-price elasticity of demand.

To gain further understanding as to why economists use this index to measure market power, we can rearrange Eqn. (10.12) as follows:

$$\begin{aligned}
\frac{p - C'(q)}{p} = \frac{1}{|\epsilon|} &= L \\
p - C'(q) &= pL \\
p(1 - L) &= C'(q) \\
p &= \frac{C'(q)}{1 - L} \qquad (10.13)
\end{aligned}$$

Eqn. (10.13) tells us that the optimal percentage markup over marginal costs that a profit-maximizing firm with market power should set equals

$$\frac{1}{1-L} = \frac{1}{1 - \frac{1}{|\epsilon|}}$$

The fairly astounding fact that a firm's profit-maximizing behavior can be determined via the market elasticity and a knowledge of the firm's marginal costs make the Lerner Index extremely useful. Antitrust authorities can measure the potential price markup due to a merger by estimating the industry's market elasticity. New-product analysts can offer insight into what the optimal markup should be in different demand conditions. In addition, the effects of new firms entering the market can be analyzed.

Entry into a Monopolistically Competitive Environment

Consider a scenario in which a firm in the BMC market suddenly faces increased competition in the form of market entrants. For instance, Apple suddenly faces competition in its iPad market from the entry of Android tablets. Using Eqn. (10.13), we can immediately determine that as the magnitude of the own-price elasticity of demand for a particular type of good increases, the incentive and ability for a firm to mark up its product over cost decreases. Intuitively, consider how a firm's elasticity will change as the number of competitors changes. In particular, for a given increase in price, as more competitors enter a market it is reasonable to assume I will lose a larger and larger number of my customers as they substitute away from my good and purchase lower-cost alternatives. Thus, entry into a market can be modeled as an increase in the magnitude of own-price elasticity. Eqn. (10.13) then implies that the firm's markup will decline and prices will ultimately drop.

In the extreme case, consider an industry in which there are a large number of firms, all firms supply identical products, new firms can freely enter the market, buyers can find sellers extremely easily, there are no network effects, and all firms can easily supply as many customers as necessary. In this case, it is reasonable to assume that a small increase in price will result in a firm losing virtually all their customers, as they will easily identify a lower-cost alternative selling an identical product. In that industry, the magnitude of the own-price elasticity approaches infinity (an extremely small price increase will cause you to lose all your customers) and the Lerner Index will therefore approach zero. In other words, in highly competitive markets we expect firms in the industry to be selling their products with essentially no markup.

10.2   Perfectly Competitive Model

To gain additional insight into the above scenario, we define an alternate model that captures the unique characteristics of a market that is highly competitive. This model is very similar to the BMC model, but differs in one fundamental aspect. In particular, firms cannot adjust their prices without losing their entire customer base. While this is effectively identical to the BMC model under the assumption that own-price elasticity approaches infinity, by modifying the model to remove a firm's incentives to change price, we can more easily focus on the quantity-selection incentives firms face.

Definition 10.9 (Perfectly Competitive Model):
The *Perfectly Competitive Model* (PC Model) is a model of profit-maximization in which

1. Consumers purchase goods according to their demand functions.

2. A firm cost-minimizes by selecting inputs according to its factor demand functions.

3. Firms select quantity to maximize their profits, where profit, Π, is measured as total revenues - total cost.

4. Firms set the same price for each customer.

5. A firm has no market power. If it increases the price of its good above the prices of the other firms, it will lose its entire customer base.

6. A firm can sell as many units as it wants as the market price.

It should be noted that these assumptions are very strict and we should not try to apply them to a wide range of industries. Instead, this is a baseline model that should be interpreted as "what behaviors should we observe in highly competitive industries, even if they aren't perfectly competitive". Alternatively, this can be used as a normative ideal, in which perfectly competitive theoretical behavior is the firm behavior which is optimal for society.[2]

---

[2] We do not explicitly discuss welfare in this book, but under a fairly intuitive definition of total society welfare, this normative ideal is reasonable.

To solve for the profit-maximizing quantity a firm will select under the PC Model, we take identical steps as when finding the profit-maximizing quantity in the BMC model. The only difference is that firms consider the market price as fixed. To justify this assumption, note that a firm cannot set price above the market price (the price other firms are setting), as it will lose all its customers. Thus, it faces the decision as to which price it should set that is not above the market price. As our final assumption states that the firm can sell as many units as it wants at the market price, there is no reason the firm would ever charge a price lower than the market price as they could sell the same amount of units (incurring an identical cost) at higher prices. Thus, each firm will set a price equaling the market price, and will view this price as given.

The steps we take to find a firm's profit-maximizing PC behavior when profit is a function of quantity are:

1. Set up the firm's Profit Function as a function of quantity with price a fixed constant.

2. Take the first order condition(s) of the firm's profit function as a respect to the variable of choice. When the profit function is a function of quantity, the variable of choice is quantity.

3. Solve the first order condition(s) to solve for the firm's profit-maximizing quantity.

4. If necessary, plug the profit-maximizing quantity and market price into the profit function to determine the profit-maximizing profit level.

As always, a firm's profits are total revenue - total cost. In the PC Model, this becomes

Definition 10.10 (PC Profit Function):
A firm's *PC Profit Function* equals

$$\Pi(q) = pq - C(q)$$

where p is the market price.

Example 10.5 (PC Profit-Maximization - General):
Question: A firm can sell as many units of a good at a market price of p per unit. The firm has a cost function of $C(q)$. What quantity level will maximize the firm's profit if we view the profit function as a function of quantity?

Answer: Following the steps above,

1. **Set up the firm's Profit Function as a function of quantity with price a fixed constant.**

Per Definition 10.10,

$$\Pi(q) = pq - C(q)$$

2. **Take the first order condition(s) of the firm's profit function as a respect to the variable of choice. When the profit function is a function of quantity, the variable of choice is quantity.**

Taking the first order condition with respect to quantity,

$$\frac{\partial \Pi}{\partial q} = p - C'(q^*) = 0 \qquad (10.14)$$

3. **Solve the first order condition(s) to solve for the firm's profit-maximizing quantity.**

As we are not given explicit functions, we cannot solve for a closed-form solution. However, we know the profit-maximizing quantity will satisfy Eqn. (10.14). Rearranging, we know the firm's quantity level will satisfy the equation

$$p = C'(q) \qquad (10.15)$$

In other words, the firm's profit-maximizing quantity level will ensure the market price equals the marginal cost of the last good produced.

Let us examine the incentives a firm faces in a PC environments versus a BMC environment. First, notice that Eqn. (10.15) implies that in a PC environment firms will not place any markup over marginal cost, the identical condition we found in the BMC model when the magnitude of the own-price elasticity approaches infinity. To further understand the incentives of a firm in a PC environment, it is useful to compare the first order conditions of a PC firm with the first order conditions of a BMC firm.

- **BMC First Order Conditions:** $\frac{\partial \Pi}{\partial q} = p'(q)q + p(q) - C'(q) = 0$

- **PC First Order Conditions:** $\frac{\partial \Pi}{\partial q} = p - C'(q) = 0$

In comparing these first order conditions, it is clear that an increase in quantity for the BMC firm affects its profits in one fundamentally different way than the PC firm. Specifically, by comparing the FOC's, we see the marginal profit due to an increase in quantity for the BMC firm involves a revenue decrease of $p'(q)q$ that the PC firm does not have to consider. Recall this term is the marginal cost of giving up revenues from existing customers a BMC firm must incur because the only way it can attract new customers is to lower its price. Because we assume PC firms can sell as many units as it wants at the market price, a PC firm does not need to consider this incentive. It is worth noting that as a BMC market becomes infinitely elastic, the price change necessary to incur any quantity change is effectively zero, making $p'(q) \to 0$. In other words, a firm in an infinitely elastic BMC firm faces identical incentives to a PC firm. As such, the BMC model can be considered a generalization of the PC model, although they tend to be treated as separate.

10.2.1 PC Market Equilibrium

In the BMC model prices are set by the firms. In the PC model prices are assumed as given, which introduces the question "what, exactly, will the market prices be in a PC industry?". We will not use a formal game-theoretic analysis, but will instead form an intuitive argument as to how this price is determined. In particular, we need to consider the incentives of individual firms and consumers at different price levels. Let us first assume the market price is such that $D(p) = a$, each firm is producing a level of output such that $p = C'(q)$, and the total output in the market (which is just the number of firms times the amount each is producing) equals $b > a$. In other words, firms are producing (in aggregate) more than consumers demand. In such a case, some firms will not be able to sell their output, as no customers will exist which want their good. In this case of a market surplus, consider the incentives of the firms who cannot find buyers. These firms will have an incentive to lower their price, as it will incentivize customers to purchase their goods as opposed to their competitors' goods. For instance, consider the discounts that car dealerships offer at the end of the model year when they cannot find a suitable number of buyers. Thus, a "stable" market price cannot be a market price which incentivizes firms to produce more goods than consumers want to purchase.

Now consider a market price such that $D(p) = a$, each firm is producing a level of output such that $p = C'(q)$, and the total output in the market (which is just the number of firms times the amount each is producing) equals $b < a$. In other words, firms are producing (in aggregate) less than consumers demand. In such a case, some consumers will not be able to purchase the good they desire, as no suppliers will exist that have any units left of the good. In this case of a market shortage, consider the incentives of a firm who has multiple customers trying to purchase its last good. This firm has an incentive to sell the good at a higher price, as one of the customers is likely to pay the higher price. For instance, consider the black-market price of tickets to the Super Bowl when there is a limited number of seats and a very large number of potential consumers. Thus, a "stable" market price cannot be a market price which incentivizes firms to produce less than consumers want to purchase.

If a "stable" price exists, there is only one possibility left. In particular, it must be the price such that the market demand exactly equals the number of units producers will provide when each is profit-maximizing via. the condition $p = C'(q)$. We call this price the *PC equilibrium price*.

Definition 10.11 (PC Equilibrium Price):
The *PC Equilibrium Price*, p_{PC} is the price at which

1. No surplus or shortage exists.

2. Mathematically, the price at which the number of units demanded, $D(p_{PC})$ equals the number of units supplied by the market. In a market with n identical firms, market supply equals n times the amount produced by each firm when each firm is profit-maximizing such that $p_{PC} = C'(q)$.

This is the mathematical formulation of the supply/demand analysis you performed in Principles of Economics. The steps we take to find a PC market's equilibrium given consumers with specified preferences and firms with specified cost functions are:

1. Solve for each consumer's demand function for the specified good.

2. Solve for the market demand function by adding the individual demand functions.

3. Solve for the quantity each profit-maximizing firm will produce at a given price.

4. Solve for the market "supply" function by adding the individual quantities each firm will produce at a given price.

5. Find the price that causes the market supply to equal the market demand.

Example 10.6 (PC Equilibrium Price):
Question: Two consumers are in a PC market. Each consumer has Cobb-Douglas preferences of the form $U(x_1, x_2) = x_1^{1/2} x_2^{1/2}$ and each consumer has an income of \$2. Forty firms exist in the PC market that produce good 1. Each firm has a cost function of the form $C(x_1) = x_1^2$. What is the equilibrium price in this market?

Answer: Following the steps above,

1. **Solve for each consumer's demand function for the specified good.**
   We know that an individual with a Cobb-Douglas utility has a demand function for good 1 of the form $x_1 = \frac{\alpha I}{p_1}$. Plugging in $\alpha = 1/2$ and $I = 2$, each consumer has a demand function of $x_1 = \frac{1}{p_1}$.

2. **Solve for the market demand function by adding the individual demand functions.**
   For a given price, the market demand will be the sum of the two individual demands. Thus, the market demand will equal $D(p) = \frac{1}{p_1} + \frac{1}{p_1} = \frac{2}{p_1}$.

3. **Solve for the quantity each profit-maximizing firm will produce at a given price.**
   Each firm will maximize profits according to

   $$\max_{x_1} p_1 x_1 - x_1^2$$

Taking the FOC's and solving,

$$\frac{\partial \Pi}{\partial x_1} = p_1 - 2x_1 = 0$$

$$\Rightarrow x_1 = \frac{p_1}{2}$$

Thus, each firm will produce $x_1 = \frac{p_1}{2}$ units of good 1 when the market price is p_1.

4. **Solve for the market "supply" function by adding the individual quantities each firm will produce at a given price.**
As each firm will produce $x_1 = \frac{p_1}{2}$ units of the good and there are 40 firms, the total market supply will equal $40\frac{p_1}{2} = 20p_1$.

5. **Find the price that sets causes the market supply to equal the market demand.**
Setting the market demand, $\frac{2}{p_1}$ equal to the market supply, $20p_1$, we can solve for the equilibrium price.

$$\frac{2}{p_1} = 20p_1$$

$$\Rightarrow \frac{1}{10} = p_1^2$$

$$\Rightarrow p_1^* = \left(\frac{1}{10}\right)^{1/2}$$

Thus, the equilibrium price in the market will equal $p_1^* = \left(\frac{1}{10}\right)^{1/2}$.

Chapter 11

Game Theory - Finite Normal Form

Until now, we have studied markets in which a firm's profit-maximizing decisions are made without considering the behavior of other firms. While, for instance, the own-price demand elasticity of a monopolistically competitive firm is strongly influenced by the number of other firms in the market, our analysis assumed that a firm sets its optimal price assuming that this elasticity is fixed. A more realistic model would incorporate the idea that one firm's actions will affect rival firms' actions, which will then affect the initial firm. For instance, if a price increase by one firm lead to a price increase by another firm, this could affect the own-price elasticity of the first firm, causing a feedback effect.

To be able to study these types of markets as well as a myriad of other strategic scenarios, economists use the tools of Game Theory. Game Theory is the study of strategic scenarios in which one individual's decision affects another individual's decision. Because most situations involve some form of strategic considerations, Game Theory has been used to make predictions in the fields of industrial organization, patent innovation, marketing, sports, politics, law enforcement, and many others.

It is important to note that Game Theory is not the study of "how to win a game". It is not the study of optimal Texas Hold'em strategies. It does not tell us how to win at chess. Instead, it tells us how a specific strategic scenario might resolve itself. For instance, assume you are a criminal engaged in the criminal act of your choosing. How much effort you put in committing the crime will directly affect how much effort the police will expend in trying to catch you.

The reverse is also true. You are both strategically responding to the other. How will this scenario play itself out? Will you extend large amounts of effort to avoid being caught making the police extend large amounts of effort trying to catch you? Will you extend large amounts of effort to avoid being caught, making the police decide it is not worth extending effort trying to catch you? Will the value of the crime affect your behavior? Will the ease in catching you affect everyone's behavior?

11.1 Normal Form Game

Depending on the application, economists have modeled strategic interactions in a few ways. The first is the *normal form game*.

Definition 11.1 (Normal Form Game):
A *normal form game* consists of

1. **Set of players:** Who is playing

2. **Strategy space of each player:** How they can play

3. **Payoff each player receives given any strategy profile:** What they will "win" given each combination of their strategy and their opponents' strategies

Example 11.1 (Normal Form Game):
Task: Consider a game of Rock/Paper/Scissors between two people in which the winner receives $1 from the loser and no money is exchanged in the case of a tie. Model this as a normal form game.

Answer: To model this game as a normal form game, we must explicitly identify the players, the strategy space of each player, and the payoff each player gets given any strategy profile.

1. The *players* are player 1 and player 2. Note if they had names, we could use their names.

2. The *strategy space* of each individual is {Rock, Paper, Scissors}. In other words, each individual can play "Rock", "Paper", or "Scissors".

3. To specify the *payoff* of each individual given any strategy profile, we need to explicitly list the payoffs of each player for every combination of their strategy and their opponent's strategy.

Define $u_1(a, b)$ as the payoff player 1 receives if he plays a and player 2 plays b.

$$
\begin{aligned}
u_1(R,R) &= 0 \\
u_1(R,P) &= -1 \\
u_1(R,S) &= 1 \\
u_1(S,R) &= -1 \\
u_1(S,P) &= 1 \\
u_1(S,S) &= 0 \\
u_1(P,R) &= 1 \\
u_1(P,P) &= 0 \\
u_1(P,S) &= -1
\end{aligned}
$$

Define $u_2(a, b)$ as the payoff player 2 receives if he plays b and player 1 plays a.

$$
\begin{aligned}
u_2(R,R) &= 0 \\
u_2(R,P) &= 1 \\
u_2(R,S) &= -1 \\
u_2(S,R) &= 1 \\
u_2(S,P) &= -1 \\
u_2(S,S) &= 0 \\
u_2(P,R) &= -1 \\
u_2(P,P) &= 0 \\
u_2(P,S) &= 1
\end{aligned}
$$

It should be clear from this example that writing the payoffs of every possibility can get tedious. As such, when there are a finite number of strategies and only two players, economists instead use a *game matrix* to represent the normal form of a game. The general form of a game matrix is shown in Table 11.1. The top

Player 2

	a	b
A	$u_1(A,a), u_2(A,a)$	$u_1(A,b), u_2(A,b)$
B	$u_1(B,a), u_2(B,a)$	$u_1(B,b), u_2(B,b)$
C	$u_1(C,a), u_2(C,a)$	$u_1(C,b), u_2(C,b)$

Player 1 is labeled on the left, with rows A, B, C.

Table 11.1: Normal Form Game Matrix

and left side of the matrix represents the players. All strategies in each player's strategy space are listed along the player's side of the matrix. In Table 11.1, for instance, Player 2 has two possible strategies: a and b. Player 1 has three possible strategies: A, B, and C. Each element of the matrix represents the payoffs each player will receive when playing the strategies corresponding to that element. For instance, the cell in Table 11.1 corresponding to Player 1 playing A and Player 2 playing a contains the payoffs to Player 1 corresponding to these strategies, $u_1(A,a)$ and the payoffs to Player 2 corresponding to these strategies, $u_2(A,a)$. Note that the first entry in the cell is the payoff to the player on the left side of the matrix. The second entry in the cell is the payoff to the player on the top of the matrix.

Example 11.2 (Game Matrix):
Question: Form the game matrix corresponding to the Rock/Paper/Scissor game described in Example 11.1

Answer: The rows will correspond to the possible actions of Player 1 {Rock, Paper, Scissors} and the columns will correspond to the possible actions of Player 2 {Rock, Paper, Scissors}. If Player 1 plays {Rock} and player 2 plays {Rock}, the game is a tie and both players receive a payoff of 0. Thus, the entry in the {Rock, Rock} cell should be (0, 0). If Player 1 plays {Rock} and Player 2 plays {Paper}, then Player 2 wins. Thus, the entry in the {Rock, Paper} cell should be (-1, 1) (Player 1 gets -1 since he lost and Player 2 gets 1). Continuing with this procedure, the full game matrix will be:

Player 2

	Rock	Paper	Scissors
Rock	0,0	$-1,1$	$1,-1$
Paper	$1,-1$	0,0	$-1,1$
Scissors	$-1,1$	$1,-1$	0,0

Player 1 is labeled on the left, with rows Rock, Paper, Scissors.

11.2 Iterated Elimination of Dominated Strategies

Having established the formal definition of a "game" (in its normal form), we can now address the issue "how will a game resolve itself". Economists have a number of solution concepts relating to varying levels of player sophistication. The first is *Iterated Elimination of Strictly Dominated Strategies* (IESDS), which assumes people behave as follows:

1. If I have a strategy that is worse than another strategy regardless of what the other player(s) do, I will never play it.

2. Knowing this, my opponents will determine if they have a strategy that is worse than any other strategy regardless of the strategy I select from those I have not eliminated. If so, they will never play it.

3. Knowing this, I will determine if I have a strategy that is worse than any other strategy regardless of the strategy my opponents selects from those they have not eliminated. If so, I will never play it.

4. And so on...

As an example, consider the game in Table 11.2. Assume you are Player 1 and ask yourself "Will I ever want to play *Top*?". If Player 2 plays *Left*, you can do better than playing *Top* by playing *Center*. In particular, you would receive a payoff of 5 versus a payoff of 3. If Player 2 plays *Middle*, you can again do better than playing *Top* by playing *Center*. In this case you would receive 8 instead of 7. Lastly, if Player 3 plays *Right*, you again do better by playing *Center* (14 versus 10). Thus, no matter what strategy Player 2 selects, you should never pick *Top* since playing *Center* guarantees you higher payoffs. Thus, when trying to determine how this game will resolve itself, we should eliminate *Top*, since it is not rational for Player 1 to play *Top* when *Center* is clearly better.

Knowing *Top* will never be played, we can now ask ourselves if there is a strategy that Player 2 should never play. Consider Table 11.3, which shows the original game with *Top* eliminated from the possible strategies Player 1 will play. Should Player 2 ever play *Left*? It should be clear that if Player 1 plays *Center*, Player 2 can do better than *Left* by playing *Middle*. Specifically, she can receive 2 instead of 1. Likewise, if Player 1 plays *Bottom*, Player 2 can do better than *Left* by again playing *Middle*. Thus, *knowing that Player 1 will never play Top*, Player 2 should never play *Left* since playing *Middle* is always strictly better. You should note that playing *Right* is also strictly better. Thus, when trying to determine how

Player 2

		Left	Middle	Right
	Top	3, 6	7, 1	10, 4
Player 1	Center	5, 1	8, 2	14, 7
	Bottom	6, 0	6, 2	8, 5

Table 11.2: Simple Game

Player 2

		Left	Middle	Right
Player 1	Center	5, 1	8, 2	14, 7
	Bottom	6, 0	6, 2	8, 5

Table 11.3: Sample Game with *Top* Eliminated

this game will resolve itself, once we have eliminated *Top* we should eliminate *Left*, since it is not rational for Player 2 to play *Left* when *Middle* is clearly better.

Knowing *Top* and *Left* will never be played, we can now ask ourselves if there is another strategy that Player 1 should never play. Consider Table 11.4, which shows the original game with *Top* and *Left* eliminated from the possible strategies that the players will play. Should Player 1 ever play *Bottom*? It should be clear that if Player 2 plays *Middle*, Player 1 can do better than *Bottom* by playing *Center*. Specifically, he can receive 8 instead of 6. Likewise, if Player 2 plays *Right*, Player 1 can do better than *Bottom* by again playing *Center*. Thus, *knowing that he will never play top and Player 2 will never play Left*, Player 1 should never play *Bottom* since playing *Center* is always strictly better. Thus, when trying to determine how this game will resolve itself, once we have eliminated *Top* and *Left* we should eliminate *Bottom*, since it is not rational for Player 1 to play *Bottom* when *Center* is clearly better. Thus, we have determined that, according to the assumptions of IESDS, the only rational strategy for Player 1 is to play *Center*.

Knowing *Top*, *Left*, and *Bottom* will never be played, we can now ask ourselves if there is another strategy that Player 2 should never play. Consider Table 11.5, which shows the original game with *Top*, *Left*, and *Bottom* eliminated from the

Player 2

Middle   Right

		Middle	Right
Player 1	Center	8,2	14,7
	Bottom	6,2	8,5

Table 11.4: Sample Game with *Top* and *Left* Eliminated

Player 2

Middle   Right

		Middle	Right
Player 1	Center	8,2	14,7

Table 11.5: Sample Game with *Top*, *Left*, and *Down* Eliminated

possible strategies that the players will play. Should Player 2 ever play *Middle*? It should be clear that if Player 1 plays *Center* (as we have predicted he will), Player 2 can do better than *Middle* by playing *Right*. Specifically, he can receive 7 instead of 2. Thus, *knowing that he will never play Left and Player 1 will play Center*, Player 2 should never play *Middle* since playing *Right* is always strictly better. Thus, when trying to determine how this game will resolve itself, once we have eliminated *Top*, *Left*, and *Bottom* we should eliminate *Middle*, since it is not rational for Player 2 to play *Middle* when *Right* is clearly better. Thus, we have determined that, according to the assumptions of IESDS, the only rational strategy for Player 2 is to play *Right*.

Under our assumptions of IESDS, we have thus determined that the game will resolve itself by Player 1 playing *Center* and Player 2 playing *Right*. It is important to note that the order of elimination does not matter. For instance, we could have started with Player 2 and ended up with the same result.

> **Example 11.3 (IESDS):**
> **Task:** Consider the game in Table 11.2. Starting with Player 2, what is the outcome of the game as predicted by IESDS?
>
> **Answer:** Eliminate *Middle* then *Top* then *Left* then *Down*. Outcome is (*Center*, *Right*).

11.2.1 Limitations of IESDS

Having established IESDS can predict the strategic outcome of a game, the natural question arises "so we are done with Game Theory, right?". Unfortunately, IESDS as a solution concept has significant shortcomings. Consider, for instance, the following scene from A Princess Bride (1987).

> **Man in Black:** All right. Where is the poison? The battle of wits has begun. It ends when you decide and we both drink, and find out who is right... and who is dead.
>
> **Vizzini:** But it's so simple. All I have to do is divine from what I know of you: are you the sort of man who would put the poison into his own goblet or his enemy's? Now, a clever man would put the poison into his own goblet, because he would know that only a great fool would reach for what he was given. I am not a great fool, so I can clearly not choose the wine in front of you. But you must have known I was not a great fool, you would have counted on it, so I can clearly not choose the wine in front of me.
>
> **Man in Black:** You've made your decision then?
>
> **Vizzini:** Not remotely. Because iocane comes from Australia, as everyone knows, and Australia is entirely peopled with criminals, and criminals are used to having people not trust them, as you are not trusted by me, so I can clearly not choose the wine in front of you.
>
> **Man in Black:** Truly, you have a dizzying intellect.
>
> **Vizzini:** Wait til I get going! Now, where was I?
>
> **Man in Black:** Australia.
>
> **Vizzini:** Yes, Australia. And you must have suspected I would have known the powder's origin, so I can clearly not choose the wine in front of me.
>
> **Man in Black:** You're just stalling now.
>
> **Vizzini:** You'd like to think that, wouldn't you? You've beaten my giant, which means you're exceptionally strong, so you could've put the poison in your own goblet, trusting on your strength to save you, so I can clearly not choose the wine in front of you. But, you've also bested my Spaniard, which means you must have studied, and in studying you must have learned that man is mortal, so you would have put the poison as far from yourself as possible, so I can clearly not choose the wine in front of me.

Man in Black: You're trying to trick me into giving away something. It won't work.

Vizzini: It has worked! You've given everything away! I know where the poison is!

Man in Black: Then make your choice.

Vizzini: I will, and I choose - What in the world can that be?

Vizzini: [Vizzini gestures up and away from the table. Roberts looks. Vizzini swaps the goblets]

Man in Black: What? Where? I don't see anything.

Vizzini: Well, I- I could have sworn I saw something. No matter. First, let's drink. Me from my glass, and you from yours.

Man in Black, Vizzini: [they drink]

Man in Black: You guessed wrong.

Vizzini: You only think I guessed wrong! That's what's so funny! I switched glasses when your back was turned! Ha ha! You fool! You fell victim to one of the classic blunders! The most famous is never get involved in a land war in Asia, but only slightly less well-known is this: never go in against a Sicilian when death is on the line! Ha ha ha ha ha ha ha! Ha ha ha ha ha ha ha! Ha ha ha...

Vizzini: [Vizzini stops suddenly, and falls dead to the right]

A critique in the same vein arises for IESDS. In particular, it requires a strong sense of "smart players", in which "I know that you know that I know that you know...". In a game with three strategies, this is possible, but for larger strategy spaces, this becomes dubious. As humans, are we able to perform the necessary mental calculations without making a mistake? Do we trust our opponent to make the same mental calculations mistake-free? To claim that games are resolved in such a manner assumes humans are smarter and more trusting than is likely warranted.

Another critique of IESDS is its lack of predictive power. Consider, for example, the simple game in Table 11.6. You should notice that no strategies can be eliminated via. IESDS. As such, IESDS predicts that any outcome is possible, giving us no predictive power. Unfortunately, this limitation of IESDS is the rule, not the exception. In most games, IESDS does not give us precise predictions.

Player 2

		Left	Right
Player 1	Top	1, 1	0, 0
	Bottom	0, 0	1, 2

Table 11.6: Game With No IESDS Prediction

11.3 Nash Equilibrium

One solution concept that addresses these critiques is the Nash equilibrium. This is perhaps the most prominent solution concept in Game Theory, and has even been given the Hollywood treatment in A Beautiful Mind (2001) (we will ignore the fact that the Nash equilibrium acted out in the bar scene is not, in fact, a Nash equilibrium). Essentially, a Nash equilibrium remains agnostic about how the equilibrium forms. It is simply a set of strategies such that if each player is playing a Nash strategy, then no other player will have an incentive to play any other strategy. While not technically exact, we can understand a Nash equilibrium by assuming a game is being repeated over and over. In each play of the game, assume the players select a strategy that is the best response to the strategy their opponent(s) played in the previous period. If, in any period, both players play the strategies as dictated by a Nash equilibrium, they will continue to play these strategies forever.

As a solution concept, the Nash equilibrium is widely heralded for numerous reasons. First, we oftentimes see strategic interactions "settle" on a particular outcome. For instance, the prices at Lenoir have been essentially stable for years. Even though the restaurants are not perfectly competitive (since they sell very different types of food), each is "happy" with their price given the prices of the other restaurants. No restaurant has an incentive to deviate and change their prices. We should be able to predict the prices each firm will offer in this "stable" environment by studying the Nash equilibrium of the price-setting game. For "observable" outcomes of strategic games, Nash equilibria offer significant predictions.

Second, the Nash equilibrium is widely accepted because it does not require excessive assumptions on the mental abilities of the players. It does not require the "I know that she knows that I know..." assumptions of IESDS. In fact, it only requires the most basic assumption that "given what my opponent is doing, I do not want to change my strategy". In addition, it does not require the assumption that humans can make significant mental calculations mistake-free.

Third, the Nash equilibrium is valuable because it offers better predictions than IESDS. In particular, the Nash equilibrium is *stronger* than IESDS. In other words, if a single IESDS equilibrium exists, then that outcome will also be the unique Nash equilibrium. However, if a single Nash equilibrium exists, it will not necessarily be the single IESDS equilibrium. As such, there are weakly fewer Nash equilibria of a game than IESDS equilibria. This is good for making predictions, in that the fewer predictive outcomes, the stronger our argument. Compare the statements "We should observe one of two possible outcomes" and "We should observe one of twelve possible outcomes". Obviously, only offering two possible outcomes is a better prediction.

Lastly, and perhaps most importantly, John Nash (1951) proved that for any normal form game with a finite number of players and strategies, at least one Nash equilibrium exists. This is an extremely useful property, in that it guarantees at least one prediction for any finite game.

11.4 NE - Pure Strategy, Finite Games

Solving for the pure strategy (we will discuss mixed strategies later) Nash equilibrium of a finite game is surprisingly easy. We will focus our attention to 2-player games so a game matrix can be used, but the underlying motivation is the same. To solve for the Nash equilibrium of a 2-player game,

1. Assume Player 2 plays one of her strategies. Underline the highest possible Player 1 payoff(s) given that Player 2 is playing this strategy. The strategy that corresponds to this payoff is called Player 1's *best response*.

2. Repeat this process until you have assumed Player 2 has played all her strategies.

3. Now assume Player 1 plays one of his strategies. Underline the highest possible Player 2 payoff(s) given that Player 1 is playing this strategy. The strategy that corresponds to this payoff is called Player 2's *best response*.

4. Repeat this process until you have assumed Player 1 has played all his strategies.

Player 2

	Confess	Don't Confess
Player 1 Confess	−6, −6	0, −9
Don't Confess	−9, 0	−1, −1

Table 11.7: Prisoner's Dilemma

5. The cell(s) that has both payoffs underlined corresponds to a pure strategy Nash equilibrium. Note there can be multiple pure strategy Nash equilibria. There can also be no pure strategy Nash equilibria.

Example 11.4 (Pure Strategy Nash Equilibrium):

Task: Consider the Prisoner's Dilemma game in Table 11.7. Find all pure strategy Nash equilibria.

Answer: Following the steps from above, we first assume that Player 2 plays *Confess*. Under this assumption, Player 1's best response is to play *Confess*, ensuring a payoff of -6 instead of -9. Underlining this payoff results in Table 11.8.

We now assume that Player 2 plays *Don't Confess*. Under this assumption, Player 1's best response is to play *Confess*, ensuring a payoff of 0 instead of -1. Underlining this payoff results in Table 11.9.

Having exhausted Player 2's strategies, now assume that Player 1 plays *Confess*. Under this assumption, Player 2's best response is to play *Confess*, ensuring a payoff of -6 instead of -9. Underlining this payoff results in Table 11.10.

We now assume that Player 1 plays *Don't Confess*. Under this assumption, Player 2's best response is to play *Confess*, ensuring a payoff of 0 instead of -1. Underlining this payoff results in Table 11.11.

The pure strategy Nash equilibrium is the outcome(s) that has both entries underlined. In this case, the unique pure strategy Nash equilibrium outcome is *(Confess, Confess)*, resulting in a payoff for each player of -6.

It is extremely beneficial to note that the Nash Equilibrium is not the best outcome for either player. In fact, another outcome would give both players a higher

Player 2

		Confess	Don't Confess
Player 1	Confess	$\underline{-6}, -6$	$0, -9$
	Don't Confess	$-9, 0$	$-1, -1$

Table 11.8: Player 1's BR to Player 2 Playing *Confess*

Player 2

		Confess	Don't Confess
Player 1	Confess	$\underline{-6}, -6$	$\underline{0}, -9$
	Don't Confess	$-9, 0$	$-1, -1$

Table 11.9: Player 1's BR to Player 2 Playing *Don't Confess*

Player 2

		Confess	Don't Confess
Player 1	Confess	$\underline{-6}, \underline{-6}$	$\underline{0}, -9$
	Don't Confess	$-9, 0$	$-1, -1$

Table 11.10: Player 2's BR to Player 1 Playing *Confess*

Player 2

		Confess	Don't Confess
Player 1	Confess	$\underline{-6}, \underline{-6}$	$\underline{0}, -9$
	Don't Confess	$-9, \underline{0}$	$-1, -1$

Table 11.11: Player 2's BR to Player 1 Playing *Don't Confess*

Player 2

Bach   Stravinsky

		Bach	Stravinsky
Player 1	Bach	2,1	0,0
	Stravinsky	0,0	1,2

Table 11.12: Battle of the Sexes

Player 2

Hawk   Dove

		Hawk	Dove
Player 1	Hawk	0,0	4,1
	Dove	1,4	3,3

Table 11.13: Hawk/Dove

payoff. In particular, if both players could agree to *Don't Confess*, they would both be significantly better off. This result underscores the strategic nature of games, where the "selfish" tendencies of individuals can result in outcomes that are worse for everyone. It also highlights what, exactly, a Nash equilibrium is. It is not the "best" outcome for any individual or society. Instead, it is simply the "stable" outcome. It is the outcome that, once reached, ensures no one will have an incentive to unilaterally deviate. In the prisoner's dilemma, knowing that your opponent is going to *Confess*, you might as well *Confess* to reduce your jail time. Another area of research called Cooperative Game Theory deals with situations in which players can commit to behave nonstrategically.

Example 11.5 (Pure Strategy Nash Equilibrium):
Task: Consider the games in Tables 11.12 and 11.13. Find all pure strategy Nash equilibria in each game.

Answer: As shown in Figure (11.14), the NE of the Battle of Sexes game are {Bach, Bach} and {Stravinsky, Stravinsky}. As shown in Figure (11.15), the NE of the Hawk/Dove game are {Hawk, Dove} and {Dove, Hawk}.

Player 2

		Bach	Stravinsky
Player 1	Bach	2,1	0,0
	Stravinsky	0,0	1,2

Table 11.14: Nash Equilibria - Battle of the Sexes

Player 2

		Hawk	Dove
Player 1	Hawk	0,0	4,1
	Dove	1,4	3,3

Table 11.15: Nash Equilibria - Hawk/Dove

11.5 NE - Mixed Strategy, Finite Games

Example 11.6 (Pure Strategy Nash Equilibrium):
Task: Consider now the Matching Pennies game represented by Table 11.16. Each player shows one side of a penny. If the sides match, Player 2 gives Player 1 a dollar. If the sides do not match, Player 1 gives Player 2 a dollar. Find all pure strategy Nash equilibria.

Player 2

		Heads	Tails
Player 1	Heads	1,−1	−1,1
	Tails	−1,1	1,−1

Table 11.16: Matching Pennies

It should be clear that this game has no pure strategy Nash equilibria. However, recall that John Nash found that all finite normal form games have at least one Nash equilibrium. To explain this apparent inconsistency, we must introduce the concept of mixed strategy equilibria.

Until now, we have focused on Nash equilibria where each individual plays a specific strategy. However, what if the players randomize over their strategies? For instance, consider a game of Rock/Paper/Scissors in which the loser must pay the winner $1. Intuitively, it should be obvious that no pure strategy Nash equilibrium will exist. No matter the outcome, one player will be the loser and one will be the winner. As such, the loser will always want to deviate. However, what if your opponent is randomly selecting between *Rock*, *Paper*, and *Scissors*? In such a situation, you have a 33% chance of winning, a 33% chance of losing, and a 33% chance of breaking even no matter what strategy you choose. As such, you might as well randomize in a similar manner. Given that you are randomizing, your opponent will then be indifferent between his strategies, meaning neither of you has an incentive to deviate. As such, this strategy profile constitutes a Nash equilibrium. Specifically, this profile is a mixed strategy Nash equilibrium.

Definition 11.2 (Mixed Strategy Nash Equilibrium):
A strategy profile in which all players are randomizing between strategies and neither has an incentive to deviate.

Note that a pure strategy Nash equilibrium is a specific kind of mixed strategy Nash equilibrium. Recall when dealing with lotteries, we discussed the degenerate lottery in which all probability is placed on a single outcome. A pure strategy is analogous to a degenerate lottery. In particular, a pure strategy is a mixed strategy Nash equilibrium in which the randomization includes 100% probability on one strategy and 0% probability on all other strategies.

While solving for mixed strategy equilibria is more difficult than solving for pure strategy equilibria, it follows a standard methodology that uses tools we have developed when analyzing uncertainty. The following steps are specific to a scenario in which each player has two possible strategies, called "action 1" and "action 2". We will not consider scenarios in which players have more than two strategies.

1. Assume Player 2 is mixing between action 1 and action 2. Specifically,

assume she is playing action 1 with probability α and action 2 with probability $1 - \alpha$.

2. Determine the expected utility of Player 1 if he plays action 1. Call this $EU^1_{\text{action }1}$. Note this will be in terms of α.

3. Determine the expected utility of Player 1 if he plays action 2. Call this $EU^1_{\text{action }2}$. Note this will be in terms of α.

4. Determine the value of α that makes $EU^1_{\text{action }1} = EU^1_{\text{action }2}$. If no such value exists, then a mixed strategy will not exist with Player 1 mixing between both strategies.

5. Assume Player 1 is mixing between action 1 and action 2. Specifically, assume he is playing action 1 with probability β and action 2 with probability $1 - \beta$.

6. Determine the expected utility of Player 2 if she plays action 1. Call this $EU^2_{\text{action }1}$. Note this will be in terms of β.

7. Determine the expected utility of Player 2 if she plays action 2. Call this $EU^2_{\text{action }2}$. Note this will be in terms of β.

8. Determine the value of β that makes $EU^2_{\text{action }1} = EU^2_{\text{action }2}$. If no such value exists, then a mixed strategy will not exist with Player 2 mixing between both strategies.

9. The mixed strategy Nash equilibrium (if it exists) will have Player 1 playing action 1 with probability β and action 2 with probability $1 - \beta$. Player 2 will play action 1 with probability α and action 2 with probability $1 - \alpha$.

Note that pure strategy Nash equilibria might not be identified with this method. This method is used to isolate the nondegenerate mixed strategy Nash equilibrium, if it exists. Also note the subtle fact that this methodology appears to have each player mixing in an effort to ensure the other player is indifferent to mixing. For instance, α is selected to ensure $EU^1_{\text{action }1} = EU^1_{\text{action }2}$. If the expected utility of both actions are identical, then Player 1 is indifferent between either action, and is therefore willing to mix. It is important to recognize that this is a trait of the solution method, and not an assumption that players are actually behaving in this manner.

Example 11.7 (Mixed Strategy Nash Equilibrium):

Task: Reconsider the Matching Pennies game represented by Table 11.16. Find all mixed strategy Nash equilibria.

Answer: Per our methodology, we first assume Player 2 mixes by playing *Heads* with probability (α) and *Tails* with probability $(1-\alpha)$. This is shown in Table 11.17. Player 1's expected utility from playing *Heads* is then

$$EU^1_{Heads} = (\alpha)(1) + (1-\alpha)(-1)$$

Likewise, Player 1's expected utility from playing *Tails* is

$$EU^1_{Tails} = (\alpha)(-1) + (1-\alpha)(1)$$

Setting these two quantities equal, we find that in order for Player 1 to mix, it must be that

$$
\begin{aligned}
(\alpha)(1) + (1-\alpha)(-1) &= (\alpha)(-1) + (1-\alpha)(1) \\
\alpha - 1 + \alpha &= -\alpha + 1 - \alpha \\
4\alpha &= 2 \\
\alpha &= 1/2
\end{aligned}
$$

Continuing with our methodology, we now assume Player 1 mixes by playing *Heads* with probability (β) and *Tails* with probability $(1-\beta)$. This is also shown in Table 11.17. Player 2's expected utility from playing *Heads* is then

$$EU^2_{Heads} = (\beta)(-1) + (1-\beta)(1)$$

Likewise, Player 2's expected utility from playing *Tails* is

$$EU^2_{Tails} = (\beta)(1) + (1-\beta)(-1)$$

Setting these two quantities equal, we find that in order for Player 2 to mix, it must be that

$$
\begin{aligned}
(\beta)(-1) + (1-\beta)(1) &= (\beta)(1) + (1-\beta)(-1) \\
-\beta + 1 - \beta &= \beta - 1 + \beta \\
2 &= 4\beta \\
\beta &= 1/2
\end{aligned}
$$

Thus, the mixed strategy Nash equilibrium has Player 1 playing *Heads* 1/2 the time and *Tails* 1/2 the time. Player 2 randomizes in the same manner.

Player 2

		Heads (α)	Tails $(1-\alpha)$
Player 1	Heads (β)	$1, -1$	$-1, 1$
	Tails $(1-\beta)$	$-1, 1$	$1, -1$

Table 11.17: Matching Pennies - Mixing Setup

Example 11.8 (Mixed Strategy Nash Equilibrium):
Task: Consider the games in Tables 11.12 and 11.13. Find the mixed strategy Nash equilibrium in each game.

Answer:
Battle of the sexes:

Assume Player 2 is playing Bach with probability α and Stravinsky with probability $(1-\alpha)$. Player 1 is indifferent to mixing if

$$
\begin{aligned}
EU^1_{Bach} &= EU^1_{Stravinsky} \\
2\alpha &= 1 - \alpha \\
\alpha &= 1/3
\end{aligned}
$$

Assume Player 1 is playing Bach with probability β and Stravinsky with probability $(1-\beta)$. Player 2 is indifferent to mixing if

$$
\begin{aligned}
EU^2_{Bach} &= EU^2_{Stravinsky} \\
\beta &= 2(1-\beta) \\
\beta &= 2/3
\end{aligned}
$$

Thus, Player 1 playing Bach $1/3$ of the time and Player 2 playing Bach $2/3$ of the time is a Nash Equilibrium.

Hawk/Dove:

Assume Player 2 is playing Hawk with probability α and Dove with probability $(1-\alpha)$. Player 1 is indifferent to mixing if

$$
\begin{aligned}
EU^1_{Hawk} &= EU^1_{Dove} \\
(4)(1-\alpha) &= \alpha + 3(1-\alpha) \\
\Rightarrow 4 - 4\alpha &= \alpha + 3 - 3\alpha \\
\Rightarrow 1 &= 2\alpha \\
\Rightarrow \alpha &= 1/2
\end{aligned}
$$

Assume Player 1 is playing Hawk with probability β and Dove with probability $(1 - \beta)$. Player 2 is indifferent to mixing if

$$
\begin{aligned}
EU^2_{Hawk} &= EU^2_{Dove} \\
4(1-\beta) &= \beta + 3(1-\beta) \\
\Rightarrow 4 - 4\beta &= \beta + 3 - 3\beta \\
\Rightarrow 1 &= 2\beta \\
\Rightarrow \beta &= 1/2
\end{aligned}
$$

Thus, Player 1 playing Hawk 1/2 of the time and Player 2 playing Hawk 1/2 of the time is a Nash Equilibrium.

11.6   Best Response Function

The Nash equilibrium is the set of strategies such that neither player has an incentive to deviate. We showed how to solve for all pure and mixed Nash equilibria using purely analytical techniques. In the case of 2 players, we can also use a graphical technique. Note that this technique is generally slower and less precise than the analytical techniques, but it offers additional insight into Nash equilibria and introduces the concept of a *best response function*.

Definition 11.3 (Best Response Function):
The *best response function* for Player i, $BR_i(s_{-i})$, tells Player i's optimal strategy given every possible strategy profile of the other players.

In the case of a two player game, for instance, $BR_1(s_2)$, tells us Player 1's optimal strategy given every possible strategy of Player 2. Likewise, $BR_2(s_1)$ tells us Player 2's optimal strategy given every possible strategy of Player 1.

As an example, consider the Battle of the Sexes represented in Table 11.12. Recall from our discussion of mixed strategies that Player 2's strategies are not only *Bach* and *Stravinsky*, but every possible mixture between the two. In other words, Player 2's strategies are fully captured by $0 \leq \alpha \leq 1$, which is the probability she plays *Bach*. If $\alpha = 1$, Player 2 is playing *Bach* as a pure strategy. If $\alpha = 0$, Player 2 is playing *Stravinsky* as a pure strategy. If $0 < \alpha < 1$, Player 2 is mixing. For every value of α, we can determine Player 1's optimal strategy, thereby forming his best response function.

In particular, note that Player 1 should play *Bach* if

$$
\begin{aligned}
EU^1_{Bach} &> EU^1_{Stravinsky} \\
2\alpha &> 1 - \alpha \\
\alpha &> 1/3
\end{aligned}
$$

Thus, for all $\alpha > 1/3$, Player 1's optimal response is to play *Bach*. In other words, play $\beta = 1$.

In addition, note that Player 1 should play *Stravinsky* if

$$
\begin{aligned}
EU^1_{Bach} &< EU^1_{Stravinsky} \\
2\alpha &< 1 - \alpha \\
\alpha &< 1/3
\end{aligned}
$$

Thus, for all $\alpha < 1/3$, Player 1's optimal response is to play *Stravinsky*, or $\beta = 0$. We determined in Example 11.8 that if $\alpha = 1/3$, Player 1 is indifferent between any strategy. If we plotted these results with Player 2's strategy (α) on the y-axis and Player 1's strategy (β) on the x-axis, we would create Figure 11.1, which is called Player 1's best response graph.

Note from this figure we can immediately determine Player 1's best response to any strategy of Player 2. If, for instance, Player 2 played *Bach* with 70% probability, then we see that Player 1's best response is to play *Bach* with 100% probability. Note when $\alpha = 1/3$, Player 1 is indifferent to all possible strategies. Thus, every

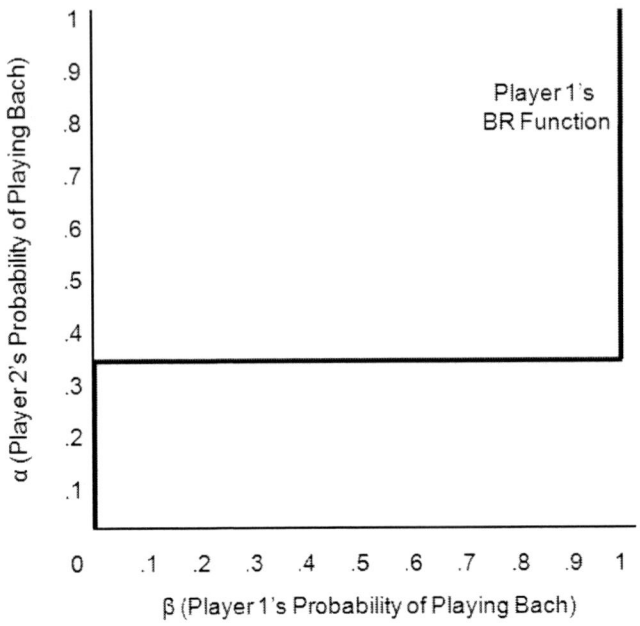

Figure 11.1: Battle of the Sexes, Player 1's BR Function

strategy is a best response.

To derive Player 2's best response function, note she should play *Bach* if

$$
\begin{aligned}
EU^2_{Bach} &> EU^2_{Stravinsky} \\
\beta &> 2(1-\beta) \\
\beta &> 2/3
\end{aligned}
$$

Thus, for all $\beta > 2/3$, Player 2's optimal response is to play *Bach*. In other words, play $\alpha = 1$.

In addition, note that Player 2 should play *Stravinsky* if

$$
\begin{aligned}
EU^2_{Bach} &< EU^2_{Stravinsky} \\
\beta &< 2(1-\beta) \\
\beta &< 2/3
\end{aligned}
$$

Thus, for all $\beta < 2/3$, Player 2's optimal response is to play *Stravinsky*, or $\alpha = 0$. We determined in Example 11.8 that if $\beta = 2/3$, Player 2 is indifferent between any strategy. Plotting these results on the same axes as Figure 11.1 results in Figure 11.2.

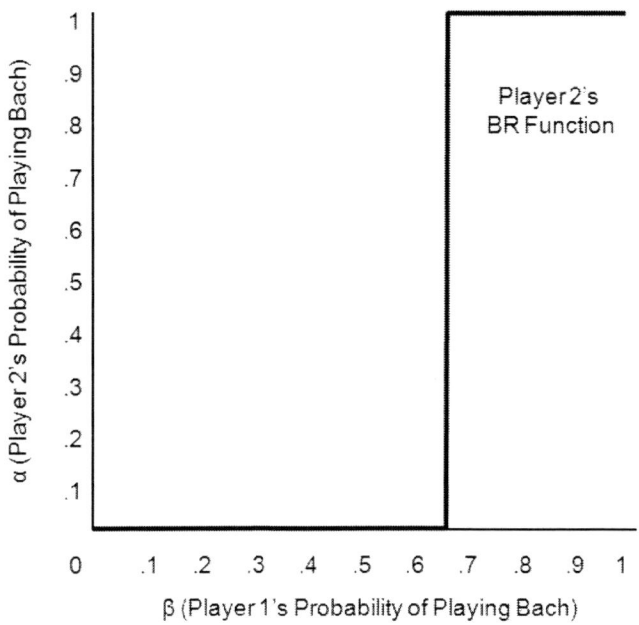

Figure 11.2: Battle of the Sexes, Player 2's BR Function

11.6.1 Nash Equilibrium

Note that in each of these best response figures, in order for a player to not deviate, his strategy and his opponent's strategy must be a point on his best response function. Consider, for instance, the point $(\beta = 2/3, \alpha = 7/10)$ in Figure 11.2. It should be clear that Player 2 has no incentive to deviate since this point lies on her best response function. We know that when $\beta = 2/3$, any strategy for Player 2 is a best response. However, Player 1 does have an incentive to deviate. As shown in Figure 11.1, when $\alpha = 7/10$, Player 1's best response is to play $\beta = 1$, not $\beta = 2/3$. Because $(\beta = 2/3, \alpha = 7/10)$ is not a point on Player 1's best response function, he will have an incentive to deviate.

That said, determining the Nash equilibrium from best response graphs is straight-forward. In particular, in order for a pair of strategies to be a Nash equilibrium, no player must have an incentive to deviate. In terms of best response functions, this means the pair of strategies must be on both players' best response functions. In other words, a Nash equilibrium is a point where the players' best response functions intersect. Figure 11.3 superimposes both Battle of the Sexes best response functions on a single set of axes. The points where the functions intersect are the Nash equilibria of the game. Note ($\beta = 0, \alpha = 0$) corresponds to both players playing *Stravinsky*. ($\beta = 1, \alpha = 1$) corresponds to both players playing *Bach*. Both of these Nash equilibria correspond to the pure strategy Nash equilibria we found in Example 11.5. Likewise, ($\beta = 2/3, \alpha = 1/3$) corresponds to the mixed strategy Nash equilibrium found in Example 11.8.

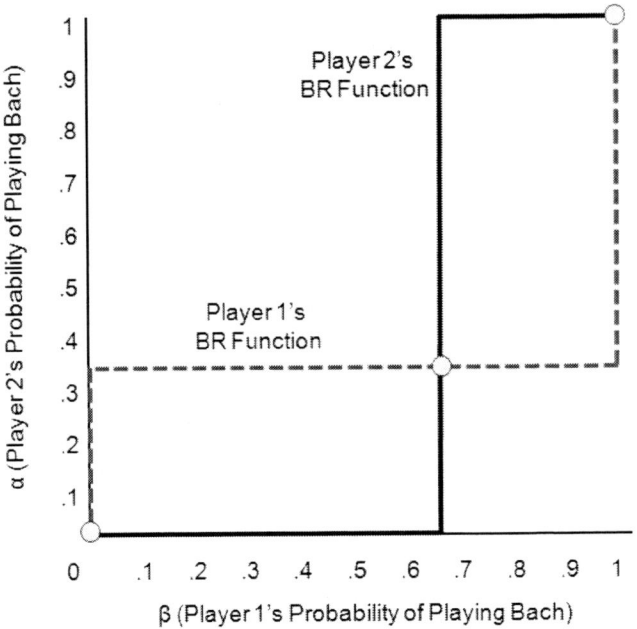

Figure 11.3: Battle of the Sexes, Combined BR Functions

Example 11.9 (Best Response Functions):
Task: Reconsider the Matching Pennies game represented by Table 11.16. Draw the best response functions of each player on a single graph and identify the Nash Equilibria.

Answer: Assume Player 2 is playing Heads with probability α and Tails with probability $1 - \alpha$. Player 1 should play Heads if $EU^1_{\text{Heads}} > EU^1_{\text{Tails}}$, or

$$
\begin{aligned}
1\alpha + (-1)(1 - \alpha) &> (-1)\alpha + (1)(1 - \alpha) \\
\Rightarrow 2\alpha - 1 &> 1 - 2\alpha \\
\Rightarrow \alpha &> \frac{1}{2}
\end{aligned}
$$

Likewise, Player 1 should play Tails when $\alpha < \frac{1}{2}$ and is indifferent to any strategy if $\alpha = \frac{1}{2}$.

Assume Player 1 is playing Heads with probability β and Tails with probability $1 - \beta$. Player 2 should play Heads if $EU^2_{\text{Heads}} > EU^2_{\text{Tails}}$, or

$$
\begin{aligned}
(-1)\beta + (1)(1 - \beta) &> (1)\beta + (-1)(1 - \beta) \\
\Rightarrow -2\beta + 1 &> 2\beta - 1 \\
\Rightarrow \beta &< \frac{1}{2}
\end{aligned}
$$

Likewise, Player 2 should play Tails when $\beta > \frac{1}{2}$ and is indifferent to any strategy if $\beta = \frac{1}{2}$.

Plotting these in Figure (11.4), we see the NE is (.5, .5), consistent with our numerical analysis.

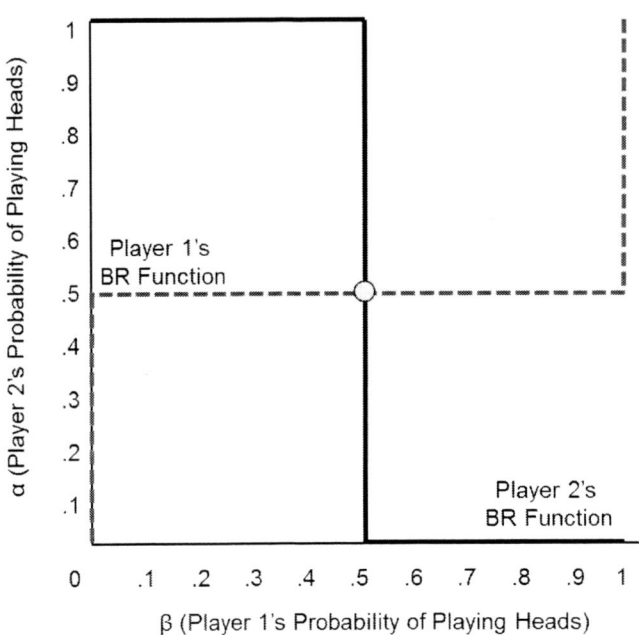

Figure 11.4: Example (11.9) - Matching Pennies, Combined BR Functions

Chapter 12

Game Theory - Continuous Normal Form Games

12.1 Normal Form and Payoff Functions

Until now, we have explicitly assumed that players have a finite number of strategies. However, this does not accurately reflect most strategic scenarios. Consider the Cournot model, which we will use as our example to demonstrate the techniques used to solve continuous games. The Cournot model is a model of oligopoly, which is a market served by a small number of firms. Unlike a monopoly, there are multiple firms competing with each other. Unlike perfect competition, these firms are large enough to affect the market price.

We will first examine the game with two firms having identical cost structures selling identical goods. The players of the game are firm 1 and firm 2. Assume each firm has an identical cost structure, $C(q) = 40q$ where 40 is the constant marginal cost. Where this game differs from a finite game is that each firm has an infinite number of strategies. In particular, each firm can select $q_i \in [0, \infty)$ units to produce. Obviously, we cannot represent this game as a game matrix, since there would be an infinite number of rows/columns. We also cannot list the payoff of every combination of strategies (i.e. $u_1(.5, 3) = 5, u_1(2, 7) = 10, \dots$), since there are again an infinite number of payoffs. Continuous games resolve this problem by representing the payoffs as a *payoff function*.

> **Definition 12.1 (Payoff Function):**
> A function that gives a player's payoff given any possible strategy profile.

The payoff function implicitly tells us the payoff for a player for any possible strategy he and his opponents select.

Our first job as game theorists is often to derive the payoff function for a particular strategic scenario. For instance, consider our Cournot example and a market in which demand follows the form $D(p) = 100 - p$. As in the perfectly competitive market, the equilibrium price will be such that the market supply equals the market demand. Recall this property holds since any other price would result in a shortage or surplus, resulting in a respective increase or decrease in prices. Mathematically, this property implies $Q = D(p)$, where Q is the total number of units produced by all firms in the market. For every possible level of output produced by firm 1, q_1, and firm 2, q_2, what payoff will each firm receive?

It should seem reasonably natural to model each firm's profit as their payoff function. Depending on the strategic scenario, other payoff functions can be used. If, for instance, the firm is concerned with environmental issues, then its payoff function might be a function related to the pollution it produces every year. In the Cournot case, as with our analysis of Production Theory, we will assume firm's are only concerned with profit.

Knowing that firm 1 produces q_1 and firm 2 produces q_2, the general profit each receives is

$$
\begin{aligned}
\Pi_1 &= q_1 p - C(q_1) \\
\Pi_2 &= q_2 p - C(q_2)
\end{aligned}
$$

Note what makes the oligopoly market different from the perfectly competitive market is that the market price is not fixed for each firm. Instead, they both affect it through the market demand function. In particular, recall $Q = 100 - p$ where Q is the sum of the outputs of each firm. Since there are only two firms, Q must therefore equal $q_1 + q_2$, meaning $q_1 + q_2 = 100 - p$, or $p = 100 - q_1 - q_2$. Plugging this into the profit function of each firm along with the specific cost functions,

$$
\begin{aligned}
\Pi_1(q_1, q_2) &= q_1(100 - q_1 - q_2) - 40q_1 \\
\Pi_2(q_1, q_2) &= q_2(100 - q_1 - q_2) - 40q_2
\end{aligned}
$$

We thus have the payoff function of each firm. Note that these functions are in terms of all players' strategies, as must be the case in the game's normal form.

Combining our results, we find the normal form of this specific Cournot game is:

1. **Players:** Firm 1 with cost structure $C_1(q_1) = 40q_1$; Firm 2 with cost structure $C_2(q_2) = 40q_2$.

2. **Strategies:** Firm 1 can play $q_1 \in [0, \infty)$. Firm 2 can play $q_2 \in [0, \infty)$.

3. **Payoffs:**

$$\begin{aligned}
\Pi_1(q_1, q_2) &= q_1(100 - q_1 - q_2) - 40q_1 \\
\Pi_2(q_1, q_2) &= q_2(100 - q_1 - q_2) - 40q_2
\end{aligned}$$

12.2   Best Response Functions and Nash Equilibria

Having formalized the normal form of the Cournot game, we can now determine the Nash equilibrium. It should be clear that the methodologies we have developed are not sufficient to determine the Nash equilibrium of this problem. Since we cannot form a game matrix, we cannot "underline the best responses" to determine the pure strategy Nash equlibria. Also, since there are an infinite number of strategies, developing a mixing strategy requires significantly more work than finding the values of α and β (in fact, finding mixed strategy Nash equilibria of continuous games is significantly beyond the scope of this course).

Luckily, finding the best response functions in continuous games can, at times, be surprisingly easy. Specifically, we use the calculus techniques we have developed throughout this course. Consider player 1's best response to a given player 2 strategy, q_2. This will be the strategy, q_1, that ensures player 1 receives the best possible payoff. Or, in other words, it is the quantity that maximizes player 1's profit function. To find this value, we need only solve player 1's first order condition treating player 2's strategy, q_2, as a constant.

$$\begin{aligned}
\max_{q_1} \, & q_1(100 - q_1 - q_2) - 40q_1 \\
\text{FOC: } & 100 - 2q_1^* - q_2 - 40 = 0 \\
& \Rightarrow q_1^* = \frac{60 - q_2}{2}
\end{aligned}$$

Thus, given a Player 2 strategy, q_2, $q_1^* = \frac{60 - q_2}{2}$ is player 1's best response function. Graphing this function results in Figure 12.1.

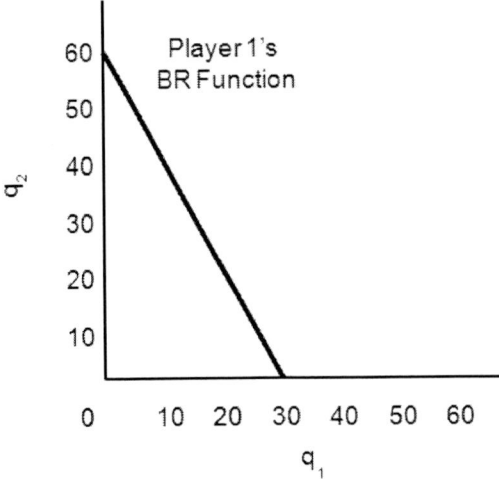

Figure 12.1: Cournot Game, Player 1 Best Response

Likewise, we can solve for Player 2's best response function,

$$\max_{q_2} q_2(100 - q_1 - q_2) - 40q_2$$
$$\text{FOC: } 100 - q_1 - q_2^* - 40 = 0$$
$$\Rightarrow q_2^* = \frac{60 - q_1}{2}$$

Plotting these results on the same axes as Figure 12.1 results in Figure 12.2.

As before, in order for a pair of strategies to be a Nash equilibrium, no player must have an incentive to deviate. In other words, a Nash equilibrium is a point where the players' best response functions intersect. Figure 12.3 superimposes both Cournot firms' best response functions on a single set of axes. The point where the functions intersect is the Nash equilibria of the game. In other words, if both firms produce 20 units of the good, neither firm will have an incentive to deviate.

In addition, note that the price they will sell their good, as determined by the market demand function is

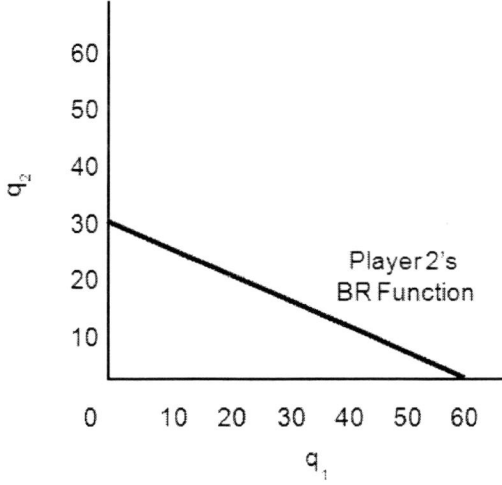

Figure 12.2: Cournot Game, Player 2 Best Response

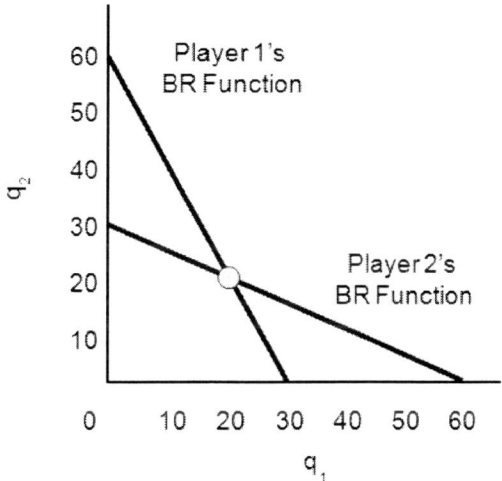

Figure 12.3: Cournot Game, Nash Equilibrium

$$
\begin{aligned}
Q &= 100 - p \\
\Rightarrow q_1 + q_2 &= 100 - p \\
\Rightarrow 20 + 20 &= 100 - p \\
\Rightarrow p &= 60
\end{aligned}
$$

With this price, the profits each firm will make are

$$\begin{aligned} \Pi_1 &= q_1 p - C(q_1) \\ \Rightarrow \Pi_1 &= (20)(60) - (40)(20) \\ \Rightarrow \Pi_1 &= 400 \end{aligned}$$

$$\begin{aligned} \Pi_2 &= q_2 p - C(q_2) \\ \Rightarrow \Pi_2 &= (20)(60) - (40)(20) \\ \Rightarrow \Pi_2 &= 400 \end{aligned}$$

12.2.1 Solving Best Response Functions Analytically

While drawing the best response functions and finding the Nash equilibria via. graphical methods gives us the correct answer, imagine the difficulty if there were three firms in the market. Specifically, we would need to draw our best response functions in three-dimensions. Even more problematic, if there were four firms in the market we could not be able to draw our best response functions at all. As always, this problem is easily remedied by using mathematical techniques.

Consider, in our Cournot example, the best response functions for each firm.

$$\begin{aligned} q_1^* &= \frac{60 - q_2}{2} \\ q_2^* &= \frac{60 - q_1}{2} \end{aligned}$$

A Nash equilibrium is a set of strategies, (q_1^*, q_2^*) that satisfy each of these equations simultaneously. In other words, when Player 1 plays q_1^*, Player 2's best response is to play q_2^*. Likewise, when Player 2 plays q_2^*, Player 1's best response is to play q_1^*. Mathematically, a Nash equilibrium will satisfy

$$\begin{aligned} q_1^* &= \frac{60 - q_2^*}{2} \\ q_2^* &= \frac{60 - q_1^*}{2} \end{aligned}$$

Notice this problem is simply solving the two best response functions for the two variables, q_1^*, q_2^*. From our Math Review, we know exactly how to do this. Plugging q_1^* into the second equation,

$$
\begin{aligned}
q_2^* &= \frac{60 - \frac{60 - q_2^*}{2}}{2} \\
\Rightarrow 2q_2^* &= 60 - \frac{60 - q_2^*}{2} \\
\Rightarrow 4q_2^* &= 120 - 60 + q_2^* \\
\Rightarrow 3q_2^* &= 60 \\
\Rightarrow q_2^* &= 20
\end{aligned}
$$

Plugging this value back into the first equation,

$$
\begin{aligned}
\Rightarrow q_1^* &= \frac{60 - 20}{2} \\
\Rightarrow q_1^* &= 20
\end{aligned}
$$

Example 12.1 (Cournot Game):

Task: Consider the Cournot game in which two firms are in the market. Firm 1 has a cost of $C(q_1) = 40q_1$. Firm 2 has a cost of $C(q_2) = q_2^2$. Both firms face market demand $D(p) = 120 - p$. Find the Nash equilibrium.

Answer: We must first form the payoff functions.

$$
\begin{aligned}
\Pi_1 &= q_1(120 - q_1 - q_2) - 40q_1 \\
\Pi_2 &= q_2(120 - q_1 - q_2) - q_2^2
\end{aligned}
$$

Solving for the BR functions,

$$
\begin{aligned}
120 - 2q_1 - q_2 - 40 &= 0 \\
q_1 &= \frac{80 - q_2}{2}
\end{aligned}
$$

$$
\begin{aligned}
120 - q_1 - 2q_2 - 2q_2 &= 0 \\
q_2 &= \frac{120 - q_1}{4}
\end{aligned}
$$

Plugging q_1^* into q_2^*,

$$
\begin{aligned}
q_2 &= \frac{120 - \frac{80 - q_2}{2}}{4} \\
4q_2 &= 120 - \frac{80 - q_2}{2} \\
8q_2 &= 240 - 80 + q_2 \\
q_2 &= \frac{160}{7} = 22.9 \\
q_1 &= \frac{80 - \frac{160}{7}}{2} = 40 - \frac{80}{7} = 28.6
\end{aligned}
$$

Example 12.2 (Cournot Game):

Task: Assume we are facing the same game as Example 12.1, but the government now offers a subsidy to firm 1. For every unit of good firm 1 sells, the government gives them \$20. Find the Nash equilibrium.

Answer: We must first form the payoff functions.

$$
\begin{aligned}
\Pi_1 &= q_1(120 - q_1 - q_2) - 40q_1 + 20q_1 \\
\Pi_2 &= q_2(120 - q_1 - q_2) - q_2^2
\end{aligned}
$$

Solving for the BR functions,

$$
\begin{aligned}
120 - 2q_1 - q_2 - 20 &= 0 \\
q_1 &= \frac{100 - q_2}{2}
\end{aligned}
$$

$$
\begin{aligned}
120 - q_1 - 2q_2 - 2q_2 &= 0 \\
q_2 &= \frac{120 - q_1}{4}
\end{aligned}
$$

Plugging q_1^* into q_2^*,

$$q_2 = \frac{120 - \frac{100-q_2}{2}}{4}$$

$$4q_2 = 120 - \frac{100-q_2}{2}$$

$$8q_2 = 240 - 100 + q_2$$

$$q_2 = \frac{140}{7} = 20$$

$$q_1 = \frac{100-20}{2} = 40$$

Not surprisingly, q_1 sells more, q_2 sells less, and (it can be shown) makes more profit. Consider this in the context of trade subsidies in an effort to keep more jobs at home.

12.3   Sequential Games

Thus far, we have dealt with games where players act simultaneously. In the Cournot game, for instance, both firms set their quantities at the same time. The definition of a normal form game, however, does not impose this restriction. In general, games can be significantly more robust, allowing players to move in a specified order. Consider the Stackelberg model, which is identical to the Cournot model except Firm 1 moves first. In our specific example, we will again assume $C(q_i) = 40q_i$ and $D(p) = 100 - p$.

On the surface, it might not appear this change will result in a significantly different equilibrium. However, consider Firm 1's decision-making process. When both firms set their quantities at the same time, Firm 1 knows the only variable he can strategically affect is the market price. For instance, if he floods the market with his product, he knows he will drive the prices down. However, when he selects his quantity first, he is also able to strategically affect another variable. In particular, his choice of q_1 will affect Player 2's optimal choice of q_2. For instance, assume Player 1 floods the market and drives the price down. He knows that Player 2, faced with an already low price, will not produce a significant amount of the good.

As such, when selecting his choice of q_1, Player 1 should take his effect on Player 2's optimal choice into consideration. He can determine this effect by solving the same problem Player 2 will solve. In other words, Player 1 knows that if he selects q_1^*, Player 2 will face the problem,

$$\max_{q_2} q_2(100 - q_1^* - q_2) - 40q_2$$

Being an optimizing agent, Player 2 will select

$$\text{FOC: } 100 - q_1^* - 2q_2^* - 40 = 0$$
$$\Rightarrow q_2^* = \frac{60 - q_1^*}{2}$$

Knowing this, Player 1 should then select q_1 to solve the problem,

$$\max_{q_1} q_1(100 - q_1 - \frac{60 - q_1}{2}) - 40q_1$$

Note that, by acting first, Player 1 is able to influence Player 2. As such, Player 1 should include this influence in his maximization problem, which is done by incorporating Player 2's best response function into Player 1's maximization problem.

Solving Player 1's optimization problem,

$$\text{FOC: } 100 - 2q_1^* - 30 + q_1^* - 40 = 0$$
$$\Rightarrow q_1^* = 30$$

which means Player 2 will select $q_2^* = \frac{60 - 30}{2} = 15$. The market price at these quantities equals $100 - 30 - 15 = \$55$ and the profits for each firm equals

$$\Pi_1 = q_1 p - C(q_1)$$
$$\Rightarrow \Pi_1 = (30)(55) - (40)(30)$$
$$\Rightarrow \Pi_1 = 450$$

$$\Pi_2 = q_2 p - C(q_2)$$
$$\Rightarrow \Pi_2 = (15)(55) - (40)(15)$$
$$\Rightarrow \Pi_2 = 225$$

Compare this to the simultaneous-move game, in which each firm produced 20 units of the good, the market price equaled $60, and each firm received $400 in profits. By moving first, Firm 1 increased its profits to $450 at the expense of Firm 2, whose profits dropped to $225. Essentially, Firm 1 flooded the market by producing 30 units of the good, causing Firm 2 to scale back production. The first player's ability to increase profits by strategically manipulating the later players' optimal strategies is referred to as the *first mover advantage*.

12.4 Nondifferentiable Payoff Functions

Until now, we have dealt with continuous scenarios where the payoff functions are differentiable, allowing us to use First Order Conditions to solve for the best response functions and Nash equilibria. Let us consider the Bertrand model, in which this is not the case. In particular, the Bertrand model assumes that identical firms with constant marginal cost do not compete in quantities, but instead compete in price. In other words, whoever has the lowest price serves the entire market.

As such, the demand each firm faces is

$$D_1(p_1, p_2) = \begin{cases} D(p_1) & \text{if } p_1 > p_2 \\ D(p_1)/2 & \text{if } p_1 = p_2 \\ 0 & \text{if } p_1 < p_2 \end{cases}$$

It should be clear that forming a differentiable profit function using this demand function will prove impossible. In cases such as this, we must use nonstandard approaches such as graphical techniques and intuition.

In the case of the Bertrand model, we will first use a graphical technique to determine the Nash equilibrium. For this specific example, assume marginal costs are $5 for each firm. To determine how the best response function for Firm 1 is derived, we have to use intuition. For instance, if $p_2 = 3$, we can ask ourselves "what is Firm 1's optimal response?". If Firm 1 sets $p_1 < 3$ (say $2.99), it will capture the full market, $D(p_1)$. However, it will be selling the good for less than it costs to produce, $5. As such, it would be better off not selling the good, which we represent on the best response function as $p_1 > 3$, since, at any price above $3, it will sell no units of the good and avoid negative profits. If $p_2 = 5$, Firm 1 will not lower the price, since it will make negative profits. If it sets $p_1 = 5$, it will make 0 profits since the price at which it is selling $D(p_2)/2$ units of the good exactly offsets the cost of making the units. If it sets $p_1 > 5$, it will also make 0 profits, since it will not sell any units of the good. Thus, if $p_2 = 5$, any $p_1 \geq 5$ is a best response for Firm 1. If $p_2 > 5$, Firm 1's best response is to undercut the price by a very small amount. If it charges more than p_2, it will receive 0 profit. If it charges an extremely small amount less than p_2, it will be selling the good at essentially the same price, but will now sell to the entire market, $D(p_2)$, instead of half the market, $\frac{D(p_2)}{2}$. Combining these results in Firm 1's best response function as shown in Figure 12.4. Identical logic results in Firm 2's best response function.

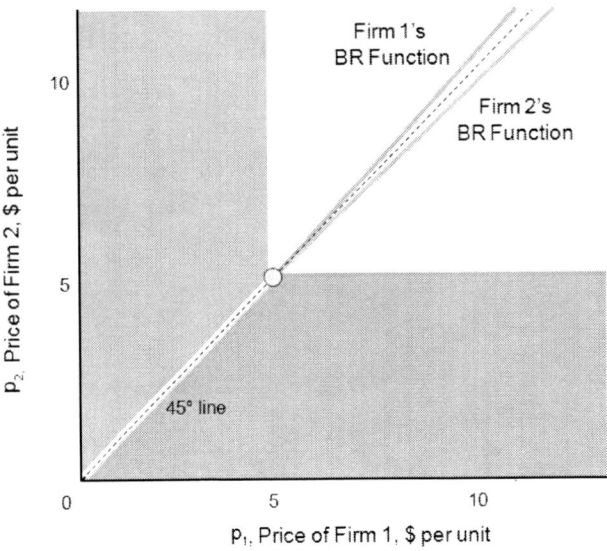

Figure 12.4: Bertrand Game, Nash Equilibrium

Combining these best response functions, we see there is only a single point where they intersect. In particular, $(p_1 = \$5, p_2 = \$5)$ is the Nash equilibrium. Note that under Bertrand competition with identical firms, the equilibrium has each firm setting price equal to their marginal cost, making a profit of 0. This is exactly the same result as in a perfectly competitive environment! This result is extremely important for optimal regulatory policy, since it shows that even when the strict assumptions for perfect competition are not fulfilled, we can still achieve a socially optimal equilibrium.

Having shown how we can derive the result graphically, we will now show how the result can be derived using only intuition. First, we can ask ourselves "would Firm 1 or Firm 2 ever set his price below \$5?". The answer should obviously be no, since any price less than the marginal cost will result in negative profits. Thus, we know than any Nash equilibrium must have $p_1 \geq 5$ and $p_2 \geq 5$. We can now ask ourselves, "is it possible to have a Nash equilibrium where $p_1 > 5$ or $p_2 > 5$". The answer is again no. If $p_1 = p_2 > 5$, then either firm has an incentive to drop the price by a very small amount, gaining the entire market (instead of only 1/2 the market). Alternatively, if $p_1 \neq p_2$, then the higher-priced firm will have an incentive to lower their price a very small amount below the other firm, gaining the entire market (instead of none of the market). Thus, we know that any Nash equilibrium must have $p_1 \leq 5$ and $p_2 \leq 5$. Since we have also determined that $p_1 \geq 5$ and $p_2 \geq 5$, the only remaining option is $p_1 = 5$ and $p_2 = 5$. To verify this is a Nash, we need only ask if either firm has an incentive to deviate. If either firm lowers their price, they earn negative profits. If either firm raises their price, they still receive 0 profits. As such, neither firm has an incentive to deviate and we do, in fact, have a Nash equilibrium.

Chapter 13

Game Theory - Extensive Form

13.1 Extensive Form

Having analyzed the concept of a Nash equilibrium, we should once again ask ourselves "so we are done with Game Theory, right?". While the Nash equilibrium is widely used and has significantly more applications than IESDS, there are still numerous strategic scenarios in which a Nash equilibrium falls short in reasonably predicting how the scenario will resolve itself.

Consider, for instance, the following game. Player 1 moves first, and selects between *Left* and *Right*. If he selects *Right*, the game ends, he receives a payoff of 1 and Player 1 receives a payoff of 2. If he selects *Left*, Player 2 then decides between *L* and *R*. If Player 2 plays *L*, both he and Player 1 receive a payoff of 0. If Player 2 player *R*, he receives a payoff of 1 and Player 2 receives a payoff of 1.

Consider the normal form of this game, in which the order of play is not considered. As with any finite game with 2 players, we can model this game as a game matrix, which is shown in Figure 13.1.

The pure strategy Nash equilibria of this game are *(Left, R)* and *(Right, L)*. Are these outcomes reasonable expectations of how the game will resolve itself? In particular, is *(Right, L)* a reasonable outcome? Since this is a Nash equilibrium, we know that **if** Player 2 plays *L*, then Player 1 should play *Right*. However, is it reasonable to expect that if Player 1 deviates and plays *Left*, Player 2 will still play *L*? In particular, since the choices are not occurring simultaneously, is it reasonable to assume that Player 1's play will not affect Player 2's decision? If Player 2 finds that Player 1 deviated and played *Left*, why would she possibly play *L*?

Player 2

		L	R
Player 1	Left	0, 0	2, 1
	Right	1, 2	1, 2

Table 13.1: Sample Dynamic Game

In particular, by playing R she can receive a payoff of 1 versus a payoff of 0 by playing L.

The normal form of a game does not take the crucial element of timing into account. For models where timing is not important, the normal form and Nash equilibria remain reasonable expectations for how the game will resolve itself. For models where timing is important, a Nash equilibrium lends itself to *non-credible threats*. For instance, in our example Player 2 can induce Player 1 to play *Right* by threatening to play L if given the opportunity. However, Player 1 should realize that once he has made his decision, Player 2 will not find it in her best interest to enact that threat. In particular, she will be hurting herself, which does not seem rational. As such, the Nash equilibrium, *(Right, L)* involves a non-credible threat by Player 2, and does not seem a reasonable outcome to this game.

To rectify this inconsistency, game theorists use an alternate game formulation with an alternate solution concept. The formation they use is the *extensive form*.

Definition 13.1 (Extensive Form Game):
An *extensive form game* consists of

1. **Set of players:** Who is playing

2. **Strategy space of each player:** How they can play

3. **Payoff each player receives given any strategy profile:** What they will "win" given each combination of their strategy and their opponents' strategies

4. **Order of moves:** The order in which players make their choices

5. **Player Information:** What each player knows when they make their choices.

Note the first three elements are identical to the normal form game. Thus, each extensive form game can be written as a normal form game. However, an extensive form game also considers the order of moves and the information each player has when moving. The information of each player plays an important role, as demonstrated in our example. If, for instance, Player 2 made her decision without knowing Player 1's decision, then Player 1's decision would not reasonably affect Player 2. As such, the order of moves would not matter and we would effectively be in a normal form game. Because Player 2 does know Player 1's decision, it can be used as a strategic device and changes the reasonable outcome of the game. The Stackelberg game, for instance, results in a different outcome than the Cournot game because the Stackelberg game has Firm 2 learning Firm 1's decision prior to making its own decision.

As the normal form game with two players has a graphical representation, so does the extensive form. In particular, we use a *game tree*. Each player is represented as a node, and his choices are represented as branches emanating from his node. Payoffs are indicated after each terminal decision, which is a decision that ensures no other decisions can be made. The extensive form of our example is represented by Figure 13.1, in which payoffs are in the form (Player 1 payoff, Player 2 payoff).

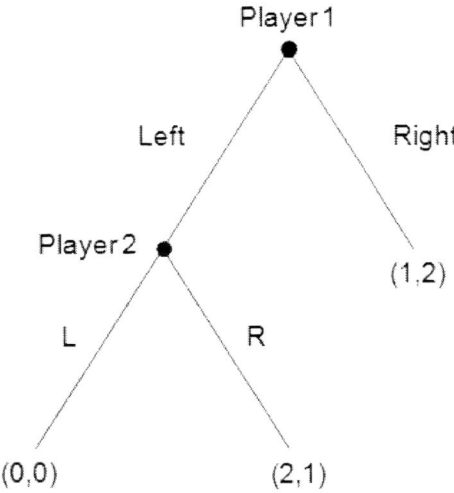

Figure 13.1: Extensive Form Game Tree

13.2   Subgame Perfection

To determine a reasonable outcome to an extensive form game, economists use the concept of a *subgame perfect Nash equilibrium*. Like the Nash equilibrium, no player can have an incentive to deviate in equilibrium. Unlike Nash equilibrium, subgame perfection also requires that when every player moves, his strategy must be a Nash equilibrium *of the remaining game*.

Consider once again our game represented in Figure 13.1. Subgame perfection requires that when Player 2 plays, her action must be a Nash equilibrium of the remaining game. The remaining game, at the point Player 2 plays, is simply

1. **Players:** Player 2

2. **Strategies:** *L, R*

3. **Payoffs:** $u_2(L) = 0, u_2(R) = 1$

The Nash equilibrium of this subgame is trivial. Since there is only one player, in order for her to not deviate, she must select the option that is best for her. In particular, *R*. Thus, subgame perfection requires that Player 2 plays *R* if given the opportunity. Knowing this, Player 1's best response is to play *Left*.

Note the method in which we used to solve for the subgame perfect Nash equilibrium. In particular, we started with the last player then worked our way backwards. This methodology is called *backwards induction*. It incorporates the idea that when making a decision, it is rational to consider how that decision will affect future players (which in turn affects you). Consider, for instance, the common parental threat "if you do _____, we'll disown you". When choosing their behavior, most teenagers do not consider this threat. In particular, they ask themselves "IF I do _____, how will my parents respond. Is it in their best interest to disown me?". Backwards induction is this process of "looking ahead" to determine how future players will respond to your actions, then choosing your optimal action.

To solve for subgame perfect Nash equilibria in games where each player knows every action played by the players who have already moved,

1. Identify every terminal decision.

2. Find each terminal player's optimal strategy at the terminal decision node(s).

3. Identify the player immediately preceding this player. Knowing the terminal player's optimal strategy, find this player's optimal strategy.

4. Continue this process, working your way backwards, until every player's optimal strategy has been identified.

To demonstrate this technique, consider the game represented by Figure 13.2.

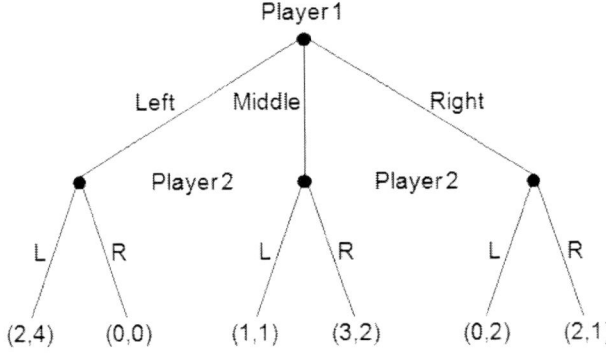

Figure 13.2: Backwards Induction

Example 13.1 (Backwards Induction):

Task: Find all subgame perfect Nash equilibrium in the game represented by Figure 13.2.

Answer: Following our steps,

1. There are three terminal nodes. In particular, the three possible decisions Player 2 can make.

2. At the left node, Player 2 plays *L*. At the middle node, Player 2 plays *R*. At the right node, Player 3 plays *L*.

3. The player immediately preceding Player 2 is Player 1. Knowing Player 2's optimal strategies, he faces the game represented by Figure 13.3. Note we have crossed out the nonoptimal strategies of Player 2. Facing only the remaining strategies, Player 1 selects *Middle*, gaining a payoff of 3.

Thus, the subgame perfect Nash equilibrium is *(*Middle, R), which gives Player 1 a payoff of 3 and Player 2 a payoff of 2.

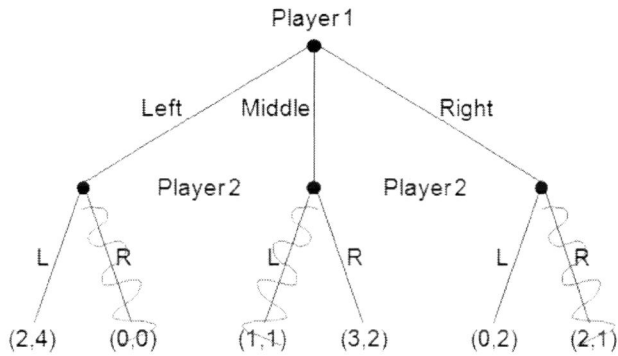

Figure 13.3: Backwards Induction

As a comparison, let us find all pure strategy Nash equilibrium. Figure 13.2 is the normal form of this game. The pure strategy Nash equilibria are *(Left, L)* and *(Middle, R)*. *(Middle, R)* coincides with our subgame perfect Nash equilibria. *(Left, L)*, however, contains a noncredible threat. In particular, Player 1 knows if he deviates and plays *Middle*, Player 2 will not enact her threat of playing *L*, since she makes a higher payoff by playing *R*.

Player 2

		L	R
Player 1	Left	2, 4	0, 0
	Middle	1, 1	3, 2
	Right	0, 2	2, 1

Table 13.2: Sample Dynamic Game

13.3 Imperfect Information

In every dynamic game we have analyzed, we have assumed players are fully aware of the actions their opponents have taken. In other words, they have *perfect information* concerning the history of the game. The extensive form of the game does not require this to be the case. In particular, we can model games in which one player has *imperfect information* pertaining to the past play of the game. In a game tree representation, we represent this uncertainty of past play as an *information set*, which is graphically illustrated as a dashed line.

Figure 13.4 represents an extensive form game with imperfect information. In particular, Player 2 does not know if Player 1 played *Left* or *Right*. Without this information, Player 1 cannot affect Player 2's decision, and the game reverts to a normal form game in which the Nash equilibria are all considered reasonable outcomes of the game.

13.4 Game Theory - To Be Continued...

At this point, it should be clear that most situations in life have some element of strategic interaction. Your decision on how much to study for an exam is directly affected by your professor's decision on how hard to make the exam. Your professor's decision on how hard to make the exam is affected by your decision on how much to study. A restaurant's decision on where to locate is directly affected by other restaurants' decisions to locate, which is in turn affected by the first restaurant's decision to locate. A CEO's decision on how to run a company is directly affected by their contract, which is directly affected by how motivated the CEO is by bonuses.

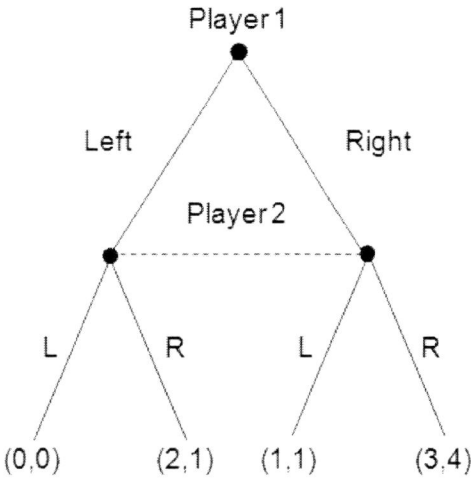

Figure 13.4: Imperfect Information

While our coverage of Game Theory has allowed us to predict reasonable outcomes of certain games, it is still far from complete. We have yet to address how to solve for subgame perfect Nash equilibria when there is imperfect information. In addition, what happens if a normal form game is repeated? Could there be strategies in which I can "punish" my opponent if they do not play in a certain way? Could that result in new predictions?

More importantly, we have not looked into scenarios where players have private information concerning their payoffs, or *incomplete information*. For instance, how would Player 1 act in any of our dynamic examples if he was unsure of Player 2's payoffs. Would a subgame perfect Nash equilibrium still predict a reasonable outcome of the game? Since most realistic scenarios involve some element of private information, formalizing games of incomplete information is necessary.

By fully developing these tools of Game Theory, virtually every strategic interaction can be studied. As such, Game Theory has been used to study politics, contract theory, patent law, sports, and of course, economics.

Bibliography

Anderson, John D. and Coble, Keith H. "Impact of Renewable Fuels Standard Ethanol Mandates on the Corn Market". Agribusiness, 2010. 26(1), pp. 49–63.

Bellemare, Marc. "How to (Maximize the Likelihood) that You Will Do Well in Your Economics Class". 2010. http://tinyurl.com/3v6du2x.

Bradbury, Hinton and Ross, Karen. "The Effects of Novelty and Choice Materials on the Intransitivity of Preferences of Children and Adults". Annals of Operations Research, 1990. 23, pp. 141–159.

Calvó-Armengol, Antoni and Jackson, Matthew. "The Effects of Social Networks on Employment and Inequality". American Economics Review, 2004. 94(3), pp. 426–454.

Crémer, Jacques, Rey, Patrick and Tirole, Jean. "Connectivity in the Commercial Internet". Journal of Industrial Economics, 2000. 48, pp. 433–472.

Economist, The. "Getting General Motors going again". The Economist, 1992. pp. 77–78.

Hayes, Dermot. "Biofuels: Potential Production Capacity, Effects on Grain and Livestock Sectors, and Implications for Food Prices and Consumers". Journal of Agricultural and Applied Economics, 2009. 41(2), pp. 465–491.

Hofstadter, Douglas. I Am A Strange Loop. Basic Books, 2007.

Huettenmueller, Rhonda. Algebra Demystified. McGraw-Hill, 2003.

Krantz, Steven. Calculus Demystified. McGraw-Hill, 2003.

Marr, David. Vision. W. H. Freeman and Co, 1982.

Motta, Massimo. Competition Policy. Cambridge University Press, 2004.

Nash, John. "Non-Cooperative Games". The Annals of Mathematics, 1951. 54(2), pp. 286–295.

Pimentel, David. "Ethanol Fuels: Energy Balance, Economics, and Environmental Impacts are Negative". Natural Resources Research, 2003. 12(2), pp. 127–134.

Prince, Jeff and Goldfarb, Avi. "Internet Adoption Patterns and Usage are Different: Implications for the Digital Divide". Information Economics and Policy, 2008. 20, pp. 2–15.

Sundaram, Rangarajan K. A First Course in Optimization Theory. Cambridge University Press, 1996.

Treme, Julianne and Allen, Samuel K. "Press Pass: Payoffs to Media Exposure Among National Football League (NFL) Wide Receivers". Journal of Sports Economics, 2011. 12, pp. 370–390.

Weinstein, Arnold A. "Transitivity of Preference: A Comparison among Age Groups". Journal of Political Economy, 1968. 76, pp. 307–311.